JACOB'S LADDER

JACOB'S LADDER

ESSAYS ON EXPERIENCES OF THE INEFFABLE IN THE CONTEXT OF CONTEMPORARY PSYCHOTHERAPY

Josephine Klein

KARNAC

LONDON   NEW YORK

First published in 2003 by
H. Karnac (Books) Ltd.
6 Pembroke Buildings, London NW10 6RE

A subsidiary of Other Press LLC, New York

British Library Cataloguing in Publication Data

A C.I.P. for this book is available from the British Library

   ISBN 1 85575 936 5

10 9 8 7 6 5 4 3 2 1

Edited, designed, and produced by The Studio Publishing Services Ltd,
Exeter EX4 8JN

www.karnacbooks.com

CONTENTS

JACOB'S LADDER

Jacob left Beer-Sheba and went toward Haran. And he came to a certain place and stayed there that night, because the sun had set. Taking one of the stones of the place, he put it under his head and lay down to sleep. And he dreamt that there was a ladder set up on the earth, and the top of it reached to heaven; and behold, the angels of the Lord went up and down on it ...

... Then Jacob awoke from his sleep and said, "Surely the Lord was in this place and I knew it not."

Genesis, Chapter Twenty-Eight

... and upon thy so sore loss
Shall shine the traffic of Jacob's ladder
Pitched between Heaven and Charing Cross.

from "In No Strange Land"
by Francis Thompson, 1859–1907

CHAPTER ONE

Introduction—Bach and Handel, transparency and quiddity

Introduction

F or whom is this book intended? Certainly for myself, and perhaps for others who, like myself, are working in the field of psychotherapy and interested in the theory behind what they are doing. By extension, it is for anyone who is interested in how people's minds work, who looks at what people experience, wonders how it all fits together, and speculates about answers in a fairly disciplined way. Because it is my own background, I propose to use the words "psychotherapist" and "psychotherapy" to cover a range of people so wide it would not do to enumerate them on each occasion that I have us all in mind: all who have to do with psychodynamics—psychoanalysts; clinical psychologists; counsellors; developmental, alternative, complementary, humanistic, and other therapists; experimental psychologists, indeed maybe anyone educated in this area of theory and discipline who wants to join our crowd. All these may be in my mind when I write "we", though of course anyone is free to opt out at any time.

The experiences that engage my interest are hard to pin down: love, wonder, awe, joy, inspiration, and particularly the feelings that seem to give us a sense that there is something beyond what we can easily find words for—ineffable feelings. Thus also hope, humility, forgiveness, emptiness fearful or bright, devotion, adoration and the desire to worship, gratitude, redemption ... the list is quite long. John Hick (1999) places them in a fifth dimension, a spiritual realm.

Definitions: the numinous, the mystic dimension, spiritual realms

The word "numinous" is not in the two-volume *Shorter Oxford English Dictionary* of 1973, though "numen" is (and so is "numismatics"). "Numen" is there said to refer to "deity, divinity, divine or presiding power or spirit". The Dictionary derives the Latin noun *numen* from the verb *nuere*, to nod the head; the Greek equivalent refers explicitly to bowing the head, "the bow that is made in the presence of superiors". "Worship" might be an easier English equivalent, and is defined in the same volume as

> to honour and revere as a supernatural being or power or as a holy thing; to regard with extreme respect or devotion.

It is Rudolph Otto, author of *The Idea of the Holy* (1917) who coined the word "numinous". He argued that "'omen' has given us 'ominous', and that there is no reason why we should not similarly form a word *'numinous'*." (p. 25 in the 1959 Pelican edition). The numinous is what we sense when we bow to what seems not to be on the human scale. In this chapter we consider how it was felt by Bach, Handel, and Gerard Manley Hopkins. In later chapters the Rev. Eli Jenkins, Ravi Shankar and many others will be cited.

Otto published his *Idea of the Holy* (characteristically, the English translation distances itself from the more direct German title *Das Heilige*) at the beginning of the twentieth century. As well as being a believing Christian, Otto was a very modern student of comparative religion, then a fashionable subject. A hundred years later, it is still a very interesting book, full of captivating ideas. Otto's psychology is so subtle, his sympathies so wide, his appreciation of aesthetics so congruent with his idea of the Holy, that his discussion of the effect of silence in music, of darkness in architecture, in conveying a sense of *mysterium tremendum* would surely still give pleasure to many readers. In his foreword to the first English edition he writes of his purpose:

> The "irrational" is today a favourite theme of all who are too lazy to think or too ready to evade the arduous duty of clarifying their ideas and grounding their convictions on a basis of coherent thought. This book, recognising the profound import of the non-rational for metaphysics, makes a serious attempt to analyse all the more exactly the *feeling* which remains where the *concept* fails, and to introduce a terminology which is not any more loose or indeterminate for having necessarily to make use of symbols. [Otto, 1959, p. 13]

I have found this an inspiring purpose. Many of us have experiences we find it hard to put it into words. The experiences of poets and mystics have, over the past century, with the development of more systematic psychological knowledge, been intellectually split off, marginalized, and left to fossilize in a language which does not work well for us now. No doubt their language expressed well enough what they wanted to say at the time, but modern psychodynamic practice make it difficult to integrate what they had to say about the psyche. I do not mean that the language needs translating, though good translations give pleasure—see for instance, the Penguin translation of Walter Hilton's *Ladder of Perfection* by Leo Shirley-Price, or Clifton Walter's translation of *The Cloud of Unknowing* (author unknown). I mean that translating what they write into twentieth-century conceptual structures might make their experiences more accessible to twentieth-century readers, and might also enrich our understanding of the processes they explored. Why should we resign ourselves to having their style of experiencing go out of fashion? They have things to say. What they have to say about love and other ineffable experiences, cast in mystical mode in terms of their experience of the love of God, may also throw light on the nature of loving and other hard-to-describe experiences, now

Their style of experience is "mystical". The *Shorter Oxford English Dictionary* defines a mystic as *inter uliu*, "one who seeks by contemplation and self-surrender to obtain union with or absorption into the

Deity, or who believes in the spiritual apprehension of truths inaccessible to the understanding, 1679". The *Dictionary* defines mysticism as "belief in the possibility of union with the Divine nature by means of ecstatic contemplation; reliance on spiritual intuition as the means of acquiring knowledge of mysteries inaccessible to the understanding". By the understanding, incidentally, is meant "the faculty of comprehending and reasoning; the intellect".

These definitions are not very much help to the run-of-the-mill intellectual style of the late twentieth century. Indeed, formal definitions are not in the contemporary style of gaining understanding. Case histories and examples may be more so, and this chapter proposes to consider some aspects of the works of Johann Sebastian Bach's *St Matthew Passion* (1729) and George Frederick Handel's (1740) *Messiah*, ten years later, with occasional sidelong glances at Joseph Haydn's *Creation*, fifty years later still (1798), to clarify what we are about.

Bach and Handel were deeply religious men, and both inspire many listeners with feelings that may be called mystical at a level "inaccessible to the understanding". Yet they are very different. That is useful for our purpose, as attending to differences, comparing, contrasting, analysing, are functions of the intellect "involving reasoning and comprehension". Also, music is less alien to modern ways than mysticism is, and may provide a smoother introduction to unfamiliar experiences "inaccessible to the understanding". The fact that Bach and Handel are so different gives us binocular vision and thus a better perspective on our subject. What might be the differences? One's first reaction might be to think of Bach as the more mystical. Yet Handel said that when he wrote the Halleluiah Chorus he saw the heavens opened and that he finished the oratorio on his knees and we can believe it. Part of the answer may lie in the very grammar of the words being used, as well as in the music, the tunes.

How Bach and Handel use language

Much more than Handel, or perhaps we should say, much more than Handel's librettist, Bach uses the first person "I", "me", "we", "us". There is not much "I" in Handel's *Messiah*, when that work is compared to Bach's *St Matthew Passion*. When Bach uses the second person, "you", the singers are usually addressing God or, less frequently, God is speaking to the listeners or the singers—God is addressing us; the third person, "he" and "they", is less used by Bach. So we, the singers and the listeners, are involved in a relationship; we are singing a relationship between God and us: you, I, we. By contrast, Handel uses the third person, "he" and "they", a good deal, both for God and, in the plural, for others, usually the heathen, or sinners. Also Handel tells us what God is doing, or did, and how the human race is responding (or not, as the case may be), using "they", not "we". The relationship between the human and the divine is commented upon, but it is not lived out within the oratorio; it is not exemplified by singers and listeners.

One can change a text that sounds like Handel into a text that sounds like Bach, by changing the grammar: by changing the personal pronouns we get a more or a less devotional-sounding text. Handel's aria "I know that my Redeemer liveth" (Isaiah) begins in that deeply personal way:

> I know that my Redeemer liveth ...

But in the very next line we are in the realm of the third person, and God is referred to as "He" and not addressed as "You":

> I know that my Redeemer liveth and that He shall stand at the latter day ...

How different it would be to hear

> I know that you live, my Redeemer, and that you will stand at the latter day ...

And, hearing another of Handel's quotations from Isaiah,

> He was despised and rejected, a man of sorrows ...
> He gave his back to the smiters—

we might feel moved in a different way if we sang, or heard the choir singing

> You were despised and rejected, a man of sorrows ...
> You gave your back to the smiters ...

There is a similar difference between Handel's

Thy rebuke has broken his heart

and what would be more like a Bach text,

Your rebuke has broken my heart.

It is, on the surface, just a question of pronouns.

In my view the German language, Bach's language, has remained an easier language in which to sound convincingly devotional. German has far fewer of the Latinate or Greek-derived word-formations, which in England do so much to alienate the English common speaker from the more educated. Equally important is the historical change in the use of those pronouns. Not only is the gender-free *Mensch* less grating to the modern ear than the harping on *Man*, but also the old intimate use of "thee" and "thou" (the old intimate second person) never got lost in German, was not split off centuries ago from the use of "you", the second person plural, which at that time was used as a mark of respect to status-superiors. (The German form of respect was the *third* person plural, "Sie".)

English opted for "you" for everyone except God, who continued to be addressed by what was, to start with, the domestic, intimate, generally-used-to-friends-and-neighbours "Thou", "Thee". As a result, when nowadays we address the Divine out loud, or discuss these matters, either we sound elevated when using "Thee", even pompous, or we sound rustic, perky, even comical in our use of "you". Both alternatives sound artificial and self-conscious, making us reluctant to address God in words at all. Social and educational class-divisions hold English devotional language in their deadly grip.

In this excursus on grammar, it is perhaps not inappropriate also to mention the personal pronouns "we" and "us", which will be more important in Chapters Eight and Nine. Mysterious concepts the more we look at them, they refer not exactly to me, not exactly to you, not exactly to either or both of us in our entirety but to something we both participate in, something that links us.

The intimate language of "you" and "I" creates a different dynamic in the heart: "we", a good feeling. But when the sense of oneness, of identification, is strong, there is also a problem, for many of us, what to do with the negative feelings. Then, if we allow it, much badness can be projected on to that third party, who is not us but them, they, him, her.

How Bach and Handel relate to the shadow side

Many of us do not know what to do with our negative feelings, our shadow side, feelings of hate or fear and such. The language of the third person allows much badness to be projected on to that third party, off our own shoulders. Handel's language allows this more easily that Bach's. Differences in the grammar used by Bach and Handel indicate two different styles of experiencing the world. Handel uses the third person singular, "he", a good deal more than Bach does, usually in referring to God as "He". Handel also uses the third person plural "they" more, because he refers more often to the bad, the sinners, the heathen, and others out of favour, as "they" or "them". In Handel's *Messiah* there is a good deal of condemnation of other people; people are more often ranged over against each other. Handel shows more rage. A famous example comes after the lovely soprano, "How beautiful are the feet of them that preach the gospel of peace and bring glad tidings of good things". Then, we have, from the Psalms, the bass singing

> Why do the nations so furiously rage together, and why do the people imagine a vain thing? The kings of the earth rise up, and the rulers take counsel together against the Lord and against his anointed.

Then the chorus,

> Let us break their bonds asunder, and cast their yoke from us.

And then the tenor,

> He that dwelleth in heaven shall laugh them to scorn; the Lord shall have them in derision.
> Thou shalt break them with a rod of iron; Thou shalt dash them in pieces like a potter's vessel.

And then everyone sings, "Halleluiah, for the Lord God Omnipotent reigneth!" from Revelations.

And again, after a heart-rending meditation on the scourging, from Isaiah,

Surely He has borne our griefs and carried our sorrows ...

and

All we like sheep have gone astray ...

we turn to fierceness again as though it is hard to sustain a quiet sorrowful mood, and the tenor and the chorus sing, from the Psalms,

All they that see Him shall laugh Him to scorn: they shoot out their
lips and shake their heads saying
He trusted in God that He would deliver him; let Him deliver him if
He delight in him.

How fierce the music is. Our momentary consciousness of sorrow and grief for sin, "surely He has borne our griefs and carried our sorrows", turns into rage and finds its outlet in the condemnation of others.

Bach takes a different line. He touches on cruelty or hate or self-deception with sorrow and shame; the consciousness of having these things in his own heart seems to weigh on his music. He identifies the bad actions of others with what is bad in his own heart. He does not use texts which isolate the badness of others as different from his own. He is as aware of sin as Handel is, but more conscious of himself as a sinner and so, when the subject comes up, it is linked with sorrow and with the hope of forgiveness, more than with anger. Thus, when Judas' betrayal is spoken of, Bach's reaction is

Break in grief, thou loving heart.

And the choir, which just then represents the congregation reliving the Passion events, sings

'Tis I, whose sins have bound Thee,
With anguish now surround Thee ...

and

The torture Thou art feeling,
Thy patient love revealing,
'Tis I should bear it, I alone.

And after the story of Peter pretending three times that he does not
belong to the group of disciples, and then hearing the cock crow as
foretold, when he goes out and weeps bitterly at his betrayal, the
music and the words combine to remind the congregation of their
own betrayals; so there is no great burst of indignation and self-
righteousness. Instead, the congregation sings:

Lamb of God I fall before Thee
Humbly trusting in Thy cross.
That alone be all my glory,
All things else I count but loss.

Bach's congregation is encouraged to identify with Peter and does
not rail against him. The depressive position, we might say. And
again, in the terrible story where Jesus appears before Pilate and we
do get opposing sides, with Pilate on the one hand and the crowd
on the other, the crowd, in that heart-stopping moment when Pilate
asks which prisoner he should free in honour of the Passover,
shouts BARABBAS, and "Let him be crucified". At that moment,
Bach's congregation is not allowed to explode into indignation, but
sings:

Oh wondrous Love that suffers this correction!
The shepherd dying for his flock" protection,
And they betray Him.

There is an exception, which is comforting to those of us who are
not as forgiving as Bach usually seems. In the story of Jesus' arrest,
the soldiers, and the elders and the usual nosy mob, come and grab
Jesus and arrest him. Bach's first response is a sad aria:

Behold my saviour now is taken ...

But then the choir bursts in with loud anger:

Have thunder and lightning their fury forgotten!

Also, to be fair, Handel does have some very tender passages, where the second person is used very touchingly, as in the passage from Isaiah,

> Comfort ye, comfort ye, my people,

and later, in another very tender aria,

> Come unto Him all ye that labour.

How Bach and Handel match words and music

Words communicate and music communicates. Some things are best expressed verbally, some things are best expressed musically. Sometimes the two together are irresistible and add to our insight. In Handel's *Messiah*, the prophet Haggai is quoted as warning the people of Israel: the Lord of Hosts will shake all nations.

> Thus says the Lord of Hosts:
> Yet once a little while and I will shake
> The heavens and the earth, the sea and the dry land,
> And I will shake all nations.

Here the instruments and the bass solo shake, fiercely, repeatedly. And the alto solo sings in response, quoting the prophet Malachi,

> Who may abide the day of His coming?
> And who shall stand when he appeareth?
> For He is like a refiner's fire.

And in many, though oddly not all, musical interpretations, the flames can be heard: zzz zzzz go the strings.

Later in the narrative, when the chorus, prompted by Isaiah, acknowledges its transgressions—

> All we, like sheep, have gone astray,
> We have turned, each one, in his own way—

we can hear the music wandering like the straying sheep over the hillside. In Handel's *Messiah* we can hear the instruments and the singers express Handel's anger at this straying. Elsewhere, sheep stray more delightfully and innocently, as in Haydn's *Creation* and in Bach's "Sheep may safely graze", yes, safely, for "flocks in pastures green abiding, safely with their Shepherd rest".

Bach can match words and tune, fact and emotion as felicitously as Handel, though his emotions and words may differ from Handel's. In the *St. Matthew Passion*, when Peter hears the cock crow, and realizes that he has been disowning his discipleship, he leaves the house, weeping bitterly, and we can hear the violin weeping bitterly around the words:

> Have mercy on me, Lord.
> Regard my bitter weeping.

But what Bach also does, is to have the music descant on the meaning, not just harmonize with it. This allows the music to comment, and to suggest meanings not carried by the words. When this happens, something changes in our perspective. Just as Bach accepts and acknowledges the shadow side of our human potential by identifying it in himself, thus providing a larger context in which events may be evaluated, so his musical associations give us room for more varied reflection. For instance, when we listen to Bach's musical comment on the woman who poured the precious ointment over Jesus' feet, the words are about sorrow, penitence and penance:

> Grief for sin, grief for sin
> Rend the guilty heart within.
> May my weeping and my mourning
> Be a welcome sacrifice.

The text is grave, the words very serious, but musically a joyful descant, a charming graceful dance-tune, starts halfway through the aria. For Bach, joy is inextricably associated with repentance, forgiveness, sacrifice—the sacrifice, in this context, may well be the giving up of self-righteousness.

Perhaps the most moving example of the music descanting on the words' meaning is Bach's treatment of Jesus' words at the Last Supper. Jesus is talking about shedding his blood for the disciples; allusively, he is talking about dying, and he says he will not drink wine again in this world. The words, and the way they are sung, are deeply solemn, for this was for long the major sacrament of the Christian churches. At the most solemn moment, which historically marks the consecration, "This is My Body", there is that little tune, dancing. The strings are celebrating.

Transparency and quiddity, words and music

We can take this difference between Bach and Handel a step further. We are exploring two musicians' manner of relating to the ineffable, the mystical regions of their experience of life, and noting that they differ in particular ways. We are working towards an under-standing of the "quiddity and transparency" of this chapter's title. We have noted that Handel focuses on the particular, the good behaviour of some and the bad behaviour of others who need correcting: Handel's perspective is active, interventionist, direct, and so is Handel's God, engaged in the day-to-day righting of wrongs. Bach's focus is wider: he sees not only the wrong-doings of the wrong 'uns, he sees how widespread wrongdoing is, and so insidious that it appears to him a general human characteristic. He presents God as a universalist too, one who relates to the whole human race and does not take sides. Bach reacts to right and wrong actions as surface phenomena, and this leads him to look more deeply into the human heart.

Handel tends to come across as reacting more immediately to the surface of life. Joseph Haydn, fifty years after Handel's *Messiah*, accomplished the same in his oratorio *The Creation*. In the Second Part, the angel Raphael describes the creation of the animals, and each named animal is accompanied by one or two bars of descriptive music. "Vor Freude brüllent steht der Löwe da"—There is the lion roaring his joy, and then we hear the roar. We have a slinking tiger next, slinking to music; we hear some bravely trotting horses in a trotting rhythm, followed by a deer scarcely noticeably flitting through the trees, then some cattle browse accompanied by a yodel or two, soft sweet-natured sheep rambling, and insects humming and zooming, and then, deep in the earth, some worms, surely giant worms, looping and weaving.

With Haydn and with Handel, we glory in a sensual experience. We identify with how we imagine it feels to be that lion, that worm, that whale; we glory in the actual, the is-ness, the thus-ness our senses report to us. We may call this their quiddity, from the Latin "quid"—this, thus. Quiddity is a good medieval word, though I would be as happy to stay with Anglo-Saxon "this-ness", thus-ness".

Bach appreciates quiddities, these sensory accompaniments of glory in nature, but he seems to see beyond them to some other glory that draws him on. For Bach, the wonders of the world are transparent windows through which he sees something at least as splendid beyond. What he sees, what we may see when a thing is transparent in this sense, is what is beyond verbal consciousness, beyond what may be achieved by the rational organization of sensory input, though not beyond poetry. The sense of the transparency of the everyday world, which directs the attention to "something beyond" is, in my view, at the heart of most mystical experiences Western, Eastern, divinely or naturally inspired, in whichever way it may be categorized.

> Two men looking at a pane of glass
> One sees dirt and the other sees stars.

Perhaps that is an oversimplification. Should we have three men facing the glass? One seeing dirt, another seeing stars—he looked *through* the glass—and one looking at and seeing the glass and saying to himself "what a wonderful substance is this glass, let's write a cantata about it"—that is quiddity. That is Handel. He rejoices in creation, in creatures. We may say that Handel tends more to celebrate the world as it appears to our senses and our intellect, and Bach tends more to see that world as transparent and to celebrate what he can see through it, beyond.

The concept of quiddity

The *Penguin Dictionary of Philosophy* (Mautner, 1997) has the entry " 'quiddity' from the Latin 'quidditas', 'whatness', n., what a thing is, its essence". The concept of quiddity goes back to Porphyry in ancient times, and was used in the Middle Ages. Thirteenth-century Duns Scotus gives it eminence as referring to the individual essence of a thing, appertaining to the question "What is it?" (*Quid est?* in Latin). The concept refers to the apprehension of a particular thing, *this* mountain, *this* horse, *this* child, often by contrast to the appreciation of mountains in general, horses, children, etc. To love a thing for its quiddity is to love a thing for its individual characteristics rather than its more general qualities. "Quiddity" passed from the Latin into the English language, first appearing, according to the *Shorter Oxford English Dictionary*, in 1539. This *Dictionary* also gives us an illustrative quote from De Quincy in the late eighteenth century: "The quiddity of poetry as distinguished from prose". Quiddity's scholastic companion "haeccity" never made it into English.

Gerard Manley Hopkins

Quiddity and haeccity were contentious topics in mediaeval discussions about the nature of reality, and the poet Gerard Manley Hopkins would have encountered these concepts during his Jesuit training. W. H. Gardner, who edited much of Hopkins' work, writes that

> in 1872, while studying mediaeval philosophy ... Hopkins came across the writing of Duns Scotus, and in that subtle thinker's *Principles of Individuation* and *Theory of Knowledge* he discovered what seemed to be a philosophical corroboration of his own private theory of *inscape* and *instress*. [Gardner, 1953, p. xxiii]

In this useful introduction to his selection of Hopkins's work, Gardner writes that Hopkins was always looking for the law or principle that gave an object "its delicate and surprising uniqueness". This was for Hopkins "a fundamental beauty which is the active principle of all true being, the source of all true knowledge and delight". Clive Bell called it "significant form"; Hopkins called it "inscape"—"the rich and revealing oneness of the natural object" (pp. xx–xxiv). In this chapter, I call it quiddity.

Later, James Reeves, another Hopkins scholar, was to write more succinctly, because there had been more time to get used to these new perspectives:

> "Inscape" is, broadly speaking, the individual and characteristic form which characterises the God-given uniqueness of a particular object or landscape, while "instress" is the intrinsic power stemming from the divine, which sustains and encompasses it, as

well as providing the communication between the observer and the observed. [Reeves, 1994, p. xii]

It looks as if quiddity provides inscape, while transparency is nearer instress. For Hopkins, quiddity and transparency are not exclusive of one another. He celebrates both. Fine things are what they are because God created them so. (We have to use theist idiom here, and often Christian idiom, because Hopkins does. It is an aspect of quiddity, of this-ness, that one has to use words at all, and this Christian idiom is the generally known one in Western culture—but it is worth emphasizing that the ideas presented here are available in other theologies and philosophies as well.) For Hopkins, appreciating a thing would lead the beholder to the thing's creator, so the thing has transparency as well. Thus in "Pied Beauty" he appears at first wholly lost in love for the world's quiddity:

> For rose-moles all in stipple upon trout that swim;
> Fresh-firecoal chestnuts-falls, finches' wings. [Hopkins, 1953]

This is a beauty all of us can see, certainly once it has been put into such words. In addition, all these beautiful things are transparent to Hopkins: in his tradition they point to a God who made these beautiful things. In another poem he writes that the world is charged with the grandeur of God, "It will flame out, like shining from shook foil". The world is charged, here, as a thing is charged with electricity, crackling with God.

Normally, Hopkins pays full homage both to creatures and to their transparent possibilities, sometimes first the one and then the other, sometimes integrally. "Pied Beauty", is an early poem, and we find the two sequentially. First, quiddity:

> Glory be to God for dappled things—
> For skies of couple-colour as a brinded cow;
> For rose-moles all in stipple upon trout that swim;
> Fresh-firecoal chestnut-falls; finches' wings.

Then, at the end of the poem, the transparency of all these things breaks upon us with poetic unexpectedness. All those beautiful things, beautiful in themselves, these, thus, are also transparent to Hopkins, charged with the God beyond.

He fathers-forth whose beauty is past change:
Praise him.

In "The Kingfisher" Hopkins integrates quiddity and transparency. First the glory of the world as it is, this, thus:

As kingfishers catch fire, dragonflies draw flame;
As tumbled over rim in roundy wells
Stones ring; like each tucked string tells, each hung bell's
Bow swung finds tongue to fling out broad its name ... [Hopkins, 1953]

He is clearly rejoicing here in things as they are, and he goes on to say so explicitly:

Each mortal thing does one thing and the same:
Deals out that being indoors each one dwells;
Selves—goes itself; *myself* it speaks and spells,
Crying *What I do is me: for that I came.*

But then Hopkins goes beyond that. The quiddities point to what he sees beyond, to what they are crackling with; they can be transparent. "I say more", he writes:

I say more—the just man justices;
Keeps grace ...

Inside each self is something beyond itself, like justice, like grace, and another reality still more deeply beyond: since "the just man justices and keeps grace", he

Acts in God's eye what in God's eye he is—
Christ.

As the Quakers say, there is that of God in every man: one gets here again that large inclusiveness that also characterized Bach. Hopkins, in a quite orthodox Christian way, maintains that this is what God sees when God looks at us, so the just man justices and

Acts in God's eye what in God's eye he is—
Christ—for Christ plays in ten thousand places,
Lovely in limbs, and lovely in eyes not his
To the Father through the features of men's faces.

C. P. Snow, a contrast

For contrast, we may take a brief look at a master of quiddity, C. P. Snow, who builds up his characters and plots through a myriad of detail: "this", "thus", like a coral reef, no word pointing much beyond itself, but the whole much more than the sum of its parts. In the early pages of *The Masters*, an academic lawyer, the narrator, describes two Fellows of his College.

> They were both genuinely humble men ... neither thought that he was anything out of the ordinary. They knew that others round them were creative, as they were not; Chrystal had once been a competent classic, was still a first-rate teacher, but had done nothing original—Brown wrote an intricate account of the diplomatic origins of the Crimean war soon after he graduated, and then stopped. They did not even think that they were unusual men. ...

> Between them, they knew all the craft of government. They knew how men in college behaved, and the different places in which each man was weak, ignorant, indifferent, obstinate, or strong. They never overplayed their hand; they knew just how to take the opinion of the college after they had settled a question in private. They knew how to give way. By this time little of importance happened in the college which they did not support.

> They asked very little more for themselves. They were neither of them ambitious; they thought they had done pretty well. They were comfortable and happy. They accepted the world around them, they believed that it was good that the college should exist, they had no doubt they were being useful in the parts they played. As they piloted their candidate through a fellowship election, or worked to secure this benefaction from Sir Horace, they gained the thrill that men feel at a purpose outside themselves ...

> ... I had never seen a pair of men more fitted for their chosen job. They were loyal to each other in public and private. If they brought off a success for the college, they each had a habit of attributing it to the other. Actually, most men though that, of the two, Chrystal was the dominating spirit. He had a streak of fierceness, and the manifest virility which attracts respect—and at the same time resentment—from other men. He also possessed the knack of losing his temper at the right moment, which made him more effective in committee. He was urgent and impatient and quick to take offence.

He gave an immediate impression of will, and many in the college used to say: "Oh, Chrystal will bring Brown with him".

I did not believe it. Each was shrewd but Brown had the deeper insight. I had seen enough of both to be sure that, in doubt or trouble, it was Chrystal who relied on the stubborn fortitude of his friend.

"How much is it likely to be?" I asked. They glanced at each other. They thought I knew something about men, but was altogether too unceremonious in the way I talked of money.

"Sir Horace hinted", said Chrystal, with a suspicion of hush in his voice, "at £100,000. I take it he could sign a check for that himself and not miss it".

"He must be a very hot man", said Brown, who was inclined to discuss wealth in terms of temperature. [Snow, 1952, pp. 33–34 in the 1956 Penguin edition of C. P. Snow *The Masters*.]

We are getting just a touch of Dickens there, always a temptation to lovers of quiddity, and Snow strives for naturalism conveyed through quiddity. Snow's accounts of the surface of things, and indeed Dickens's accounts, are so multi-faceted that the characters, their reactions and ways of relating, are both unexpected and expected. Snow is a master of quiddity, but by the use of so many facets he points our attention beyond; we go beyond the detail to the character himself. Thus at length the effect, built up by a myriad quiddities, has a transparent effect; the whole is greater than the sum of its parts, and so, as we proceed through the novel, we do see a "whole man" emerging. That this is not an inevitable process is shown, in my view, by Snow's less than felicitous characterizations of women, and it is interesting to compare him to a nineteenth-century author also interested in power relations described in the quiddity mode, Anthony Trollope, whose women seem to me to carry greater conviction. Roy Calvert is another character who never achieves whole-person status in my eyes. Either Snow's selection of Calvert's quiddities must have been mistaken or my psyche does not sufficiently resonate to them.

Snow's lack of recourse to conventional academic or clinical psychological categories in describing character has given rise to a

charge of lack of subtlety, but in my view only in the minds of those
too devoted to the "transparency" mode of novel writing.

Clinical considerations

What is the relevance to psychotherapists of the two trends
contrasted in this chapter? Intentionally or unintentionally, psychotherapists make decisions from time to time either to deal with
the this-ness and thus-ness of what the patient presents—anger with
a spouse, fears at work, anxieties when travelling—or else to deal
with the underlying processes of which the anger, fear, worry, are
examples or manifestations, causes or effects. One could say that at
any time, psychotherapists deal either with the patient's quiddities
or they treat these quiddities as transparent, leading to phenomena
that lie beyond them. Our psychotherapy training will have made
us variously responsive to our patients, pulling us in one direction
or the other. At the beginning of our career we might be tempted to
concentrate on one direction at the expense of the other. We might
concentrate on the quiddity of the actual events the patient is
relating to us, or, if trained in another tradition, we might
concentrate on the quiddity of what we believe to be going on in
the consulting room at that moment—the transference. Or, if trained
to be more drawn to transparency and what is beyond the this-ness,
we might occupy ourselves with what we guess to be the dynamic
drives, or perhaps the phantasies, behind what the patient is saying,
concentrating on processes we believe to be behind the patient's
choice of these particular things that are being said, processes of
which the patient is also as yet unconscious.

Staying at the level of concreteness at which the patient comes to
the treatment might be seen as first of all a form of respect,
validating the patient's experience. Confused and under-confident
people need to have confirmation that they are allowed to feel what
they do feel, and to describe it in the words that come naturally to
them. Patients who tend to experience in quiddity mode require to
be treated with tact, especially as regards timing, before they are
helped to look at the more unconscious or less easily uttered
underlying trends which their this-and-thus accounts may indicate
to the therapist's mind. Otherwise we run the danger of alienating

them from the day-to-day level of experience at which their
conscious life is lived.

On the other hand, staying at this level too long may keep
patients from understanding the more unutterable, less conscious
meanings that everyday events have for us below the surface. Yet
these underlying meanings are part of how we experience our lives,
and determine how we act and react. Patients' fears of getting into
waters too deep for them have to be respected, but patients are
entitled to reminders that they may be missing a grasp of important
trends in their lives.

While some patients will be presenting themselves as in general
more captivated by this-ness and thus-ness, others come to us
preoccupied by a sense of the transparency of things and events.
These patients are entitled to meet in their psychotherapist an
attitude of acceptance that there is usually more to events than
meets the eye, that there are meanings beyond everyday consciousness to be talked about and made more conscious and manageable.
Yet staying at this more elevated level for ever will impoverish the
patient's experience of the natural world, the world of creatures, of
easy contact with people and things, since the patient, following the
therapist's example, will not have much interest in what is
happening at the obvious sensory or everyday level.

We find a similar contrast in the ways in which clinical work is
reported. At one extreme we find punctilious quiddity: we know
almost precisely what the patient said, what the psychotherapist
said in response, and when, and how. At the other extreme we find
the patient described and presumably understood in the abstract
terms of theoretical formulations. At one extreme we may be left
puzzled about the reason why the therapist (or the patient) said
what he or she is reported as saying. At the other extreme we are left
wondering on what basis the psychotherapist arrived at the
conclusion he or she reports.

Finally, what should be the clinician's reaction to the patient's
explicitly spiritual material? Occasionally, patients bring a strong
sense of that kind of transparency to the session. It has to be faced,
no subtlety will get us round it. We do not know and cannot know
whether we are dealing with derivatives of infantile object-relations
or are learning something of someone else's encounter with
ineffability: experiences that remain stubbornly themselves and

irreducible. Just as a person may have lived for decades not knowing that a particular feeling was his or her way of feeling grief or anger because, in their environment, grief or anger was never expressed in this way or named, so a person can have experiences which may be variously described as being in touch with one's deepest self, as attending to one's breathing preparatory to meditation, or as the beginnings of awe and reverence in the face of an encounter with an Other. When patients bring a strong sense of this kind of transparency into their sessions, psychotherapists may treat such offerings either in terms of the unconscious as they have been taught to think of it, positivistically, or, if this seems to go against the obvious evidence, they may ignore what is being said.

Are psychotherapists allowed to consider the role of the ineffable, as we have been doing in this chapter? Once the question is faced, it is not so difficult to answer, provided we do not look for certainties or absolutes, and, particularly, provided we make an effort to avoid the ready-made oft-chewed responses of those who come at these questions from the viewpoint of religious controversy—either for or against. It is not the responsibility of psychotherapists to decide whether or not there is an ineffable reality out there independent of our subjectivity; psychotherapists have to avoid taking sides on this issue just as they have to avoid taking sides for or against a patient's spouse or boss or political affiliation. The psychotherapist's responsibility is to help patients explore, to free them for choices. The psychotherapist's views are to be expressed only in an extreme case, say to avoid a suicide or murder.

Steering that careful course, it may be said first of all that there is nothing too challenging in what we have been considering; it is consonant with our training whether strictly psychoanalytic or generally psychodynamic or attachment-based or academic experimental or perception-and-learning or neurological theoretical. Our methods rely basically on pursuing associations of ideas: that is the fundamental process we all work with. That notion is two hundred years old at least. Events experienced as having something in common, or close together in time, or space or the conceptual realm, tend to become associated. The association of ideas goes on all the time. It is what experience is built up from.

But we cannot tell from the association of our ideas whether there is a God or not, whether I am talking to God when praying, whether God responds to me, whether there is an Eiffel Tower in Paris or a crocodile in the airing cupboard. Pursuing the associations between ideas in the mind can only tell us what is in a person's mind, and that is what psychotherapists must work with. We know people differ according to the ideas they associate. One person easily associates the smell of roses with sad solitude in a garden, because of past experiences; another associates the smell of roses with blissful solitude in a garden, because of past experiences; yet another associates the smell of roses with the safety of a loved grandmother's lap. One person easily associates Mighty Otherness with God but does not easily associate God with everyday life. Another person, such as Bach, also associates God with closeness and intimacy in everyday life. Really, nothing of this ought to present intellectual problems or novelty from a clinical point of view.

It is perhaps more interesting to assert that psychotherapists ought to stay neutral in this debate, though of course supportive, while patients sort out their associations and inclinations. I do not think we always do stay neutral. I think that some of us really approve much more when patients have positivistic orientations, seeing it as a sign of health when patients do not rely on what they and we consider baseless phantasies to support the self. Freud saw it that way. But then, some other psychotherapists are pleased when patients do have a sense of something beyond, and see *that* conviction as strengthening the self. And, of course, there is a large category of psychotherapists who politely ignore any reference our patients may make to what they feel to be their spiritual life. But this needs careful examining too. It may be difficult to talk with patients about such experiences without committing oneself to either confirming or else denying these experiences' objective existence, but hardly more difficult than sitting with a patient who complains about their badly-behaved, or else their idealized, spouse, parent or child.

Currently, too many of us have been too ready to ignore references to this whole set of experiences, just as we for long ignored references that should have alerted us to the possibilities of sexual abuse in childhood. It is not that patients suddenly began to talk of this: it is that we suddenly began to hear what they might be saying. Uncomfortable, we left it alone. Such a stance cannot be defended for long. It is usually in our patients' interest if we encourage them to explore their feelings and beliefs in ample ramification, without steering them this way or that. We have no right to foreclose their exploration.

To the extent that we do foreclose on our own or our patients' explorations of experiences of transparency, we deprive ourselves and them, and our world, of valuable knowledge. Nineteenth-century positivism has been a valuable debunker of religiosity and sentimentality, but it has no business to hinder any exploration of experience, though we have perhaps allowed it to do so out of shyness, or because we had more urgent preoccupations, or whatever. Maybe we can do better in this century.

CHAPTER TWO

Methodology, language, focus, limits, assumptions, method

A sense of transparency is found in many cultures—a vague feeling not everyone has but almost everyone knows about, that there may be a veil, or more than one way of experiencing the world, or something to be contained that is bigger than the containers we have or are. Such feelings may have their origin in baby-experience—babies must surely feel something like this many times, not as yet having the equipment to conceptualize precisely—but on the other hand, perhaps there are also other sources for these intimations. At the start of the twenty-first century it may be interesting to go back over the centuries and consider some earlier specialists in mental processes, particularly mystics and poets, to see what they made of phenomena we think of in a post-Freudian psychodynamic way. Poets and mystics are more likely to have this sense of transparency, indeed perhaps that is how they became poets and mystics: the others may have been busy with other worthwhile pursuits. Many mystics were the psychological experts of their day, with a sophisticated knowledge of people; they were spiritual directors and counsellors. Their language, their concepts, their aims and interests, are not exactly like those used by professionally interested people nowadays—counsellors, psychotherapists, and psychologists—but, like us, they were trying to understand people. What did they see? And what theories structured what they saw? Where might they set us thinking new thoughts? What were they writing about that might escape us as incidental or unimportant or not our concern, like, say, awe? love? wonder? mystery? We can reduce their way of looking at the world to the bits our current theories can easily incorporate, or perhaps we can modify our theories to be more hospitable, more inclusive.

What have been some of the reasons for the relative neglect of this kind of material by later systematic thinkers? Besides a fear of being thought airy-fairy, I think we can blame the cruder kinds of nineteenth-century positivistic mechanistic scientism and indeed still earlier handicaps to meticulous thought. But before looking at these more epistemological reasons, it has to be said that one reason comes from the undeniable fact that some exponents of the spiritual life are repulsive. They literally tore the hearts out of living people dozens at a time and they burnt people alive saying it was for their own good; to this day too many of those in charge of publicly spiritual affairs pick bits out of their holy scriptures about sexual and other domestic matters, but not the bits about social justice and jubilee years, often holding forth with a smugness or a sentimentality that can drive other people crazy with irritation. But there are also more intellectually-based reasons, like misunderstandings about the nature of theories and the use of definitions, our preference for nouns rather than verbs, and our relatively poor vocabulary for feelings.

The nature of theories

Among the intellectually-based reasons for psychotherapists' neglect of the more ineffable experiences of transparency, is the fact that the growth of understanding has its own dialectic; in order thoroughly to understand one particular process we often have to exclude some other process from consideration, at least for a while, so as to free ourselves from its inconvenient presumptions.

Freud had to try hard to free the psychoanalytic from the purely fantastical; he set himself to be scientific, though no one at the time seems to have been very clear what made a procedure "scientific". But Freud would oppose anything that appeared to him anti-scientific, and, in reaction, many people more sensitive to transparency at that time declared themselves to be against the "deadening influence of science". For the sake of preserving what they saw as the scientific approach, the earlier Freudians (and their more devout successors) may have felt that they should not pay too much attention to love, wonder, and other ineffable experiences.

Ideas about the nature of theories have changed since Freud's day. Like other systematic thinkers, psychotherapists see patterns in at least some aspects of human experience. These patterns form the basis of theories, built up partly from our own ideas about life and partly from our selection of theories we have read or heard about and found congenial. These theories broaden the language in terms of which we do our thinking: this is how we come to favour certain words to think with. What I have no words for, I cannot say. Thus we are extended, but also restricted by the theories that enable us to think in an orderly fashion. Learning more languages, we learn more theoretical languages and this broadens our understanding and excites our imagination.

The more we talk to each other, the more we learn each other's languages, the more we use commonly agreed definitions and assumptions. We develop a common language. But soon this language, such a convenience to us, acts as a barrier which discourages other people from joining our exploration. People who come from a different starting point have a different perspective because they think with different concepts. And vice versa: the barrier is mutual. If we want to join a debate seriously, we have to learn a common language. If we avoid those who do not use our language, or whose language is alien and perhaps repugnant, we may lose potentially useful ideas about matters which are obscure to us, but which their language may have helped them to understand. Bliss, meaning, laughter, anything beyond common sense and the senses—the languages psychotherapists use at present do not allow much attention to such experiences.

Definitions

"Cats are not dogs". There is only one place where you can hear good things like that thrown off quite casually in the general run of conversation, and that is the bar of the "Angler's Rest". It was there, as we sat grouped about the fire, that a thoughtful pint of bitter had made the statement just recorded.

Although the talk up to this point had been dealing with Einstein's Theory of Relativity, we readily adjusted our minds to cope with the new topic. Regular attendance at the nightly sessions over which Mr Mulliner presides with such unfailing dignity and geniality tend to produce mental nimbleness. In our little circle I have known an argument on the Final Destination of the Soul to change inside forty seconds into one concerning the best method of preserving the juiciness of bacon fat. [Wodehouse, 1933, "The story of Webster"]

Before we discuss anything serious, we have to agree on the meaning of key words. One might have thought that nineteenth-century positivism, which has merits as much as shortcomings, would have put a stop to endless quarrels about what things "really" are, but alas we still need to be reminded that the name we give an object or a process is conventional—it is something we agree together, after we have talked about what we will call by that name and what we will not. We should have scraped off an adherence to the essentialist fallacy of the Middle Ages but no, we still find ourselves arguing about what love "really" is, what life "really" is. A waste of time, but the temptation is there, especially when we take an interest in ineffabilities. We ought to keep in mind that definitions are conventional. We agree them, we do not discover them.

We need to remember that nothing in nature comes neatly labelled: the cows do not walk about with c.o.w. stencilled on their flanks. Definitions and names are useful when it comes to defining the outlines or boundaries of the matter under discussion. Sometimes it is enough to agree that a cow be called a cow. Sometimes we have to be more precise: shall we call this here a cow, a heifer, or an Ayrshire? Some concepts, and some phenomena, are of such a kind that at some definite moment we have to say "Here is a boundary, a limit—overstep it and what you are pointing at needs a new name. It was a calf, now it is a cow. It was drizzling, now it is raining". Sometimes it is pointlessly time-consuming to argue too much about what we should call our cud-chewing friend in the meadow and we can just agree on a convention. But sometimes we have to work hard at a definition in order to avoid later trouble. We may have to make our definitions so carefully circumscribed that no serious or mischievous logician can trip us into inconsistency.

And all the time we need to be aware that, far less often than we assume, there may not be a nicely outlined phenomenon for us all to see the same way—and it never has its name printed on the side. Cats are not dogs but they carry no label c.a.t. As for an ineffable like love,

> love is more thicker than forget
> more thinner than recall
> more seldom than a wave is wet
> more frequent than to fall
>
> it is most mad and moonly
> and less it shall unbe
> than all the sea which only
> is deeper than the sea
>
> love is less always than to win
> less never than alive
> less bigger than the least begin
> less littler than forgive
>
> it is most sane and sunly
> and more it cannot die
> than all the sky which only
> is higher than the sky [e.e.cummings 1960]

This whole issue is further discussed in Chapters Seven and Eight—there are no pencil lines around things, around people, between people—much depends on definitions.

Nouns and verbs, words for things and words for processes

We can at times be ill served by the language we use to give expression to our experiences. For instance, many single words do not stand for one thing or one process but for more. A word is often a *bundle*, containing so many elements that a selection of them will suffice for useful communication. "Cleaning" is not one action but several, and for most purposes we do not need to know which particular cleaning activities the speaker may have in mind.

"Amusing" similarly has a number of diverse elements. "Dog" can cover spaniels, Dobermans, Pekinese. "House", "muck", "grieving", "deserving"—what we mean by these, what we have in mind when use the words, is, like a bundle of sticks, a bundle of feelings and thoughts. Of course, the more we want to understand, the more we shall want to look at many components or elements, to add, to qualify, to enrich. What is usually not useful is to spend time arguing whether this is "really" love, or should be in some other bundle.

Keeping in mind that sometimes bundle words are the best means of accurately describing something, helps us not to ask ourselves what a phenomenon "really" is, or whether it is "this kind of thing" rather than "that kind of thing". And not only that: what we are discussing may not be a thing at all but a *process*. Both the general climate of present opinion and the language of psycho-therapists tend to be in terms of objects, things, and not in terms of processes, and this can impair our sympathy with some ways of thinking, and is not always convenient for clarity. We are not always aware that we are discussing not things or bundles of things, but processes or *bundles of processes*.

If we are to speak about processes, we need sentences with *verbs*; nouns will not do it. And this helps our thinking in two ways. One: the more we use nouns rather than verbs, the more abstract we become. We do not walk away, we "take our leave"—what did we actually *do*? People no longer talk to each other, they have a conference; they do not play together, they have "quality time"— what do they actually do? By the same token, loving is an active process, not an abstraction. "Do you love me?" is a question that has meaning, so is "Is this a loving action?", and "Is this a loving person?". We may be able to answer such questions once we have agreed on definitions. But, "What kind of thing is love?", is too abstract to tackle.

For, secondly, we could talk forever if we do not agree to *operationalize* our terms: what activity shows an action to be loving? What processes are we talking about? The great ineffables may be a little less ungraspable if we think not in terms of things but in terms of activities.

Can we define God? What might be the problems? What could we agree on? In the Western tradition, God is thought of as a person and a person is not a thing, nor an abstraction, but a set of active processes, whatever else a person may also be. Formulations in terms of processes, of verbs, will direct our attention more to what people do, to what they say they do, to what they say about their thoughts and their feelings, to how they live and what they say about their life's experiences. These communications can to some extent be subjected to rational systematic examination. Instead of asking, "What kind of thing is, say, awe?" or "What kind of thing is God? How can we define God?", we might ask, "In what kind of experience or situation is awe involved or encountered?" and "In what kind of experience is God described as having been encountered?" and "How do people react when they say they feel awe, or meet God?" That will keep our focus within manageable limits and confine our attention to mental processes, some of which—in principle at least—we can subject to systematic study and rational discourse. It should protect us from controversy about matters that may be beyond our comprehension by definition.

> My brother kneels, so saith Kabir,
> To stone and brass in heathen wise,
> But in my brother's voice I hear
> My own unanswered agonies.
> His God is as his fates assign,
> His prayer is all the world's—and mine. [Rudyard Kipling's, "The Prayer" from *Kim*, 1901]

Words for feelings: category affects and vitality affects

Words for emotions are notably restricted by the culture. Emotions, we learn as soon as we learn another language, are not neatly packaged entities universally and uniformly recognizable like cats or dogs or cows. We come to recognize that many different experiences and combinations of experiences are covered by such words as love or God or agony. Also, different cultures collect different combinations of affective experience for naming: each culture has words for some emotional experiences that other cultures simply neglect and perhaps even remain unaware of.

In our culture, we have names for feelings like love, hate, fear, comfort, need, greed, longing, gratification, and many more. When asked how we feel we can say "happy" or "cross" or "alright". For greater subtlety we may use sensation-words like "blue", "sweet", "irritated", etc., using our culturally accepted words for aspects of colour, taste or touch to increase our descriptive vocabulary. We can thank poetry and music for supplying us with the means to extend our range of expressiveness yet further. We may also sigh, yell, groan, and gasp—and the mystics do a good deal of this—but even so there are experiences for which we have no words. We tend not to talk about these, having no language for them that communicates easily, and we may remain wordless and unconscious of them. They are there, potentially at least, perhaps even vividly, but, unaccompanied by conceptual or verbal processes, they remain unnamed and undefined, waiting for cultural recognition and definition.

The languages that psychotherapists use at present may not allow much attention to some important experiences, but every now and then someone finds new concepts to organize hitherto ineffable aspects of life, giving us verbally-labelled recognizable patterns of experience. We are indebted to Daniel Stern for giving us the concept of "vitality affects" to help us think more clearly in one such area. In our culture we describe our emotional experiences in such terms as love, hate, fear, hope, guilt, and so on. Stern calls these feelings *category affects*. For the emotions which accompany variations of excitement, variations in tension, and other feelings for which we have no single words, Stern uses the term *vitality affects*.

> What do we mean by this, and why is it necessary to add a new term for certain forms of experience? It is necessary because many qualities of feeling do not fit into our existing lexicon ... These elusive qualities are better captured by dynamic, kinetic terms such as "surging", "fading away", "fleeting", "explosive", "crescendo", "bursting", "drawn out", and so on. [Stern, 1985, p. 54]

Other possibilities easily come to mind: rhythm, shape, intensity, abruptness, closure. Emde (1981, 1990) suggests variations in constriction or limitation, and we may add variations in the sense of buoyancy, of well-being, or risk, or excitement, and so on; the new concept invites us to be inventive. Brazelton *et al.*, writing as long ago as 1974, wrote of amplitude, direction, variations in attention, variations in receptivity—these are vitality affects noticed before the time came to name them.

From an early infancy we have these feelings. We pick them up from others. The way mother pushes the pram, the way father carries the baby, the tones and rhythms of the voices that speak, all these tell the infant something about the world, and the infant in turn jumps and stiffens and relaxes and coos in ways which affect the world around it. We communicate with vitality affects as we do with words, whether or not we intend to or know about it. Here is, in fact, a means of communicating what may be difficult to put into words. The lion's roar, or my groan when you ask me how I am, may be communications worth a hundred words. That I groan tells you something, how I groan tells you more. Many things that are hard or uneconomical to put into words, may be communicated through intonation, body language, colour, or sounds.

Music, because non-verbal, operating with non-verbal meanings and a non-verbal logic, can more easily communicate the ineffable. Listening to music one finds oneself full of feelings for which there are no words, for which there is no name. We should be thankful for music, painting, dance: by their means what is verbally inexpressible has been preserved and not destroyed by "being put into words" like being put into a cage. Emotions lose something when packaged (Stern, 1985, p. 74ff.).

Vitality affects make non-cognitive patterns. They are not part of our language, so these qualities of our experience are less accessible to conscious thought. All this is relevant when we try to understand what mystics were describing and how we and they are handicapped in understanding what was going on with them. Indeed, psychotherapists have somewhat similar troubles because of these limitations in the words for what their patients are engaged in.

The scope of this investigation and its limits

Given the elusive nature of the topics to be discussed, how can we proceed to consider them in an orderly fashion? It is not possible in one book to do justice to the great variety of phenomena that might be included. The more representative the range of phenomena selected, the less justice can be done to detail. In any case, the phenomena one selects can only be studied from a limited perspective; this is how it is in any field that has no natural boundaries. For instance, nature mysticism has been largely omitted —though it is pleasant to quote C. S. Lewis on the topic here (without committing ourselves wholeheartedly to his perspective on the matter).

> If you take nature as a teacher she will teach you exactly the lessons you had already decided to learn; this is only another way of saying that nature does not teach. The tendency to take her as a teacher is obviously very easily grafted on to the experience we call "love of nature". But it is only a graft. While we are actually subjected to them, the "moods" and "spirits" of nature point no morals. Over-whelming gaiety, insupportable grandeur, sombre desolation are flung at you. Make what you can of them, if you must make at all. The only imperative that nature utters is, "Look. Listen. Attend".
>
> The fact that this imperative is so often misinterpreted and sets people making theologies and pantheologies and antitheologies— all of which can be debunked—does not really touch the central experience itself. What nature lovers—whether they are Words-worthians or people with "dark gods in their blood"—get from nature is an iconography, a language of images. I do not mean simply visual images; it is the "moods" or "spirits" themselves— the powerful exposition of terror, gloom, jocundity, cruelty, lust, innocence, purity—that are the images. In them each man can clothe his own belief. We must learn our theology or philosophy elsewhere (not surprisingly, we often learn them from theologians, and philosophers). [Lewis, 1960, p. 23]

Secondly, the book confines itself mainly to theistic experiences, drawing moreover mainly on Western Christian writers, with particular insights and blind spots. It gives no access to the treasures of the great Jewish, Muslim, and Far Eastern mystics—this compiler has heeded Gita Mehta's warning that we must not pretend to an understanding we do not possess.

> No one heeded Ravi Shankar when he pleaded with his audiences: "Get high on the *music*, it is enough!"
> Nothing was enough for those who had heard the sirens scream Turn On, Tune In, Expand your Mind.
> Alas, the mind can be expanded until it bursts, and when it does

there stands an Indian parental type saying, Oh yes, this is common mind-expansion problem, bursting. It has been going on in our country for about four thousand years. [Mehta, 1979, p. 29]

Friends brought up in Jewish or Muslim traditions, or who have adopted Hindu or Buddhist ways of thought, can match many of the insights quoted in the present volume and bring treasures of their own. But cultures are deep and complex processes that deserve more than an occasional learned reference. No disrespect is implied by either selection or omission.

Within the Christian tradition the book is impoverished by the lack, for a variety of reasons, of representative material on what has for centuries been called the Dark Night of the Soul, the shadow that is thought by many to be an inevitable companion to the experience of light. Beside the accounts of rapture and bliss, there should be explorations of doubt, emptiness, depression, and lack of feeling. But this task also has had to be left to other hands and other times, though an interesting chapter might have been written, starting from the premise that these grim episodes in most mystics' lives need not be attributed to God's direct intervention or purpose, as is generally thought. Might we, in the twenty-first century, call them depressions, or anxiety attacks? An argument might be developed that, until recently, neither the concept of psychologically-rooted illness, nor the concept of distress beyond the control of our conscious wishes, was available in the main stream of Western thought: everything used to have to be attributed to Providence or else to sinful disobedience. In those conditions, mental distress can only be understood either as the result of sin or as sent by a benign if mysterious Providence for our own good, and, either way, to be welcomed. The twentieth-century French intellectual and mystic Simone Weil (1950) suffered often from severe attacks of what she called "le malheur" (perhaps most appropriately translated as "affliction") but, in keeping with twentieth-century thinking, she did not attribute these painful episodes to God, as previous generations might have done. In physical pain, and unable to feel the presence of God as she had recently begun to experience it, she set herself to survive and await better times—she never thought of them as sent by God.

Another omission, less obvious in the current climate, may well disturb some practising Christians. There are no references to the redemptive implications of the crucifixion and resurrection of Christ, either on a personal level or at the interpersonal level in terms of what has come to be called the Social Gospel or, more recently, Liberation Theology.

On the other hand, also excluded is astrology, as it appears to lack the important human element of agency: to consider it would take us too far into psychopathology. In general, occult experiences, whether benign or malign, are excluded, though they might throw light on the psychopathology of envy, ill will, and ill doing. William James (1902) thoroughly documented those very wild shores of mysticism. The present volume draws mainly on writers for whom it is easier to feel respect.

Before the end of this sub-section it may also be appropriate to be reminded not to assume that mystical experiences naturally make people sensible rather than crazy or bad, or that they are for the educated and well-bred only.

> "Let us not speak, for the love we bear each other—
> Let us hold hands, and look".
> She, such an ordinary little woman;
> He, such a thumping crook;
> But both a little lower than the angels
> In the tea-shoppe's inglenook. [Betjeman, 1958, "In a Bath Teashop"]

One cannot make easy assumptions about the goodness or morally elevating value of ineffable experiences. The whole of *Under Milk Wood* (1954) is suffused with mysticism, as are many of Thomas' other poems, yet this major poet, like many others, lived his life in no more orderly or edifying a manner than the rest of us manage. The best that can be said for mysticism as a moral force is that it sometimes encourages people to adopt a quietist position which prevents them from allying themselves to violent religious, political or other mass movements. But quietism in the presence of major injustices may not have great moral merit either. And, of course, some very well-known mystics, sure of God's approval, have headed movements which permitted the most inhuman atrocities. Those with mystical experience cannot claim higher intellectual or moral or spiritual ground than others. But they have characteristics worth exploring.

Western, Judeo–Christian, assumptions

Most of the material in this book comes from Western culture, with its successive Christian influences, Catholic and Protestant, with Jewish influences woven in, and occasional Rationalist–Humanist or Anti-clerical tones. Each of these strands contributes its unique sensitivity both to the everyday world and to the ineffable. Other cultures, with their own sensitivities, may now be appearing in this complex web, and other writers are needed to explore these newer developments. What the source-materials of the present book have in common is a set of assumptions (or reactions against these assumptions) that there is—or is not—a God, whom we did not create but who created us, that there is only one God, and that God is perfect. This idea, of monotheism and a morally unassailable God, may be seen as a major achievement of civilization, though of the Middle East rather than the West—especially when we call to mind the very dubious preoccupations of the Greek gods.

Also, this God was until recently generally believed to be a person, not a natural or supernatural force or anything so vague: this God is a person, if rather different from a human person, and takes a personal interest in history, society, and people. In Western Judeo–Christian culture, people may believe in God, or not believe in God, but they have an ingrained notion that God should be well-disposed toward the human race, a person who loves, and until recently was also thought to hate and, from a while further back still, to be jealous. God is not thought to be a neutral, impassive, colourless person: God acts and reacts. God is not an impersonal force, God has a will and wishes and we think we should act on these and we think God should act on ours, or at least that he could if he wanted or thought it right. God has conversations with people. God is vulnerable when things go badly. God has purposes and intentions. God is thought of as a creator who wants contact with what has been created. And since God is moral, God expects morality from people.

It is characteristic of the Western tradition, taken for granted by Western mystics, that God is a perfect and loving moral person who loves people and can be loved by them, however imperfectly. All this is shared by the whole Western tradition, and much of it also by Islam.

Persons relate; the idea of a relationship is included in the idea of what it means to be a person. Indeed Buber, whose ideas appear at various places in the present book, maintains that relationship is the essential characteristic for being a person (see pp. 186–190). In the Christian tradition, there are relationships not only between God and God's creation, but also within God. This is not so very out of the ordinary, since the idea of a person in any case includes the idea of personality structure and personality organization. So God is thought to be a good father and God is also thought to be an obedient son who does what his father asks of him and this gives rise to a third element: in much Christian theology, the dyad Father–Son is thought insufficient to describe what can be known about the structure of God and so, thirdly, God is also the love between Father and Son, a relationship who is also a Person—the Third Person of the Trinity (see also pp. 140–144). It is interesting that the old theologians resisted the temptation to construe the divine personality-structure on the model of earthly nuclear families, though the pressure to do so must have been very strong at times. The Holy Spirit is not modelled on maternal lines.

A Jewish mystical tradition holds that from the beginning there was a female side to God—Wisdom—and in some Christian sub-cultures the mother of Jesus has since the Dark Ages been elevated to the status of mother of God, thought in some ways more approachable than the original divine persons, but the official declarations of the Christian creeds never supported this.

It may be said, however, that it is a matter of regret to many people that God is normally imagined as a male, not just as a person but as a male person (Clark, 1998). God may be more than a man, or a man as well as other things, but without a doubt most people in the West picture God as a kind of superlative male, usually quite old. The idea that God may as well be thought of as a mother has of late been causing anger and also distress in circles literate and illiterate alike. And as for the idea that the second person of the Trinity is as much a daughter as a son ...

The fourteenth-century Lady Julian of Norwich was an exception: in her prayers and meditations she seems to have had no problems in addressing God as Mother when motherly behaviour is what she experienced in her revelations.

What does Jesus, our true mother do? Why, she, all-love, bears us to joy eternal. [*Revelations of the Divine Love*, "About certain things in the previous fourteen revelations", Chapter 60]

Mother says it is going to be alright. You shall see for yourself, everything will be alright. [*ibid*. Chapter 63]

All shall be well, and all manner of thing shall be well. And it may be noted that when mainstream Western mystics describe their experiences, there is hardly ever anything in their descriptions (as distinct from their pronouns) which indicate that their God is gendered. There is rarely anything to make it unimaginable that on some other world that Person might be female, a mother, a Martian, or an elephant on Alpha Centauri, but in the Western Christian imagination, at the centre of the unseen realm, is a male.

Problems of selecting from so many sources, and problems of authenticity

Police, journalists, juries, psychotherapists, all know the difficulty of getting accurate accounts of people's experiences; we really only know what people report. Similarly we only know what mystics wrote about their experiences, or what was written down by those who heard them. I have worked on the assumption, which is open to question, that the least fancied-up authentic material is to be found in what these mystics, or those they talked to, wrote down when they were close to the ineffable experiences we are trying to understand better. By authentic I mean likely to have come from the heart and nerves rather than the head. Of course, everything we think, say, write, is likely to come to us in the thought-forms of the contemporary culture; nevertheless we probably get nearest to a faithful account of an experience from those who were actually there.

Not quite so uncontaminated, more vulnerable to being brought into line with how the culture determines that we should see, feel, think, are the later, more reasoned, accounts we give of what happened to us or to others. More vulnerable still to being streamlined in terms of the thought-forms of our culture, is what we write about our experiences, especially when we try to tell others how to behave if they want to have a similar experience, as spiritual directors sometimes do. Finally, there the later generalizers and popularizers, like myself, who may not have much experience of what they are writing about, but who are trying to make sense of it for themselves and perhaps for like-minded people who want to understand. Although these accounts are the least trustworthy, it would be a pity to exclude us altogether, especially when the writing seems to issue from careful thought, even if it is the thought of the later commentator. I find many of them admirable, moving, helpful, and sincere. Nevertheless, their accounts are most likely to be tainted by the intellect that told them how it must have been, drawing on history, drawing on theory, comparing, contrasting, and generally making more of a mixture.

Ninian Smart (1996, p. 69) has some admirably English pragmatic things to say about authenticity. He holds that the less general, abstract, or rarefied the language describing the mystical experience, the more directly descriptive of the experience we may assume it to be. In the same way as "I saw a white sail" takes less for granted than "There was a yacht on the other side of the lake", so "It was a dazzling darkness" may be taken to be a more reliable description than "It was the birth of the Trinity of the soul". This does appear a useful guideline in general, though there is no reason why Hamlet should not see his father's ghost just as it was described by Shakespeare.

But is getting a grasp of the phenomena no more than a question of getting our language sorted? How sure can we be that different writers are just using different words for the same phenomena? Smart seems very sure—

> The ways different people experience sex, a sailor in Milwaukee, a newly-wed in Ghana, an adept in the Himalayas, are different, but do we doubt that the basic sensation is the same? [Smart, 1996, p. 169]

I do doubt it. Admirably robust and pragmatic, Smart is here considering the relevance of the cultural context, and his answer is "The basic sensations are the same". Not everyone will find this answer altogether satisfying. Are our basic sensations really so pure and unaffected by our thought-forms? Can all agree with Smart's belief that our "basic sensations" of sex are the same in different moods, or with different partners or the same partners in different moods? And even if we do agree with that, would we agree that the "basic sensations" in encountering God, or any other ineffable, are always the same? That a major scholar should come to such a conclusion is a warning to the rest of us. If there are experiences that are ineffable, that is, if something about them eludes precise description, we must exercise discretion lest we theorize too confidently beyond unshakeable facts.

Perhaps the eighteenth-century rationalist Alexander Pope managed the final verdict best:

> Know then thyself, presume not God to scan,
> The proper study of mankind is man. [Pope, 1688–1744, *An Essay on Man*]

Or, in more modern idiom,

> Best not to theorise about God's features,
> But study our own ways and other creatures'.

CHAPTER THREE

To sing in the presence of a lion—
to talk about the ineffable

I n spite of the problems of expressing what we mean and
defining what we are talking about, we seem compelled to try.

Summer, thought Jachin-Boaz ... There is no magic; nothing and no
one to help me. Cool before the morning I must do it alone, up from
nothing, out of nothing. In his hand was the rolled-up master-map.
Across the street stood the lion ...

"No meat", said Jachin-Boaz to the lion. He turned and walked
toward the river. The lion followed ... Jachin-Boaz came to the
bridge, turned right, walked down the steps to the part of the
Embankment below street-level ... The lion followed. Jachin-Boaz
turned and faced him ...

"Lion", said Jachin-Boaz, "you have waited for me before the
dawns. You have walked with me, have eaten my meat. You have
been attentive and indifferent. You have attacked me and you have
turned away. You have been seen and unseen. Here we are. Now is
the only time there is ... There are no maps   No way back ..."

As long before, words appeared in his mind, large, powerful,
compelling belief and respect like the saying of a god in capital letters:

TO SING IN THE PRESENCE OF A LION

Jachin-Boaz was not trembling. His voice was firm ... He sang. [Hoban, 1974, pp. 187–189]

We may also be heartened by a quotation from Harold Searles' early book *The Non-Human Environment in Normal Development and in Schizophrenia.*

> My colleague Joseph H. Smith has made to me the following valuable suggestion: the very fact that it proves difficult to define the mature person's attitude towards the non-human environment is itself of deep significance; it may well be that maturity involves *a readiness to face the question* of what is one's position about this great portion—by far the greatest portion—of one's total environment, rather than fleeing to some pat explanation (such as primitive peoples' regarding this environment in an animistic light or modern-day psychiatry's predominantly assuming it to be only a frame for psychologically meaningful human living, rather than an—in many respects—integral part of such living). True maturity probably involves a large, livelong measure of open interest in, or seeking and questioning, the meaning which this facet of one's life holds. [Searles, 1960, p. 101]

But how can we talk about the ineffable? By definition we cannot encompass the ineffable in words. "Ineffable" means, in the words of the *Shorter Oxford English Dictionary*, "unspeakable, inexpressible, that which cannot be expressed in words". "Ineffable" comes from the Latin "effari"—"to speak out". "Whereof we cannot speak, thereon we must be silent", wrote Wittgenstein (1922). We can have sympathy with the inane babble that the Gospel writers attribute to Peter when he saw Jesus with Moses and Elijah in unearthly light on the Mount of Transfiguration. We may want to talk, but sometimes nonsense is all we can utter. The fourteenth-century author of *The Cloud of Unknowing* asserts repeatedly that, "He may well be loved, but not thought. By love he may be gotten and holden, but by thought never" (1961 edition, Chapter 6). Poets and mystics through the ages may have communicated their meaning tellingly, but if we want to do more logically connected work, we are apt to go astray. Some theologians may not have done too badly, but mainstream psychotherapists—except for Jungians—are only beginning to attempt the enterprise.

Our intellectual endeavours are handicapped not only by language problems and by awe, but also by the emotional impact of unfamiliarity. It is demoralizing to be addressing problems we have already discovered to be insoluble by ordinary rational approaches. Conventional logical thought becomes counter-intuitive, and we drift off, discouraged.

> "The cow is there", said Ansell, lighting a match and holding it out over the carpet ... He waited until the end of the match fell off. Then he said again, "She is there, the cow. There, now".
> "You have not proved it", said a voice.
> "I have proved it to myself".
> "I have proved to myself that she isn't", said the voice. "The cow is *not* there". Ansell frowned and lit another match.
> "She's there for me", he declared. "I don't care whether she's there for you or not. Whether I'm in Cambridge or Iceland or dead, the cow will be there".

> It was philosophy. They were discussing the existence of objects. Do they exist only when there is someone to look at them? ...

> Ricky, on whose carpet the matches were being dropped, did not like to join in the discussion. It was too difficult for him ... Was she there or not? The cow. There or not. He strained his eyes into the night ...

> If she was there, other cows were there too. The darkness of Europe was dotted with them, and in the Far East their flanks were shining in the rising sun. Great herds of them stood browsing in pastures where no man came, nor need ever come ...

> Yet ... suppose the cow not to be there unless oneself was there to see her. A cowless world, then, stretched round him on every side. Yet he had only to peep into a field, and click! It would at once become radiant with bovine life. [Forster, 1907, *The Longest Journey*, pp. 3–5]

Attempting a natural history of lions: monism and theism

To make a start, we may examine some of the categorizations that have found favour among the scholars, in their attempts to trap the lion in order to study leonine features. (Until the middle of the twentieth century, most "natural historians" took it for granted that you had to trap and kill your specimen before you could study it. With some honourable exceptions, the practice of studying live lions in their natural habitat—or living butterflies or flowers—is not yet a hundred years old.) To categorize living phenomena is not easy. Not only are we put off by the magnitude of what may be before us, it may also not be in their nature to be categorized by our senses. But John Hick's book *The Fifth Dimension* (1999) provides an interesting detailed and very modern example of such an attempt to establish that the cows are there in a context that accepts that we do not know much about them. It is a pleasure to read Hick wrestling with the problems of identifying for his readers what it is he wants them to address, and an added pleasure that he takes pains not to confine himself to Western Judeo–Christian nomenclature or phenomena. He uses such untendentious terms as "the Fifth Dimension", "Transcategorical Reality" and the "Real", avoiding "God" as carrying too many connotations now a hindrance to thought. For example:

> As well as being intelligent animals, we are also "spiritual" beings. I am using this term here to refer to a fifth dimension of our nature which enables us to respond to a fifth dimension of the universe. In this aspect of our being we are—according to different versions of the religious picture—either continuous with, or akin to and in tune with, the ultimate reality that underlies, interpenetrates and transcends the physical universe. [Hick, 1999, p. 2]

In a nutshell, he argues that

> The fifth dimension of our nature, the transcendent within us, answers to the fifth dimension of the universe, the transcendent without ... The mystics of the great traditions affirm almost unanimously that the Real is beyond human conceiving. It is ineffable or, as I prefer to say, transcategorical—outside the scope of the categories with which we think. It (though "it" is as inappropriate as "he" or "she") is what it is, but what it is does not fall within the scope of our human conceptual systems.

> This notion of concepts not applying to something is a familiar one. Philosophers speak of category mistakes. It does not make sense, for example, to ask whether a molecule is intelligent or stupid, because it is not the sort of thing that could be either. And nor is the Real.

Indeed, it is not a kind of thing at all ... So human language can
describe the various forms taken by the "impact" of the Real upon
us, but not the Real as it is in itself.

This impact upon us might legitimately interest the psychotherapist
(among others, of course). He concludes that

> It follows at once that the descriptions of ultimate reality treasured
> by the different religions do not apply literally to the Ultimate in
> itself ... They are personal and impersonal manifestations of the
> Ultimate as it impinges upon our different religious mentalities,
> with their associated spiritual practices, as these have developed
> within the great historical traditions. [*ibid.*, pp. 8–10]

R. C. Zaehner, at one time Professor of Eastern Religions at
Oxford and a Fellow of All Souls (yes, truly, a good joke, this), in his
book *Mysticism, Sacred and Profane* (1957), not surprisingly notes
transparency as one common element in many mystical experiences.

> The person who has had the experience feels that he has gone
> through something of tremendous significance beside which the
> ordinary world of sense perception and discursive thought is almost
> a shadow of a shade ... [p. 199]

For Zaehner, an experience of something transparent in this way
is associated with a sense of unity, of union, of merging.

> ... sense perception and discursive thought are transcended in an
> immediate apperception of a unity or union which is apprehended
> as lying beyond and transcending the multiplicity of the world as
> we know it. [pp. 198–199]

Within this general field, Zaehner identifies three different types
of experience. Simplifying grossly, there is Nature Mysticism—
experiencing all things in nature as being somehow one, without
necessarily involving a sense of divinity (p. 50), and Monism, and
Theism. According to a monist's understanding of mystical
experience, a person who encounters the All, merges with the All,
and has no sense of being separate: the person is of the same
material, as it were, though what is encountered and merged with
seems not to be nature as we commonly understand it. On the other
hand, theists consider that there is an encounter with someone or

something Other; there may be an experience of union but not of merging, and it is with an essentially Other. Zaehner contrasts theism and monism, respectively, seeing

> ... an unbridgeable gulf between all those who see God as incomparably greater than oneself, though He is, at the same time, the root and ground of one's being, and those who maintain that soul and God are one and the same and that all else is illusion. [p. 204]

Zaehner opposes those who obscure the difference, quoting fourteenth century Gerhard Ruysbroeck who, with practical good sense, objects that monists ...

> ... must think that they had reached the highest possible mystical state, what the Hindus call *parma qatih*, whereas they had only reached the state of self-isolation, of rest and "emptiness" within themselves. Believing this to be union with God, they were prevented from taking any further step because they believed there was no further step to take. This, for Ruysbroeck, as for any Christian, was manifestly absurd, for how, as Abu Yazid once said, could one ever come to the end of the Godhead? [p. 204]

Writing forty years after Zaehner, Ninian Smart (*Dimensions of the Sacred*, 1996, Chapter Four on "The experiential and emotional dimensions of the sacred") provides interesting descants to Zaehner's position and of course brings new erudition and argument to it, but he does not change the essential distinctions.

Ninian Smart, as well as distinguishing monism from theism, contrasts two types of experiences of the sacred also in another way. On the one hand there is the *contemplative* or *mystical* experience, which does not postulate an other and hence cannot be theist: there being no self and no other in the experience, the event must be "inner" and subjective. This is in contrast to the experience Smart calls *numinous*, which is an encounter and hence dualist and indeed theist. Smart has wider general knowledge than was available to Zaehner, particularly of mysticism beyond the West, but unfortunately it seems to lead him to play down some important features of Western mysticism. He maintains, perhaps too logically, that people in cultures whose mystical experience holds no concept of the Other can have no sense of encounter, let alone union or communion: they will only have a sense of the loss of a self-other (subject–object) differentiation.

Although they have some purchase on reality in the history of religions, both Schleiermacher's sense of dependence and Otto's sense of the numinous are ultimately too narrowly conceived. It is not easy to see the manifestation of a *mysterium tremendum et fascinans* as present in purely mystical experience, for instance in that of the Buddha attaining enlightenment. This seems a different phenomenon from the apprehension of the fearful Other such as one finds in the prophetic experience of Isaiah or Paul's vision on the Damascus Road. Putting the contrast rather crudely, the numinous experience so evocatively described by Otto as of an Other, while often mystical, is delineated as non-dual, as if the subject-object duality disappears. The one is *tremendum*, to be shuddered at, and the other is supremely serene. [Katz, 1978, p. 167]

Robert Gimello has commented on this distinction, and amplified it:

Numinous experience is of an encounter with a being wholly other than oneself, and altogether different from anything else ... gratuitous in the sense that those subject to it are not themselves responsible for its occurrence ... it is typically described as both overwhelming and self-authenticating.

The *mystical* experience by contrast is not so much an encounter ... as it is the interior attainment of a certain supernatural state of mind ... the result of the subject's own efforts in following a certain contemplative discipline or method. [Gimello, 1978, p. 172]

These are interesting arguments but perhaps they illustrate the dangers of being captivated by questions of definition and classification; they are perhaps too severely, too unimaginatively logical about the probably inevitable imprecision with which people experience their feelings and use their words. To build our knowledge of the world too assertively on the foundation of a couple of concepts we ourselves have just constructed could be futile. We shall never get acquainted with the lion by caging him in categories. Mystics of all kinds write of their experiences in terms of, say, plenitude and emptiness, in the same short paragraph, without a care for terminological contradictions. In my view, this is necessarily so, and this whole discussion is an example of how irresistible it is to go on being logical about events that cannot be pinned down one way or the other. Studying them is legitimate;

coming to conclusions purporting to be logical, is not always so. In an enchanting if laborious paper in the same volume, Katz (1978) considers to what extent or in what sense we can say that the experience of one mystic is like—or even has something in common with—the experience of another. He comes to the conclusion that, "what we say about mystical experience cannot be made to prove anything about the natural world" (p. 177).

My Lion? Yours? Ours? Positivism and other stances

A colleague wrote to me:

> As I see it, the problem of making the psychoanalytical world safe for mysticism is fascinating. Can something seen in the consulting room as a reaction to deprivation or trauma be the springboard to a valuable experience which the well-structured Freudian ego, built around good experiences and objects in childhood, cannot reach?

> One of the main problems about a discussion of mysticism—particularly in its more ecstatic forms—in a psychoanalytical context is that many people see it as divine madness, i.e. as pathological; either manic, psychotic, hysterical (with sexual implications) or narcissistic, with God as a projected grandiose self, or as a regressive collapse of the ego into the original fusion state before differentiation. Can a genuine mystical experience exist? The Martin Buber experience, it might be argued, is far more real. A horse is Out There, God is in your head, mystics just relate to themselves, the argument goes.* And they might continue: the whole psychoanalytical project is aimed at helping the patient develop a relationship with the world, at growing away from overcathected subjectivity of the sort typified by mysticism. [Robert Royston, private communication, February 1997]

This is indeed one of the problems: Did we create the Other in the course of thinking about our ineffable experiences, or did God create us and is that why we get these intimations? If we are to understand other people's experiences this must be left an open question, lest we use the wrong criteria in judging the accuracy of

---

*Buber's experience with the horse is to be found on pp. 236–237.

their reports. Naturally the more religiously oriented would tend to assume that mystical experiences have to do with encounters with an Other, and the positivistically oriented would assume such experiences to be the outcome of something that happened exclusively in a person's mind, no "Other" being involved. Zaehner's enthralling book painstakingly analyses similarities and differences between these possibilities. In his introduction, Zaehner declared himself a believer, having converted to Roman Catholicism in 1946 (p. xiii). Scholarly and respectful as a rule, he is nevertheless inclined to believe that those who have no Other in their experiences are all rather alike, whether they are poets like Wordsworth and Jefferies, or people experimenting with drugs, or afflicted with a mental disorder; he starts his chapter on "Integration and Isolation" with a fairly tendentious pronouncement:

> In our study of nature mysticism we have been forced to the conclusion that this experience is, if not identical with the "manic" state in the manic-depressive psychosis, then at least it is its second cousin. [Zaehner, 1961, p. 106]

Actually, this sentence does not do justice to the painstaking pages preceding this odd excursus, but even in the more careful earlier pages, he does not allow for the possibility that there are states of mind—under the influence of stress, drugs, madness or other as yet unidentified "transports"—when our normal defences against Lions are weakened. An interesting reflection comes from Karen Armstrong, a very articulate modern scholar who spent years in a convent but eventually left it; she wondered, at the end of her auto-biographical *Beginning the World*:

> My neurologist once told me that people with temporal lobe epilepsy are often intensely religious. Certainly just before I have a *grand mal* fit I have a "vision" of such peace, joy and significance that I can only call it God. What does this say about the whole nature of religious vision? Certain episodes in the lives of the saints have acquired new meaning for me. When Theresa of Avila had her three-day vision of hell, was she simply having a temporal lobe attack? The horrors she saw are similar to those I have experienced, but in her case informed by the religious imagery of her time. Like other saints who have "seen" hell, she describes an appalling stench, which is part of an epileptic *aura*. Is it possible that the

feeling I have had all my life that something absolutely unimaginable but almost tangibly present, is simply the result of an electrical
irregularity in my brain? It is a question that can't yet be answered,
unless it be that God, if He exists, could have created us with that
capacity for Him, glimpsed at only when the brain is convulsed.
What I can say, however, is that if my visions have sometimes led me
into "Hell" they have also given me possible intimations of a Heaven
which I would not have been without. [Armstrong, 1983, pp. 237–238]

For our purpose, the focus has to be not on the Unknowable—
almost all authorities define God as unknowable by the intellect—
but on people, who are at least to some extent knowable, and the
way they have described their experiences.

What is a lion—really? A religious entity? A collective representation? What?

For psychotherapists there seem to be two main positivistic
approaches, plus Winnicott who, as so often, is at right angles to
every one else and has to be considered separately in Chapter Nine.
One line of positivism aims to explain mainly mystical moods, and
feelings of a *merging* kind. In the old psychoanalytic tradition, these
states are attributed to the infant, or to the mother–infant dyad,
whence these feelings are thought to have first arisen. And so they
may have. It is of course also possible to turn this notion on its head
and to speculate that these writers had experiences of a particular
kind that they could only conceptualize or put into words by
projecting them on to the defenceless infant of their phantasy, who
is in no position to contradict them. In considering ineffable
phenomena, one constantly finds oneself in this situation: either
there is something there, and that is why we have these inklings, or
we had certain experiences in early childhood and, catching up with
them in recollection, we are now trying to account for them in the
idiom of our adult culture.

The psychotherapists' other major positivistic line aims to
account mainly for the sense of *otherness*, and explanations tend to
be in terms of the more conscious parts of our mind being
confronted in a new way by something that had hitherto been
unavailable to conscious thought. This is the main Jungian position.

I tend to regard religious experience, in the first instance at least, as part of the "non-I" part of the Self entering or becoming known to the "I" part. [Redfearn, 1985, p. 48]

This, and similar views, are further explored in Chapter Nine.

More tentative but more detailed is the kind of positivist approach put forward by David Black (1993) who asks "What sort of thing is religion?". Current psychoanalytical theory tends to work with the concept of "internal objects"—imagined figures, shaped partly from memories, who people our inner world and carry an emotional and cognitive load. It seems an easily understood process.

If I am taken over by rage in battle and "cease to be myself", there must be another being, the God of War, who has inspired me. If I am overcome by sexual desire, Eros has controlled my limbs. If I panic in the lonely woodland, I have met Pan who presides over wilderness. The feeling precipitates the entity. [Black, 1993, p. 618]

The feeling precipitates the entity, a good positivistic notion. Black proposes that we should regard religious entities, such as the Buddha or the Christ, as internal objects that some of us create from what we feel about ourselves and others.

Like analytical internal objects, religious objects have a heuristic function but no material existence. Unlike analytic objects, they are derived from a definite cultural tradition ... They may be understood to have a function of containing the feelings, thoughts, and phantasies arising in individual practitioners, and of making these experiences comprehensible. These objects then enable the believer to speak more truthfully of, and relate more fully to, the larger world within which the human world is situated. [ibid., p. 624]

We do not, of course, experience internal objects as having been created by us; we experience them as given. Black calls them "instruments to think with". For some of us they appear divine, and Black suggests that they embody our need for something or someone strong and safe to contain and understand our frailties, our hopes, fears, and pains, which the people we care about may not wish to take on as roles for them to fulfil. Religious entities can do more than ordinary people can: they may forgive, rescue, even redeem. Black considers the evolution of people's ideas about the

Buddha; he concludes that the Buddha is an internal object that is experienced as accepting whatever is projected on to him, and thus a person can feel understood and recognised and accepted.

> ... Bion has spoken of the experience—a "disaster"—that a baby or a patient suffers if he meets an object which denies "the normal employment of projective identification" (Bion, 1967 p. 92). The tolerance and kindness of the all-encompassing central object of Mahayana Buddhism, like the "forgiveness" of the central object of Christianity, is a device that, in principle, allows everything to be acknowledged, with affect, and every sort of experience to be placed and understood. [*ibid.*, p. 621]

Black says we use internal objects as instruments to think with, and this puts him in a corner—a new, psychoanalytic, corner—of a larger sociological/anthropological field whose tradition goes back at least as far as Durkheim (1858–1917), widened and modernised in the 1930s and 1940s by Abram Kardiner and his school of "Cultural Anthropology". These positivistic sociological/anthropological theories recognize that, in every culture, people elaborate the shapes of their world, and attribute meanings to them.

Kardiner and his school were especially interested in the intimate correspondence between child-rearing practices and their effects on the ways in which a culture explains why the world is as it is and imagines the world beyond, to which the everyday world is to some extent transparent. Philosophical, religious, and moral ideas and feelings are distinctive parts of people's cultural heritage as much as their buildings, their agriculture and their child-rearing practices. Culture is what Durkheim thought of as the realm of "collective representations" and Kardiner and his school as the realm of cultural elements: facts of life that people would experience as external to themselves and given, facts they would be as powerless to alter as the weather, and yet entirely "in the mind". Accordingly, it is because of what Durkheim would call a collective representation that, for instance, people in our culture can recognize a gun as a phallic symbol. Freud did not invent this idea—he noted and remarked on it. Just so are bags and pockets evocative of female genitalia in more than one culture, and just so, in our culture at least, we find a pervasive general something that gives our psychotherapists the confidence that our patients' dreams might have sexual implications even before we have explored them in detail. Sociologists, following Durkheim, would give the term "collective representations" to such population-wide attributions of symbolic meanings. Other examples might be the Oedipal overtones of all triangular forms, and the significance of the female breast as the source of goodness. But consider also Simone Weil's conclusion:

> Foolish as the theory of Durkheim may be in confusing what is religious with what is social, yet it contains an element of truth; that is to say that the social feeling is so much like the religious as to be mistaken for it. [Weil, 1950, p. 15]

Is the lion an animal? A symbol? Either? Both?

Language is what we use to communicate, and to communicate clearly we need to agree on definitions. But if we define too strictly, or prematurely, or too concretely, we get stuck in unprofitable debates. Sometimes symbols, having less rigour about them, help our thinking. Might they help capture our lion? A symbol is "... something that stands for, represents, or denotes something else", says the *Shorter Oxford English Dictionary*. That sense of transparency, of something beyond the concrete, gives emotional impetus to our use of symbols.

> A symbol may be a word, a picture, a sound, or any other thing. What it is in itself is not important except in its capacity of being a vehicle for the meaning of the concept it conveys. In itself, it acquires a kind of transparency, so that we see through it to what is meant. [Wright, 1991, p. 90]

The nature and use of symbols has been discussed by philosophers at least since Plato. Rather more recently, psychology has begun to take an interest in this aspect of our communications. A good background history is to be found in Kenneth Wright's *Vision and Separation* (1991), which also makes some highly original contributions to the topic.

Psychoanalytic orthodoxy holds that our capacity to use symbols begins with the infant's experience of the mother (M. Klein, 1930; Segal, 1957), or perhaps rather more with the infant's experience of the absence of mother (Winnicott, 1974, pp. 13–17 and pp. 104–105; see also J. Klein's comments in 1987, Chapter 14).

According to Winnicott, the infant's sense of "something missing" gives it something—almost an idea, almost a concept, almost an inward image of wanting something that is not there. That experience, of something that should be there but is not, takes the infant out of a stream of events experienced one by one, into a world where it knows of an event that is not happening—the infant is experiencing the absence of what is desired. And thereby the process of symbol formation has started.

So there is a sequence of development and of gradual separation, from actually being with the mother in an unquestioned unproblematic way, to forming a notion of a mother who is present when needed, to missing mother when she is needed and not there, to expecting mother, recalling to mind the mother who is not there, and then to imaging the mother whether she is there or not. There may be a number of expectations or images of mother, each in a particular role and aspect. However that may be, the images or expectations of mother stand for or represent the mother in the mind. That is, they are symbols of her.

The fortunate infant, with a well-attuned mother, finds often that, at the very moment when the image of the mother arises in its mind, mother has indeed come. (For an elaborate description of this process, see J. Klein, 1987, Chapter Fourteen, on symbols.) The "hallucinated" breast of Winnicott's theory can coincide with the breast presented by the mother at the very moment at which the baby desires and imagines it. At that moment, infant and breast are at one subjectively, and almost so objectively. The symbol and the action are at one, writes Meissner (1994, pp. 389–390), a Jesuit psychoanalyst who considers this event to be analogous to the mystical religious experience. There is an intersect of two realms (see Chapters Eight and Nine, where, however, this view is examined critically).

Of course, this process allows for a lot of what statisticians call "error". The infant's imagery of the mother is likely to be much affected by what is important for the baby, so the symbol lacks whatever does not matter to the baby just then. Fears and hopes will creep into that picture, making it richer by all these associations, more and more part of one person's reality, but less and less part of what Winnicott was the first to call "shared reality". Much of psychoanalytic psychotherapy consists of teasing out these associations that have accrued around the mother, say, and distinguishing between what probably originated with the mother, and what probably got there by way of associated events. Associations make a symbol immensely rich, so rich and complex that it cannot be easily put into words. Moreover, the origins of many symbols lie in the time when the infant had no words yet, only emotions and bits of sensory experiences like sights and sounds and contact. Added to this are the consequences of all the vitality affects and attunements that never got put into words. We carry within us these complex unnameable mental entities.

Ritual

Ritual, relying as it does on symbolism, may be better than anything at communicating ineffable possibilities. Consider the devout orthodox Jew, his head enveloped entirely in his prayer shawl, for that moment alone with his God, before he arranges the shawl round his shoulders so as to be visibly a member of a visible community of men, all similarly attired. Ritual garments are a means of expressing the inexpressible. In other religious circumstances, based on other associations, there will be sounds—perhaps Gregorian chant, perhaps wordless yells—to convey solemnity, joy, exaltation and so on. Many objects, like statues, paintings and icons, and above all many physical movements like bowing the head, rocking, clapping the hands, genuflecting, kneeling and prostration, symbolise our connection to the Lion, and indeed often bring about a sense of contact and heightened awareness.

Ritual is not confined to the religious sphere. In our culture, as in many others, our possessions carry a symbolic burden. We make our statements less by bowing or wearing hats, more often by keeping our bathroom furniture up to date, treating our visitors to boars-meat sausages, holidaying in Thailand. The sense of significance and well-being that such things convey is unmistakably based on what these things symbolize. Whether a Lion is involved in these rituals might be interesting to debate.

Is the Lion for specialists? Via negativa and via positiva

Over the centuries, two traditions of mystical practices—two approaches to the Lion—have evolved in the West, one very much against bathroom furniture and boars-meat sausages, the other less bothered.

Via negativa recommends giving up anything that might distract the attention away from the Lion; the idea being that the Lion is so other, so difficult to approach, so fierce, that one has to get into training to venture near it. This leads to a class of Lion-specialists, a spiritual elite. The other perspective, *via positiva* or *affirmativa*, has easier and more casual access to Lions, in an air that may be breathed in a more democratic style. So, on the one hand, Andrew Marvell, in seventeenth-century London, gives us a sense of how easy and natural an ineffable experience can be:

> Here at the fountain's sliding foot,
> Or at some fruit-tree's mossy root,
> Casting the body's vest aside
> My soul into the boughs does glide;
> There like a bird it sits, and sings,
> Then whets and combs its silver wings;
> And, till prepared for longer flight,
> Waves in its plumes the various light. [Marvell, 1621–1678, *The Garden*]

On the other hand, we find the view that

> Mystical experience is ... only attained by the denial of all that we commonly call experience. A new world is discovered which is so different from our familiar one that all our words drawn from our ordinary and familiar experiences fail to describe it. They would seem bound in fact to give the wrong impression, as they make us think of what we know instead of this new unknown ... It could not be that experience if the words used to tell of it were common to it and what we already know. [D'Arcy, 1951, p. 4]

There are experiences we find it hard to put into words; we say that words fail us. How to describe a landscape ... the taste of a meringue ... our reaction to Solti's Sibelius? There is nothing morally meritorious in being able to describe a lion, though it is nice if one can do it and sometimes pleasant for others. But it should not be confused with being on good terms with lions. There is in general a tendency in our culture to confuse having an experience with being able to describe it in well-chosen words. A parallel may be seen with the situation of excellent clinicians who cannot put together convincing papers about their work, though their patients thrive. The rest of us lose the benefit of their clinical talents because we tend to privilege those who write impressive papers. It is a mistake easily made by intellectuals, to confuse the ability to communicate on any subject with the ability to perform or to be receptive or even to experience. And so with Lions: long ago the tradition evolved that you have to get into training to meet those.

The anxiety aroused by this kind of elitism may be tempered by allowing that there are experiences not easily put into common language. There need be no implication that a person is not good enough to appreciate lions. There is a Jewish tradition, commended by Buber (1946) for its realism, that Moses stammered; the choice of Moses as God's mouthpiece shows that perfection is not required for encounters between the Ineffable and the human. (I am indebted to another colleague, Estelle Roith, for this insight.)

The title of a fourteenth-century book, *The Cloud of Unknowing* (edited, e.g., by Clifton Walters, 1961), comes from the unknown author's belief that

> When you first begin, you find only darkness, and as it were a cloud
> of unknowing. You don't know what this means except that in your
> will you feel a simple steadfast intention reaching out towards God.
> Do what you will, this darkness and this cloud remain between you
> and God ... For if you are to feel him or to see him in this life, it
> must always be in this cloud, in this darkness. [*The Cloud of
> Unknowing*, Chapter 3]

This author presents a more benign form of *via negativa*: if you try to get to know God intellectually, all you get is a cloud. The author is not so much anti-enjoyment or anti-intellectual, as anti-obsessional: he writes to a perhaps notional correspondent who had asked how he might get closer to God that "He may well be loved, but not thought. By love he may be gotten and holden, but by thought never." (Chapter 6). Like other spiritual directors, the author instructs his correspondent—many mystics wrote in this instructional style—not to do this, or think that, or persist in the other. But then he corrects himself:

> Do what you will, this darkness and this cloud will remain between
> you and God, and stop you from seeing in the clear light of rational
> understanding. [*ibid.*]

Later he writes the same in a different context: do not direct yourself to God "up there", or "in here", or at any other location.

> Well, you will say, where am I to be? Nowhere, according to you. And you will be quite right. Nowhere, is where I want you. [*ibid.*, Chapter 68]

> Where another man might tell you to withdraw all your powers and thoughts within yourself, and worship God there—and he would be saying what is absolutely right and true—I do not care to do so, because of my fear of a wrong and physical interpretation of what was said. [*ibid.*]

And there it is. Experience of the ineffable depends not on how clever or good we are, but on quite other qualities, of which a hint may be caught here and there on other pages of this book, scrappy and self-contradictory though it is. Climbing mountains, making huge sacrifices, plumbing depths, studying hard, none are guaranteed to lead to one's Lion. Better to respect Bottom, the weaver in *A Midsummer Night's Dream*, hardly a sophisticate, not short on narcissistic traits, but too jaunty a character to believe in the value of suffering, able to accept good fortune when it comes:

> I have had a most rare vision. I have had a dream—past the wit of man to say what dream it was. Man is but an ass if he go about to expound this dream. Methought I was—there is no man can tell what methought I was, and methought I had—but man is but a patched fool if he will offer to say what methought I had. The eye of man hath not heard, the ear of man hath not seen, man's hand was not able to taste, his tongue to conceive, nor his heart to report what my dream was. I will get Peter Quince to write a ballad of this dream; it shall be called Bottom's Dream, because it hath no Bottom. [Shakespeare, *A Midsummer Night's Dream*, Act IV Scene I]

CHAPTER FOUR

The experience of the Holy:
Mysterium Tremendum et Fascinans

> Let all mortal flesh keep silence
>   And in fear and trembling stand;
> Ponder nothing earthly-minded,
>   For with blessings in his hand
> Christ our God to earth descendeth
>   Our full homage to demand.

Hymn from *The Liturgy of St. James*

A we, and pondering nothing earthly-minded, is a sponta-
neous response to the ineffable. But so is the wish to tell
people about the encounter, and how it felt. The opening
sentence of the *London Quarterly Review*, quoted on the inside cover
of the Pelican Paperback edition (1959) of Rudolph Otto's 1917 book
The Idea of the Holy (in German the title is simply *Das Heilige* but the
otherwise excellent English translator's culture-bound urges digni-
fied the subject into abstraction) begins:

> Before religion became "morality touched with emotion" it was the
> emotion itself.

Emotions were Otto's starting-point, making the translator's "Idea"

61

of the holy a contradiction of Otto's theme: *Mysterium Tremendum et Fascinans*. Otto identified some common elements in how people reported what had happened to them—they *trembled* as Dante did when he met Beatrice and understood that his life was to be transformed, and they were *fascinated*. Otto listed aspects of this experience: the sense of being in the presence of power and majesty, the awe and fear that spring from this, also the accompanying sense of energy and vitality and excitement, as in the presence of a lion, as in the first bars of Verdi's *Dies Irae*.

Otto began his investigation of our emotions by looking at an element that he called "creature feeling": "the feeling some people have that they owe their being, and every moment of their continued existence, to something or someone they therefore naturally stand in awe of". A famous example is St Augustine's exclamation to his God: "Thou hast made us for Thy Self, and our hearts are restless till they find their rest in Thee". It is easy for us post-Freudians to discern parent–child echoes here, feelings of "you-big, me-little"; "you-rich, me-poor", but that is not the point here. Otto came to the concept of creature-feeling via Schleierma-cher's concept of "dependence" (1821–1822), which Otto did not quite like. For Otto considered our response, when faced with something very other and very powerful—as it might be a lion—as so deep and strong and suffused with awe, that "dependence" is too human-scale an analogy, losing the essence of it, much as "fear" is a weak word for describing "awe". Also, Otto considered "dependence" a word to be used when our attention is on our side of a relationship; "creature-feeling" is the word to use when we are out of our depth faced with a lion on the loose, something huge and compelling that makes us tremble: *mysterium tremendum*. Isaiah trembled:

> In the year that King Uzziah died, I saw the Lord sitting upon a throne high and lifted up; and his train filled the temple. Above him stood the seraphim ... And one called to another and said:
>
> Holy, holy, holy is the Lord of hosts,
> The whole world is full of his glory.
>
> And the foundations of the thresholds shook at the voice of him who called, and the house was filled with smoke. And I said:
>
> Woe is me for I am lost ... for my eyes have seen the King, the Lord of hosts. [Isaiah, Chapter 6, vv. 1–6]

In a more recent idiom:

> Thou mastering me
> God! giver of breath and bread;
> World's strand, sway of the sea;
>   Lord of the living and dead;
> Thou hast bound bones and veins in me, fastened me flesh,
> And after it almost unmade, what with dread,
>   Thy doing; and dost thou touch me afresh?
> Over again I feel Thy finger and find Thee.

>   I did say yes,
> O at lighting and lashed rod;
> Thou heardst me truer than tongue confess
>   Thy terror, O Christ, O God ... [Hopkins, 1953, *The Wreck of the Deutschland*]

Mysterium is *tremendum*. It is also *fascinans*—fascinans describes the spell-binding quality of the bond. Fascinum, the *Shorter Oxford English Dictionary* tells us, is Latin for spell. To fascinate, according to the *Dictionary* is to "deprive a victim to the power of escape or resistance by one's look or presence"—"especially of serpents" it adds rather disconcertingly for the present purpose—and it thereupon also offers "attract irresistibly, enchant, charm". Chapter Five, on Love, will offer examples of the power of the Holy to captivate. *Mysterium* is hugely attractive, hard to turn away from once it has caught your eye. In his "Canticle to the Sun", St. Francis is just carried away, transported:

> Most high, omnipotent, Good Lord,
> Thine are all praise, glory, honour, and all benedictions.
> To Thee alone, most High, do they belong,
> And no man is worthy to name Thee.

> Praise be to Thee, my Lord, for all thy creatures,
> Especially Brother Sun,
> Who is our day and lightens us therewith.
> Beautiful is he and radiant with great splendour;
> Of Thee, Most High, he bears expression ...

and so do Sister Moon, the stars, Brother Wind, the clouds, the Weather, Sister Water, Brother Fire, and Mother Earth. St. Francis cannot stop talking for rapture (1964, pp. 127–131).

The daemonic-divine object ... allures with a potent charm, and the creature, who trembles before it, utterly cowed and cast down, has always at the same time the impulse to turn to it, nay even to make it somehow his own. The "mystery" is for him not merely something to be wondered at but something that entrances him; and besides that which bewilders and confounds, he feels something that captivates and transports him with a strange ravishment ... [Otto, 1959, p. 45]

Mysterium tremendum, and worship

Otto quotes from the Book of Job which in his view is

not so much concerned with the *awefulness* of the majesty of the numen, as with its *mysteriousness*: it is concerned with the non-rational ... , with sheer paradox baffling comprehension, with what challenges the "reasonable" and what might reasonably be expected, which goes directly against the grain of reason. [*ibid.*, p. 116]

These reactions chime with Otto's conception of the Holy:

It will be our endeavour to suggest this unnamed Something to the reader as far as we may, so that he himself may feel it ... the Hebrew *qadosh*, to which the Greek *hagios* and the Latin *sanctus* and, more accurately still, *sacer*, are the corresponding terms. [*ibid.*, p. 20]

Otto quotes Martin Luther on the experience of awesome majesty:

Yea, He is more terrible and frightful than the Devil. For He dealeth with us and bringeth us to ruin with power, smiteth and hammereth and payeth no heed to us ... In His Majesty He is a consuming fire ... For therefrom can no man refrain: if he thinketh on God aright, his heart is struck with terror ... Yea, as soon as he heareth God named, he is filled with trepidation and fear. [*ibid.*, p. 115]

For, writes Otto:

... that before which his soul quails again and again in awe is not merely the stern Judge, demanding righteousness ... but rather at the same time God in his "unrevealedness", in the awful majesty of His very Godhead; He before whom trembles not simply the transgressor of the law, but the creature, as such, in his "uncovered" creaturehood. [*ibid.*, p. 114]

Otto comments that this "is the absolute numen, felt here partially in its aspect of *maiestas* and *tremendum*", "the non-rational aspect of the Deity, which has no need to be subject to our ideas of or preference for rationality" (p. 116). Otto also warns us that all this energy and force must not simplistically be assumed to be moral, or, if moral, not necessarily on a human scale. Among our contemporaries Bion, Eigen and Grotstein (*viz.* pp. 175–178) illustrate this, as did much in William James' *Varieties of Religious Experience* (1902).

Luther, awed and terrified, put his hopes of safety in his faith in God's Grace, holding on to the belief that God will be gracious to His creatures if they put their trust in Him, whatever else may be true of *mysterium*. How else could a person survive in that Presence? Evelyn Underhill comments:

> Lutheran worship, originating in its founder's temperamental reaction to Reality, and conditioned by its historical and religious environment, still bears the marks of its descent ... Luther's subjective sense of sin and need, his craving for personal assurance, liberation, peace, his robust love of human life and revolt from monastic asceticism, are reflected in its emphasis on the Divine mercy and grace, the saving and releasing love of God, meeting his creature here and now on its own ground. [Underhill, 1936, p. 283]

and

> Luther, warm-hearted, vehement, uneasy, vigorously alive on every level, passionately desired to bring the supernatural grace and mercy within the reach of every needy soul ... For him the message of the Gospel was liberation and assurance, and worship was man's grateful response. Loving confidence in the Divine generosity was its essential mood ... [*ibid.*, p. 286]

It may at first glance be surprising that Underhill considers the uproarious overpowering sense of God's majesty compatible with the quieter and more unassuming kinds of holy living that Lutheran ideas fostered. But Underhill sets the great terror that God's majesty inspires in the context of the great gratitude people may feel when they learn that God may be safely approached under stated conditions.

> Such worship is essentially receptive and responsive. In it one aspect of man's relation to the Holy—his humble and creaturely confidence—is given adequate expression. [*ibid.*, p. 286]

Quiet, humility and modesty are seen as the expressions, in "holy living", of a cast of mind whose other aspect is "the adoring recognition of mystery, of the Inaccessible Light before which even the seraphs veil their eyes" (*ibid.*, p. 283). Underhill contrasts Luther (1483–1540) with Calvin (1509–1564):

> For Calvin, the supreme religious fact was God's unspeakable Majesty and Otherness, and the nothingness and simplicity of man. In the type of worship which he established, we seem to see the result of a great religious experience—the impact of the Divine Transcendence on the awe-struck soul—and the effort towards a response which is conditioned by a deep sense of creaturely limitation but deficient in homely and child-like dispositions. [*ibid.*, pp. 286–287]

Underhill sees Lutheran worship as relatively lacking in "the adoring recognition of mystery, of the Inaccessible Light before which even the seraphs veil their eyes", while Calvin lacked "humble and creaturely confidence", and "homely and child-like dispositions".

In his final novel, *Sick Heart River* (1941), John Buchan, a twentieth-century writer of exciting thrillers (we must forgive him the unfortunate cultural assumptions he grew up with—he was inevitably a man of his times) describes a man's conversion from the Calvinism of his youth to the rather more merciful creed we may consider nearer to a Lutheran view of the world, writing so simply and lovingly it is surely autobiographical. The stoic Scottish lawyer Leithen, one-time Attorney General in a British Cabinet, dying of tuberculosis caused by gas inhaled in the First World War, searches the Arctic wastes of Canada for a friend's friend lost in temperatures of minus forty. The passionate unconscious nature-mysticism alive in many of Buchan's favoured characters expresses itself in the quotation which follows. Leithen, apparently prompted by a change in the weather, finds he has moved has moved from *via negativa* to *via affirmativa*.

> ... The blizzard died away, and there followed days of sun, when a rosy haze lay on the hills, and the air sparkled with frost crystals. That night Leithen was aware that another thought had stabbed his dull mind into wakefulness.

> When he left England he had reasoned himself into a grim resignation. Life had been very good to him, and, now that it was

ending, he made no complaint. But he could only show his gratitude to life by maintaining a stout front to death. He was content to be a pawn in the hands of the Almighty, but he was also a man, and ... must die standing. So he had assumed a task which interested him not at all, but which would keep him on his feet. That task he must conscientiously pursue, but success in it mattered little, provided always he relaxed no effort ...

He had welcomed the North because it matched his dull stoicism. Here in this iron and icy world, man was a pigmy and God was all in all. Like Job, he was abashed by the divine majesty. He asked for nothing—not "nut in the husk, nor dawn in the dusk, nor life beyond death". He had already much more than his deserts: and what Omnipotence proposed to do with him was the business of Omnipotence; he was too sick and weary to dream or hope. He lay passive in all-potent hands.

Now there suddenly broke in on him, like a sunrise, a sense of God's mercy—deeper than the fore-ordination of things, like a great mercifulness ... Out of the cruel North most of the birds had flown South from ancient instinct, and would return to keep the wheel of life moving. Merciful! But some remained, snatching safety by cunning ways from the winter of death. Merciful! Under fetters of ice and snow there were little animals lying snug in holes, and fish under the frozen streams, and bears asleep in their lie-ups, and moose stamping out their yards, and caribou rooting for their grey moss. Merciful! And human beings, men, women and children, fending off winter and sustaining life by instinct as old as that of the migrating birds ... Surely, surely, behind the reign of law and the coercion of power there was a deep purpose of mercy.

The thought induced in Leithen a tenderness to which he had long been stranger. He had put life away from him, and it had come back to him in a final reconciliation. He had always hoped to die in April weather when the surge of returning life would be a kind of earnest of immortality. Now, when presently death came to him, it would be like dying in the spring. [1941, pp. 162–163]

Mysterium tremendum, quietism and holy living

The second millennium of the Christian era—until in the eighteenth-century the Age of Enlightenment channelled these dangerous phantasies into political channels—saw great outbursts of religious ecstasy and terror in Europe, and the kind of witch-hunt that the idea of a God beyond common morality and decency seems inevitably to inspire. In reaction naturally there spread a longing for quiet holy living as a proper response to the *Tremendum*, which was, after all, thought to be tempered by gracious condescension to human littleness.

This reaction, favouring a quiet life of humility and service, was of course not a Protestant invention—in the fourteenth century the Lady Julian of Norwich, and the author of *The Cloud of Unknowing* are among the many Catholic exemplars—but it was more visible in Protestant settings because people did not usually segregate themselves in convents to practise it. And an especially Protestant version of the quietist tradition prospered not long after Luther, among learned and unlearned both.

Lancelot Andrewes' domestication of the mountainous heights and steeps of Luther's vision flourished at the turn of the sixteenth and seventeenth centuries. Immensely learned, it was said of him that when he was a Fellow of Pembroke College, he applied himself to learning a new language every year. Andrewes contributed greatly to the *King James Authorised Version of the Bible*, and to the beautiful prayers in the Anglican *Book of Common Prayer*. In these, and in his own collection, *Preces Privatae*, he consistently directs attention first to God and away from self, and then on to what needs doing next, with much fine poetry and a sturdy disregard of the anxious preoccupations of *via negativa*. His tomb rests in London's Southwark Cathedral (Higham, 1952).

In *Preces Privatae* there are prayers for every day of the week, often beginning with a Prayer for Grace, i.e. for acceptance by the *Tremendum*, then perhaps a confession of having fallen short, then some expressions of praise and worship, and often an intercession for other people. Thus Monday's prayers begin:

> My voice shalt Thou hear betimes, O Lord;
>   Early in the morning
> Will I deliver my prayer unto Thee
>   And Thou wilt look upon me.
>   Blessed art Thou, O Lord,
> Who didst create the firmament of heaven ...
> The waters above the heavens, mists and exhalations,

For showers, dew, hail, snow as wool,
Hoar frost as ashes, ice as morsels,
Clouds from the ends of the earth,
Lightnings, thunders, winds out of Thy treasures, tempests;
Water beneath the heavens,
For drinking and for bathing.

And Saturday's Prayer for Grace

Guard Thou my soul, stablish my body, elevate my senses, direct
my converse, form my habits, bless my actions, fulfil my prayers,
inspire my holy thoughts, pardon the past, correct the present,
prevent the future.

Here, and in the *Book of Common Prayer*, are neither the wild
torments and frantic strivings of the darker mystic experiences, nor
the rather dry superego-bound versions of holy living that, for
instance, William Law presents some generations later (*viz.* pp. 71–
73, 246, 251–252). This is the more remarkable because Andrewes
lived in a time of religious and social turmoil, when those in power
felt they could only be kept safe by the torture and murder of their
religious opponents. But before considering William Law, we may
pause to enjoy another master of English prose, John Bunyan (1628–
1688), who was imprisoned for preaching his beliefs without
permission from those in power at the time. Very much in the
Protestant tradition, he is alive to the *tremendum* but writes not so
much of God's majesty as of his conviction of his own sin, and the
guilt that makes him tremble. In *The Pilgrim's Progress*, a novel in
verse, a travel epic that is still beguiling, first published in 1678,
Bunyan's hero, Christian, goes on pilgrimage to the Heavenly City
from the City of Destruction where he lived with other sinners, and
he encounters characters bad and good. The latter are all much
preoccupied with their own and other people's consciousness of sin
and with stories of how they were redeemed. As in novels for
centuries to come, there are meticulous examinations of people's
motives, and insights into the way their minds worked. Thus, one
evening on his journey, Christian

... lifted up his eyes, and behold there was a very stately Palace
before him, the name of which was *Beautiful*; and it stood just by the
High-way side ...

Two lions confront him, but Christian gets to the Porter, who asks him what he wants and interrogates his motivation. The Porter judges him sound.

> So *Watchful* the Porter rang a bell, at the sound of which came out at the door of the house a grave and beautiful Damsel named *Discretion*, and asked why she was called. The Porter answered, This man is on a Journey from the *City of Destruction* to *Mount Zion*, but being weary and benighted, he asked me if he might lodge here tonight; so I told him I would call for thee, who, after discourse had with him, mayest do as seemeth thee good, even according to the Law of the House ...

> So when he was come in and set down, they gave him something to drink, and consented together that, until supper was ready, some of them should have some particular discourse with *Christian*, for the best improvement of the time; and they appointed *Piety*, and *Prudence*, and *Chastity* to discourse with him, and thus they began:

> *Piety*: What moved you at first to betake you to a Pilgrim's life?
> *Christian*: I was driven out of my native country by a dreadful sound that was in mine ears: to wit, that unavoidable destruction did attend me, if I abode in that place.
> *Piety*: But how did it happen that you came out of your country this way?

Christian tells her but, as the side-rubric explains, "Piety makes Christian talk", like an overeager psychotherapist learning how to assess a prospective client: "Did you not come by the House of the Interpreter?", "Did you hear him tell his dream?", "Was that all you saw at the House of the Interpreter?", "And what else did you see on the way?" and so on. When Piety is finished with him, the side-rubrics indicate that Prudence next sounds out his spiritual state and when she has done, Charity "discourses him about his love to his family": "Why did you not bring them along with you?", "But did you tell them of your own sorrow and fear of destruction? For I suppose that destruction was visible enough to you?" "Yes", answers Christian,

> Yes, over and over and over. They might also see my fears in my countenance, in my tears, and also in my trembling under the apprehension of the Judgement that did hang over our heads ...

But Charity persists, perhaps not too charitably, "What could they say for themselves, why they came not?" And then Christian has to explain that his wife and children were too consumerist to care, whereupon Charity asks

> But did you not, with your vain life, damp all that you by words
> used by way of persuasion to bring them away with you?

All this provides everyone with much opportunity to sort out the Divine Purpose, in a quiet sort of way, before supper. Satisfied, they ask him to stay a few more days to engage in further pious discourse.

William Law's *Serious Call to a Devout and Holy Life* first appeared in 1728, a century after Andrewes was writing. He is of the same learned Protestant tradition, with almost the same talent for language, but of a different temperament. Perhaps in eighteenth-century reaction to the excesses of mystic fanaticism and martyrdom, Law couches his ideas of happiness in terms of effortless obedience to Divine Providence, a favourite eighteenth-century theme: we have a duty to believe Providence to be bountiful. Indeed, Providence was a preferred name for the Divine.

> First, every man is, by the law of his creation, by the first article of
> his creed, obliged to consent to and to acknowledge the wisdom
> and goodness of God in His general Providence over the whole
> world. He is to believe, that it is the effect of God's great wisdom
> and goodness, that the world itself was formed at such a particular
> time and in such a particular manner; that the general order of
> nature, the whole frame of things, is contrived and formed in the
> best manner. [Law, 1728, 1961 ed., p. 227]

> It is very common for people to allow themselves great liberty in
> finding fault with such things as have only God for their cause.
> [*ibid.*, p. 228]

He instances, at this point at least, only one example: the climate!

> Everyone seems to consent to this, as an undeniable truth, that all
> things must be as God pleases; and is not this enough to make every
> man pleased with them himself? [*ibid.*, p. 229]

No, it is not, thought Law's contemporary, Voltaire, philosophical representative of quite another eighteenth-century tradition, lampooning every new instance of disaster met by the eponymous hero of *Candide* (1759), who had been led to believe by the clergy that "all's for the best in the best of all possible worlds".

Law's superego-mindedness obscures a conviction generally embraced by mystics, and perhaps especially by mystic martyrs, that nothing falls outside God's Providence. Much more than Andrewes, Law wants to push people into a particular frame of mind "so as to increase the spirit of devotion". While Andrewes expresses himself in prayers that people can adopt if they wish to, Law addresses himself more directly to those who, in his view, need to reconsider how they live. He uses not prayers but exhortation, in a mixture of common sense and humour and shame, so as to get people to behave well.

> I take it for granted, that every Christian, that is in health, is up early in the morning, for it is much more reasonable to suppose a person is up early because he is a Christian, than because he is a labourer, or a tradesman, or a servant, or has some business that wants him. We naturally conceive some abhorrence of a man that is in bed when he should be at his labour or his shop ... Let us therefore conceive how odious we must appear in the sight of Heaven, if we are in bed, shut up in sleep and darkness, when we should be praising God. [*ibid.*, p. 119]

Nevertheless, his instructions allow us glimpses of his own warmly devout feelings.

> Begin, therefore, with words like these: O Being of all beings, Fountain of all light and glory, gracious Father of men and angels, whose universal Spirit is everywhere present, giving life, and light, and joy, to all Angels in Heaven, and all creatures upon earth, etc. [*ibid.*, p. 127]

Law's fervour does not always appear, and one may feel it is rather a come-down to read him straight after Andrewes. But he is often shrewd and amusing, and he entertains himself and us by telling us of the good and less good practices of such citizens as Penitens, Callidus (lukewarm), Miranda, and Paternus, who all live a good life in some ways, but who do not pay proper attention to other requirements of holy living. Matilda, for instance, though devout, directs her daughters' attention to trivia like clothes (p. 182). Mundanus though conscientious about saying his prayers, still prays as he did when he was six years old (p. 132).

> Flavia would be a miracle of piety, if she was but half so careful of her soul as she is of her body. The rising of a pimple on her face, the sting of a gnat, will make her keep her room two or three days, and she thinks they are very rash people who do not take care of things in time. This makes her so overcareful of her health, that she never thinks she is well enough; ... it costs her a good deal in sleeping draughts and waking draughts, in spirits for the head, in drops for the nerves, in cordials for the stomach, and in saffron for her tea.
> [*ibid.*, pp. 52–53]

Such stories keep us on the right path, and they are interspersed with more solid advice on the upbringing of children, the running of a Christian household and the exposition of some theological tenets. Nineteenth century Florence Nightingale drew her strength from this tradition, spending some months in Kaiserswerth on the Rhine, where deaconesses in pursuit of holy living were bravely founding a nursing order at a time when nursing was an occupation for drunks and derelicts.

Worship

> For giving me desire,
>   An eager thirst, a burning ardent fire,
> A virgin infant flame,
> A love with which into the world I came,
> An inward hidden Heavenly love,
> Which in my soul did work and move,
>   And ever ever me inflame
> With restless longing. Heavenly avarice,
>   That never could be satisfied,
> That did incessantly a Paradise
> Unknown suggest, and something undescried
>   Discern, and bear me to it, be
>   Thy Name for ever praised by me ...

This soaring, sacred thirst,
Ambassador of bliss, approached first,
   Making a place in me
That made me apt to prize, and taste, and see.
   For not the objects but the sense
   Of things doth bliss to souls dispense,
   And make it, Lord, like thee.
Sense, feeling, taste, complacency, and sight,
   These are the true and real joys,
The living, flowing, inward, melting, bright,
And Heavenly pleasures; all the rest are toys:
   All which are founded in desire,
   As light in flame and heat in fire [Traherne, "Desire" 1636?–1674]

The *Shorter Oxford English Dictionary* defines desire as

unsatisfied appetite, longing, wish, craving.

The somewhat more generous *Concise Oxford Dictionary* adds that it is

that emotion which is directed to the attainment or possession of some object from which pleasure or satisfaction is expected.

And defines "to worship" as

to honour and revere as a supernatural being or power or as a holy thing; to regard with extreme respect or devotion.

The word *numen* comes from the gesture of awe and respect that makes us bow the head, writes the *Shorter Oxford Dictionary*. To bow the head may seem the natural accompaniment to *mysterium tremendum*. And it is interesting to speculate that in cultures that insist, on principle, that nothing can be mysterious, and certainly not tremendous, the impulse to bow down and worship appears fitful and weak. Whoever has a sense of *mysterium* inevitably worships: it is intrinsic to that state of mind. Symmetrically, those in whom the desire to worship is strong, will be looking for *mysterium* to fill that need. For Otto, worship seemed a natural almost inevitable response to the Holy—the *mysterium* is *fascinans* as well as *tremendum*.

Clinical considerations

An interesting aspect of this desire to worship, as of the sense of the Holy, is that some people have it strongly and others not. We must perhaps look to differences between cultures to account for this variability, for the trait seems no more evident in one personality configuration than in another: easily depressed people may have it, or not; anxious people may or may not; so may those plagued with obsessions or compulsions; some diagnosed as hysteric show it, others not; people deprived or greatly damaged in childhood, and fortunate people wholesome as apples, any of them may or may not be susceptible to the fascination of the Holy.

The need for closeness with (preferably benevolent) parental figures may well be something we get addicted to if we have much of it in the first years of life. If we add, to closeness at that time, circumstances that rightly or wrongly lead children to extremes in regarding their parents as powerful and adorable and always to be kept in mind, we may make a little sense of the fact that some people are more vulnerable to experiencing *mysterium* as powerful and non-rational and non-moral, like their parents, to be worshipped but with rather strange forms of love. Others will find it natural to love *mysterium* in less authoritarian ways. Moreover, while some people love according to their own experience of having being loved, others love according to the words which were used to instruct them on how to love, and yet others, fortunate in some as yet unspecifiable way, seem to have been able to invent a good way of loving, from the way they feel love should be, constructing it from their very experience of its absence. In that sense, the desire to worship becomes a search for a good object and a resolution to stay in touch with it, a possibility further explored in Chapters Nine and Eleven.

Second among clinical considerations that come to mind, we might think it amazing that the experiences discussed in this chapter, which are not so very rare, are normally not regarded in the consulting-room—unless they can be called psychotic, of course. Their exclusion shows also in the lack of reference to them in the indices of the *International Journal of Psychoanalysis* and other mainstream psychotherapy journals—no mention there of awe, worship, numen, devotion, etc. Yet these feelings exist and are presumably at times both felt and spoken about in psychotherapeutic sessions. Alas, perhaps we stare out of countenance the feelings that do not fit easily into the theories we have so far constructed.

How can a psychotherapist deal with this wish to relate to an object that seems to require worship? How can the psychotherapist respond to people who say they have been in the presence of *mysterium tremendum et fascinans*? It seems important not to be simply reductionist and see it all in terms of transference: "You are re-living an experience you had with your parents"; "It is me you are really feeling like this about". Some innovators with perhaps better ideas are discussed on pp. 176–184.

Enough of polemics. The chapter may fitly end with a brief glance at some settings in which both worship and psychotherapy often take place: dimly lit spaces, and silence:

> ... in neither the sublime nor the magical, effective as they are, has art been more than an indirect means of representing the numinous. Of directer methods our Western art has only two, and they are in a noteworthy way negative, *viz. darkness* and *silence*.

> ... The semi-darkness that glimmers in vaulted halls, or beneath the branches of a lofty forest glade, strangely quickened and stirred by the mysterious play of half-lights, has always spoken eloquently to the soul, and the builders of temples, mosques, and churches have made full use of it.

> Silence is what corresponds to this in the language of musical sounds. "Yahweh is in His Holy Temple: let all the earth keep silence before Him" (Habakkuk ii 20). Neither we nor (probably) the prophet any longer keep in mind that this "keeping silence", if regarded from the historical "genetic" standpoint, springs from the fear of using words of ill omen, which therefore prefers to be altogether speechless. It is the same with Tersteegen in his "God is present, let all in us be silent". With prophet and psalmist and poet we feel the necessity of silence from another and quite independent motive. It is a spontaneous reaction to the feeling of the actual *numen praesens*. [Otto, 1959, pp. 83–84]

From here, Otto goes on to note that at least Oriental art, and possibly all art, knows a third direct means of producing a strongly numinous impression, *emptiness*.

In these ways, we may think, an ambience is created in which either of two things may come about. Either the dimness, the silence, the emptiness, may be found to contain a *mysterium* worth being in the presence of, or else the darkness, the silence, the emptiness, may be experienced as containers able to hold something that we have put there, some part of ourselves needing just such a frame. Or, of course, our sensitivities may not extend into this dimension at all.

CHAPTER FIVE

Unselfish love—some theories

A story from the days of sail. Voyages took years. One ship's voyage is uneventful except that an albatross has adopted it and followed it for days. This powerful and beautiful bird lightens the unvarying burdensome routine of the crew's days. They make a pet of it and apprehend, without thinking much about it, that it stands for something important and good. Then, says the mariner who is telling the story, without explanation or warning,

> With my cross-bow, I shot the albatross.
> [The Rime of the Ancient Mariner, Coleridge, S. T., 1772–1843]

It is as though a hate for something good and beautiful came unexpectedly from the unconscious depths of the mariner's mind and expressed itself in action. The crew is shocked and angry, and they hang the inert symbol of play and promise round the guilty man's neck. All the crew die one by one, even the wind dies. The sea dies.

> The very deep did rot: O Christ!
> That ever this should be!
> Yea, slimy things did crawl with legs
> Upon the slimy sea.

About, about, in reel and rout
The death fire danced at night;
The water, like a witch's oils
Burnt green, and blue, and white.

For a long time the mariner is alone. He sees Death-in-Life.
Everything is still. Then, with equal suddenness, there is a reversal.
Out of the mariner's depth, from which the murderous impulse had
sprung, comes an impulse to love. Something beautiful captures his
imagination and his love: it is a swirl of colour and movement—the
sea serpents at play, weaving in and out, and these are the same
monstrous slimy things that had filled him with so much horror in
another mood.

Within the shadow of the ship
I watched their rich attire:
Blue, glossy green, and velvet black,
They coiled and swam; and every track
Was a golden fire.

Oh happy living things! no tongue
Their beauty might declare;
A spring of love gushed from my heart,
And I blessed them unaware.
Sure my kind saint took pity on me,
And I blessed them unaware.

Coleridge is describing something about the movements of love
and hate. He does not explain—he describes. After gruesome
suffering and loneliness, a new event. When the Mariner sees the
watersnakes again, he is not the same man. A spring of joy is free to
gush from his heart, whence a shudder of disgust had sprung at the
start of his ordeal. Why? The spring of love is not explained, but its
effect is dramatic.

The selfsame moment I could pray;
And from my neck so free
The Albatross fell off, and sank
Like lead into the sea

The Mariner had no practical use for the serpents; he was not
aware of needing them; there is no question of them loving him back.

It is the selflessness of that moment that is the crucial element in one kind of love worth exploring in the language of psychotherapy, unselfish love.

Likierman (1989) writes that Kant describes beauty as the aspect of form which is not concerned with functionality or purpose, a view also voiced by Freud (1950b), whom she quotes:

> the aesthetic attitude towards an object is characterised by the condition that we do not ask anything of the object, especially no satisfaction of our serious needs. [Freud, 1950b, pp. 10–11]

Unselfish love

"What is love?"—not a useful way to approach the topic. There are so many kinds, so many aspects to love, so many combinations of aspects. It is not usually profitable to involve oneself in an argument about who has the best definition.

It is surprising when one first begins to notice, how many people love others in the same way as they love Black Forest Gateau—for consumption, for possession. Freud (1914) called this anaclitic love. The kind of love here to be considered, on the other hand, is romantic but not too romantic. It has elements of wonder and of worship in it, and an element of identification, as well as a search for gratification. It is probably more mature than what we are born with. What encourages its growth and what inhibits it? From the point of view of psychodynamics, maybe it can be said to be born at that moment when we no longer habitually place ourselves in the centre of the universe—it is this, among other things, that happened to the Mariner when he lost himself in the beauty of the serpents. We no longer inhabit the centre of our universe and we like it that way. We live with more humility. This kind of love takes the depressive position in its stride. The seeds of this capacity are available from quite an early age—some of the infants in Winnicott's consulting room wanted to share the shiny metal thing on Winnicott's desk with Mother—but many of us may not love like that until very much later. Being a parent may have pushed some of us into it, perhaps to our own surprise. How many people never love like that, or only rarely?

We are not considering here the unselfishness of the you-have-the-last-chop-dear kind. We are thinking of a style of living which recognizes that other people have the same rights, the same position in the universe, as oneself, and that they suffer and rejoice as much, as fiercely, as really, as oneself. Stated like this, it is obvious that such a style of living requires the operation of sophisticated ego-processes: this kind of recognition does not comes from the id-impulses with which we are born. So we are exploring what may happen in the course of life, that shifts us out of the centre of our universe.

What are the ways in which unselfish love becomes part of the psyche? How does it come about that we do not hate, fight, and compete all the time, and how does it come about that we are able to regard each other with respect, liking and love?

Psychoanalytic ideas

Freud and later Klein and others put their main efforts into understanding selfish love. If we are interested in the roots of well-being, we find that the body of theory on unselfish love, which on the whole is the poets' and mystics' kind, is a little thin.

For classical Freudians, appetites and drives are primary, tenderness an outcome of aim-inhibited sexuality, of sublimation. Sexuality is an instinctual drive, an irreducible motivation; tenderness comes about when that drive is thwarted. Obviously tenderness is only one of a number of outcomes of frustrated sexuality; rage could be another, repression another, and so on. So when would a person turn to tenderness rather than these? Freud (1924b) proposed identification was a way out of complete self-centredness.

Identification, of the kind Freud had in mind, is wanting to be like, and feeling oneself into being like and behaving like, what the other is imagined to be feeling. The boy, in classical psychoanalytic theory, gives up his anaclitic object—the mother whom he had wanted to possess—and identifies with the father whom he wants to be like because the father seems to the boy to be a person who could be expected to be in possession of the mother. Is it possible to understand further how this process works? For Freud it was an irreducible. Not for us, necessarily. But the whole theory creaks a bit, excellent beginning though it was a hundred years ago. Freud was thinking of a boy around four, for instance, by which time a lot of mental processes have already been established. But we can imagine identification—wanting to be like—at an earlier age than four and for girls as well as boys. We can imagine a younger child grateful for some good thing the parent has given, and wanting to be a person who evokes this loving gratitude in others. Winnicott observed—indeed any of us may observe—that babies only just capable of grasping a spoon will move to feed the mother. The seeds of unselfish acts are there then.

For Melanie Klein, to treat her equally briefly, anaclitic love arouses and is bound up with guilt and fear. The savage rage consequent on not being able to rely absolutely on the breast that is so needed, brings fear that one's rage might destroy that essential comfort and also brings fear of retaliation from the outraged owner of the breast. The idea that the much needed and passionately loved breast might be destroyed alongside the needed but hatefully absent breast gives rise to concern, another possible start for unselfish love.

The fear of retaliation was of course also important to Freud, though he was thinking of toddlers rather than nurselings. It was bound up with the fear of castration, this fear leading the toddler to cease competing with the father and to identify with him instead.

Meira Likierman (1993), in some valuable textual research into Melanie Klein's developing thoughts on love, thinks that perhaps there has come to be an undue emphasis on Klein's ideas about destructiveness. Likierman points to an element in Klein's thought that other writers were also groping after at the time, an element through which, from the infant's very beginnings, an idea of love gradually crystallizes in the psyche, based on good experiences but going beyond them. She writes: "By 1957 the libidinally invested breast was felt by Klein to be a principle of fulfilment that reflects the power of the life instinct, and is a boundless, ideal source of mental sustenance". She quotes:

I would not assume that the breast is [to the infant] merely a physical object. The whole of his instinctual desires and his unconscious phantasies imbue the breast with qualities going far beyond the actually nourishment it affords. [M. Klein, 1957, p. 180]

So Klein, writes Likierman, "not only added early love to her theory, she also gave it a central place in infantile mental life, and showed how the object on which identity is modelled is none other than the good object" (Likierman, 1993, p. 249). The breast, in any case normally a word used by Kleinians to describe all nourishing, exciting, supportive aspects of the person who is mothering, is here given a further transparency. Through experience of the breast, we glimpse, or perhaps create, goodness "far beyond the actual nourishment it affords".

It may be that this theory, which allows for goodness far beyond the actual nourishment, can be taken one step further, towards an explanation for the surprising frequency with which we meet loving and unselfish people whose history includes very little experience of a "good breast". How is it that these amazing people were able to construe, from minimal enjoyment of goodness, from excessive submission to badness, nevertheless an idea, an ideal, of what a loving person could be, and were able to identify with that ideal and grow such goodness within themselves? Something like idealization through contrast must play an important part in such development. How? Much more thought has to go into that, but see M. Likierman (1989) and Chapter Nine.

To return to less problematic ground. Winnicott (1974, p. 105) presents a softened version of Klein. For him, concern, or "ruth", modifies the infant's rage at frustration, much as Klein's fear of retaliation does, but for him, love and gratitude follow the child's discovery that the good object, the good breast, the parental figure, has not been destroyed by the child's angry reaction to frustration. Nor is the child destroyed by having asserted its wishes in opposition to the grown-up. Winnicott's infants and toddlers, in their different ways, can be as selfish as may be, can give expression to their unpleasant impulses and, when not retaliated against, find themselves loving the tolerant generous grown-up. Gratitude comes again into the picture, and recognition that *someone* has not been selfish: Winnicott believes that love comes from having felt another's love. Alas, many a frustrated parent knows that this cannot be the whole story, having tried it and landed up with some very demanding, selfish, and thoughtless offspring. But still, what a beautiful thought, if we could just refine it into being invariably true, that we gain in love and selflessness by means of the love and selflessness of another person. The whole point of this kind of love is that it is a recognition of the other person as other, and as valuable even when not of use to us, like the Mariner's serpents.

Beatrician moments

The ancient mariner's hate and love came appropriately from the depths—of the sea, of the psyche. They do not yield to any easy explanation. Dante, the great poet of love divine and human, also tells of these movements which come from depths beyond our command, from some place which is unexpected and unpredicted.

Dante first sees Beatrice when they are both about nine years old, and she becomes for him all that is lovely and good. He writes (later, of course, in the appropriately named *Vita Nuova*—New Life) that his heart trembled and said, "Here is a power stronger than you" and his mind said, "This is for you the meaning of life and blessedness", literally, "Here and now your beatitude is manifest" ("Iam apparuit beatudina vestra"). He recognizes what she is to be to him, but, equally, he recognizes who he is and what, for him, is "blessedness". During the next decade he occasionally sees her about Florence, but not to speak to until he is nineteen. This second crucial encounter further defines him, how he is to be, how he is to live his life and what her significance is to be in his life. Charles Williams, a twentieth-century poet and writer, calls that moment of encounter a "Beatrician moment". Dante stops writing elegant conventional Latin verses for his aristocratic public and his fellow poets, and writes elegant Italian verses instead, in a new style, many around Beatrice and the nature of love, but also long and weighty ones on the nature of the state, and on right politics and right action. He sees both kinds of verse as glorifying Beatrice and the divine source from which he believes her beauty and goodness to derive. Nowhere, by the way, is there any reference to the possibility that Beatrice is in love with Dante or that he expects her to be. As far as we know she was a respectable married woman when she died, still in her twenties. What we are looking at here is the glory of loving, of living in a wonderful world where a wonderful person called Beatrice is also alive. We are looking at that aspect of love which has to do with feeling that there is meaning in the world, and that that meaning is somehow proved by the fact that there is someone in the world who is to be loved.

The Divine Comedy is one result, written in Dante's middle years. It describes Dante's visit to other worlds in the company of another poet, Virgil, who stands for goodness and truth and poetry in the classical world, before the revelation of God's incarnation as a man, which, in the world in which Dante lived, changed the nature of goodness and truth. The role of poets in the world is crucial in all this. Dante meets many on his way through Hell, Purgatory and Heaven and he and they recognize each other and own their indebtedness to each other, and we in turn are indebted to him and to them. The notion that, one way or another, all people of goodwill are indebted to each other, is another of Charles William's concepts, and very much to do with love; Chapter Nine considers this idea at greater length.

Dante is led by Virgil through Hell and then through Purgatory. He meets some of his contemporaries, and so he comes to recognize his own nature in the persons of those he has loved or hated. Eventually he comes out onto a meadow, where Virgil has to leave him, as classical virtue cannot get you into the Christian Heaven, but here is Beatrice, perfected. She has been in Heaven all this while. And here is another Beatrician moment, for Dante does not immediately recognize her, both are so changed by their experiences since last they met; he is dazzled, at a loss, who she is, who he is. She sees this and addresses him in a memorable phrase that expresses something about love that to my mind is as profound as anything can be. She says, "Yes. Look at me. It *is* me. I *am* Beatrice".

Guardate ben. Ben sem, ben sem Beatrice.

To know and be known, an ecstatic and frightening aspect of love. To recognize and be recognized for what one is, and what the other is.

Recognition: I am known and can know

The Mariner did not recognize the albatross for what it was: he had no sense of its significance for him, so shooting it appeared to have no great meaning either, at the time. By contrast, when he saw the sea-serpents, he recognized something about them. To use a metaphor from Chapter One, they were transparent to him. On the occasion of his first sighting, he saw in them the horror of evil, and later, innocent joy.

Not that the albatross was anything but an albatross, and the sea-serpents were nothing supernatural. But they stood for something the Mariner could recognize. Herman Melville's *Moby Dick* was a white whale but for Captain Ahab he stood for something too immense to be put into words, something ineffable, *fascinans*. Ahab recognized it and insisted on recognition from it; he could not let it be, he hunted it (Melville, 1851). We want to be recognized. We get a sense of significance from our mutual recognition. Jacob wrestled with an angel all night to know its name, or perhaps its nature, another *mysterium fascinans*. The next day he changed his own name and found his nature changed. There are "recognition" stories in many scriptures. Therapists recognize their patients in this sense; we recognize their potential health and goodness, as well as the horror of their evil potential. That is part of the healing process: patients gain from our recognition. And they come to recognize us—we gain significance from their recognition—we get as well as give. In Chapter Eleven this theme is pursued as it affects the psychotherapy of people with strong narcissistic traits.

Kenneth Wright's contribution

We can come at this important concept of recognition from another direction, drawing on the writings of Kenneth Wright, who was influenced by Winnicott and built on his foundations. In his as yet unpublished paper, "Recognition and Relatedness", Wright first commends Freud for his thorough exploration of one valid way in which love is experienced, based on the body and the pleasures it affords. Then, however, he turns to other phenomena to which we must do justice, not reducible to the anaclitic, not easily derived from obvious physical urges. These Wright attributes to an aspect of mother–infant relatedness unique to the human species—its larger capacity for symbolizing. "Symbolising enables us to imagine the world as well as to act in it". And this, Wright proposes, comes "from the specific kinds of relatedness in which the human baby is bathed. From the beginning the human mother not only feeds and protects her baby; she wraps the baby in a garment of imaginary forms which furnish a kind of substrate for symbolic development". Inspired by Winnicott, he considers the mother gazing at her baby, and the baby gazing at the mother and deriving from the contemplation of the mother's changing features (the first television Wright called it in a discussion) a sense of self and of the other too, a recognition. And then he takes a daring leap.

> The baby's first relation is not, as object-relations theory would suggest, with the mother's breast, or at least not only with that. It seems to me at least equally with the mother's face. The infant's relation with the mother's face is apparently based on an inborn disposition to relate to faces, and to relate to them in ways that are independent of the instinctual excited relation to the breast. [Wright, unpublished]

The infant's interest in faces evolved, Wright imagines, to contribute to the survival of the species. He postulates a useful mechanism built into the human mind so that the baby knows, or perhaps learns, that *this* mother, with *this* face, *these* features, is uniquely appointed to look after this baby, and is worth recognizing, clinging to. And so the argument returns to the importance of recognition in love.

> It is the mother's knowing and recognising of the baby in all his quirky specificity [i.e. of quiddity, j.k.], and her communication back to the baby of this knowing, in her quirky and specific fashion, that ultimately gives to the baby a maternal (i.e. an accepting and containing) place to be.

This kind of love, Wright points out, is relational. It is "about things that go on between people which do not have a concrete result but are more a kind of communication".

At the same time, Wright reminds us that the mother's features, however loveable, cannot be possessed, cannot be controlled.

> The face is a very peculiar kind of object and if we understand this we begin to understand why it is so important in human relationships, and particularly in loving. It is the only object in the infant's world which can never be fully appropriated concretely ...

... that very specific constellation of features which is essential to the infant's bond with the mother from the start ... can only be apprehended visually, in a non-appropriative, non-tactile mode.

As Michael Balint (1959, pp. 62 ff.) pointed out, sight is a distal sense. What we see cannot be grasped or ingested by the act of seeing; it cannot be swallowed. What cannot be appropriated cannot be controlled (see also J. Klein, 1987, Chapter 13). So we have here a very early experience with another person who is more than a symbol, about whom we may have illusions and any number of phantasies, but who cannot be controlled by the pictures in our head, who is not subject to our omnipotence. It is a relationship in which we are, in a sense, subject. And here Wright takes another leap:

It is gradually becoming appreciated that this experience of being recognised and known is centrally important in the process of being a self. It is as though I can only become the self I am through your recognising ... in some way that I am that self.

This rather stands on its head Winnicott's idea of the use of an object. Winnicott (1974, Chapter 6) writes that mothers may emerge as separate persons in their child's consciousness because they survived the child's rage and displeasure. But here Wright considers another plausible and equally Winnicottian possibility, that mothers emerge as separate beings in their child's consciousness because the child gets a sense of its uniqueness from her, and this is how the mother, or the carer, becomes unique, in turn, as the one whose respectful and loving eyes, voice, hands, the baby recognizes.

In another paper, "Looking after the self"(1996), after paying proper dues to Brazelton (q.v.) and Stern (q.v.), Wright explores the extent to which the development of the sense of self is encouraged yet limited by this recognition from the other. He looks at the experience of finding an other who gives back to us what we now recognize more clearly to be essential to our nature, an other who reflects what we feel and are and think. Recognition means mutuality here, responsiveness, identification, naturally coloured by gratitude for the feeling of rightness and acceptance here and now. It is interesting that Wright does not refer explicitly, or at least not at length, to love. His topic is recognition here. But surely that feeling we have, that accompanies the sense of "Ah, I've found you, *that* is what I must have been searching for", that feeling is love and that situation, that moment, generates love and perhaps recalls the moment when the mother's face is seen for what it means to the infant. Meltzer and Harris Williams (1988) make this the central experience of the apprehension of beauty, of love, of meaning. In a personal communication Wright confirms this idea. "I think that what I am saying is an alternative to the anaclitic view of love 'I love you because you first *fed* me'. I think am saying 'I love you because you first *recognised* me and *answered* me and gave me a place where I could be' ".

A form answering to his subjectivity is what Beatrice was to Dante; she gave him a place where he could be. For lovers, to look at each other's faces, to look in each other's eyes, can be an act of love as deeply significant as the act of sex or nursing (not indefinitely of course, but that is true of sex and food as well). Seeing is a distal sense: the more closely we possess, control, ingest each other, the less we can see of each other. We need the distal senses to know we are loved, that there is someone *not us* who finds us loveable.

Hearing is the other distal sense, and it is useful that Wright brings in Stern's descriptions of mothers' and babies' attunement by means of vitality affects (see pp. 31–33), as the forerunners of later more verbal forms of mutual understanding, adaptation, and communication. Through humming and nonsense sounds, through subtle inflections in words and sentences whose intonation goes well beyond what the words convey, we communicate with babies and with each other, using all sorts of hard-to-specify implications and rhythms. The music of our conversation is not only Handel, it can also be Bach.

We are beginning to get an idea of how we develop that talent in childhood or, if we really put our minds to it, later in life. The key concept is "attunement".

Recognition and affect-attunement

The long tradition of mother-and-baby games and songs is evidence that matching of vitality-affect is enjoyable. It stands to reason that when two people's inner worlds are brought into harmony, both enjoy it. Attunement is two people dancing together. It can be a simple dance, when the two harmoniously do much the same thing at the same times, or it can be complex, as when they jazz it, with counterpoint and variations.

Daniel Stern (1985) considers in detail how we learn to recognize one another in wordless ways and learn to attune ourselves to one another, through the often unconscious matching of vitality affects. Stern describes how the baby learns this, with the essential assistance of a mother or other carer who is well attuned to the baby and its affects.

A nine-months old girl becomes very excited about a toy and reaches for it. As she grabs it she lets out an exuberant "aaaah" and looks at her mother. Her mother looks back, scrunches up her shoulders and performs a terrific shimmy with her upper body, like a go-go dancer. The shimmy lasts only about as long as her daughter's "aaaah" but is equally excited, joyful and intense. [1985, p. 140]

The nine-months old boy bangs his hand on a soft toy, at first in some anger but gradually with pleasure, exuberance and humor. Mother falls into this rhythm and says "kaaaaa-*bam*, kaaaaa-*bam*", the "*bam*" falling on the stroke and the "kaaaaa" riding the preparatory upswing and the suspenseful holding of him arm aloft before it falls. [*ibid.*, p. 140]

Stern points out that:

What is being matched is not the other person's behaviour *per se*, but rather some aspect of the behaviour that reflects the person's feeling state. The ultimate reference for the match appears to be the feeling state (inferred or directly apprehended), not the external behavioural event. Thus the match appears to occur between the expressions of inner state. These expressions can differ in mode or form, but they are to some extent interchangeable as manifestations of a single recognisable internal state. [*ibid.*, p. 142]

The concept of matching our affects, of affect-attunement, opens up new worlds to rational discourse, both in the world of parenting and among clinicians. A person who missed early training in attunement may be blind and insensitive to what is obvious to more fortunate people. The link with empathy and intuition is obvious here. Also, therapists with poor attunement skills are at a disadvantage in the consulting room; is it possible to consider whether training of some kind might improve their performance? By the same token, might patients be helped to improve their attunement skills so that they can make better use of whatever else the therapy has to offer? Examples of help of this sort may be found in the clinical records of child analysts already:

> More helpful than interpretation of his conflicts over destructive-ness was a game which emerged in the course of the second year of treatment. David wished to repeat it day after day for months. The game consisted of David and his analyst making notes on "what I think you think I am thinking about you today". Increasingly he would call for a round of the game at times of heightened anxiety during his session. The content of what the analyst and the patient wrote evolved to include a large variety of feelings, wishes and phantasies. The useful aspect of this initiative was that David became better able to differentiate fears and wishes within himself and between himself and his analyst. [Fonagy & Moran, 1991, p. 17]

"David" was seven at this time; "Rebecca" was five:

> The bulk of Rebecca's treatment consisted of a single game, with many variations. In the game, she is a somewhat older girl, Hannah, who has a father, which is my role. Hannah and her father (Peter) had many adventures, most of which involved visiting Hannah's friend, pretend Rebecca, who (in the game) had a father, Jeff. Jeff was a pathetic figure who frequently got things wrong, and on such occasions would be often unceremoniously dismissed, mostly by mother and sometimes by her. Hannah would intercede with pretend Rebecca and Rebecca's mother on Jeff's behalf: "You don't understand him!" she berated pretend Rebecca on one occasion, "He is only upset because you told him off for making a mess". [Fonagy, 1995, p. 40]

"Michael", aged eight, experienced Mrs Baradon's attunement as love, and was able to respond with love:

> I was again positioned in the corridor, and Michael left the toilet door ajar. While I waited for him my mind drifted. I was, I think, doing a mental checklist of my day in which Michael, of course, featured, but not as the sole focus of my preoccupation. After a few

minutes I collected my thoughts and raised my eyes to check on him. I saw him peering at me from behind the toilet door. Obviously he had seen me deep in thought. I wondered if he felt I had left him ... and I felt guilty about this and feared that he would regress. Yet I also thought that perhaps he would be able to tolerate my being with him in a more limited way. In the event, I did not offer an interpretation of abandonment but merely reflected what had occurred: "I was thinking and you were watching me". Then I added: "Perhaps you were wondering what I was thinking?" Michael responded by throwing himself at me in a rough embrace. [Baradon, 1998, p. 161]

Idealizing, and loving what is

Alice Balint's chapter "Love for the mother and mother love", first published in 1939 and later included in the newly enlarged edition of Michael Balint's *Primary Love and Psychoanalytic Technique* (1965), provides a useful summary of orthodox psychoanalytic thought up to that time. She adds at least one thought of her own, about solipsist "archaic" loving *versus* loving within a shared reality.

There exist an archaic form of love of which the essential determinant is the lack of reality-sense toward the love object ... The development of the socially higher forms of love derives as a consequence of adaptation to reality. This classification is closely related to Freud's distinction between sensual and aim-inhibited love, for aim-inhibition is indeed the most important of the factors, originating in the influence of the external world, which brings about the development of emotional life; pure sensuality, on the other hand, knows solely "the erotic reality sense" and can exist, in relation to the partner, fairly comfortably coupled with naïve egoism. [Balint, M., 1965, pp. 105–107]

Alice Balint defines the sense of reality in terms of what it is not: where it is "scanty", "the object is recognised but not its self-interest". An admirably succinct dictum, it defines one kind of loving—cupboard-love: I love Black Forest Gateau and do not consider whether the gateau may have views on the matter. Or, as between people, "I love you so much, you just have to go to Paris with me". By contrast, what Balint calls "reality-sense" requires us to acknowledge that the loved one, however loving, may have wishes that run counter to our own. Our reality-sense requires us to recognize that other creatures have lives of their own, and we may wish to respect that: that is a way of loving them.

Idealizing is what we do when we love our own phantasized creations. It can be contrasted with our love for what we have not created and have no control over. We may be more ambivalent about loving what is not under our control, because it is often so inconvenient, but it may be a more desirable way of loving and being loved, at least for some people: more reliable through ups and downs, with more mutual recognition. Oscar Wilde's "An Ideal Husband" is based on this idea. Lady Chiltern loves her husband for all kinds of qualities which that all too human man does not possess. Trouble ensues. Fortunately all gets voiced and sorted at the end of *Act Two*, never mind the absurd genderism of the time:

Lady Chiltern:	... The world seemed to me finer because you were in it, and goodness more real because you lived. And now—oh, when I think that I made a man like you my ideal! The ideal of my life!
Sir Robert Chiltern:	There was your mistake: There was your error. The error all women commit. Why can't you women love us, faults and all? Why do you place us on monstrous pedestals? We have all feet of clay, women as well as men; but when we men love women, we love them knowing their weaknesses, their follies, their imperfections, love them all the more, it may be, for that reason ... Women think that they are making ideals of men. What they are making of us is false idols merely ...

Much has been made of the psychotherapists' hate for their patients (Winnicott, 1947), because recognition of its existence ensures that we do not omit to work constructively with those aspects of our patients that evoke hate in others. But therapists also love their patients (Gerrard, 1996). They love them for all sorts of human reasons as well as for their obviously loveable qualities, but also they love them for qualities which they do not yet possess but which they are capable of, given good therapy and some luck. People can be loved for their potential. Both reality-sense and a kind of idealization are involved in this attitude—see also Chapter Eleven.

Love, affect-regulation, and the reality of other people's rights

What distinguishes loving-what-is from idealizing love is the recognition, with as little self-deception as can be managed, that the other person is as he or she is. Affect-attunement can be very conducive to this clearer sight. From affect-attunement to affect-regulation is a natural step. Allan Schore (1994) in his monumental *Affect-Regulation and the Development of the Self*, writes *inter alia* about the role played by the reality-sense in the development of the more unselfish elements in love. He makes affect-regulation the centre of social motivation and behaviour and control: infants, and then children, and finally we adults, are more or less well-trained to pick up minute clues as to what pleases mothers and others and to act accordingly. Affect-regulation is the means by which mothers or others give clues to the child, very much in the way described by Stern, as to what suits the (m)other's feelings of the moment, and what is a bit of a shock to her; or is really unpleasant. This runs side by side with, and sometimes counter to, what she actually says.

Mothers and others communicate what they want, relying on the child's attunement, and, at the same time, the best of them are habitually attuned to the infant and react appropriately to the fortunate growing child. But after infancy, the better mothers are not pushovers: their responses to what they pick up from the child in their attunement may be pleasure or displeasure, approving or disapproving, and these responses are in turn picked up by the child, because the child is attuned to them. So the adults make their mark on the child, and this mark is among the consequences that the child experiences as a result of what it did. In a wordless, often unconscious way, the child learns what keeps it in other people's good books.

What is so very original about Schore is that he adduces a neurological groundwork for the processes that make the (m)other's influence very nearly permanent. Unfortunately for the present purpose, he substantiates his thesis with such solid detail that brief illustrative quotations are not easily extracted.

Schore's is a very developed theory, ranging from neurology to psychoanalysis but, essentially, affect-regulation is the means by which children in felicitous circumstances come to appreciate, without too much resentment, that there are other people in the world much like themselves, and that these others are not just competitors and rivals but have equal rights to a place in the world. Good attunement is the means by which such desirable personalities come into being.

Almost all children sooner or later discover that they are not in control, that there are limits to what they can have. Their reaction to that discovery may be matter-of-fact; or happy, interested and playful; or reluctant and resentful. In unfortunate circumstances, there may be insane reactions like denial, pretending it is not happening and turning away from the reality of the experience; or perversion, where the evil is seen as the good. Which reaction eventuates would depend on a number of variables: the strength of the child's impulse, the child's ability to cope with delay and frustration, the suddenness and cruelty of the child's discovery of its limitations, and so on. Interestingly, these variables reflect Kernberg's ego-strength variables: tolerance of frustration and uncertainty, flexibility, sound impulse-control and, not surprisingly, good contact with the realities we share with others. (Kernberg, 1984, Part Two). There are ample case-histories in the literature of psychotherapy, and particularly of child psychotherapy, to illustrate all of these reactions and their consequences.

The role of the father in the development of unselfish loving and living

There has been a tendency among psychotherapists to represent the father as the mediator of the discovery of an uncontrollable objective world "out there". This is not surprising, but it may be questioned; as far as I can discover, the men we know do not seem noticeably more realistic than the women we know. The theory may owe something to the fact that men get into print relatively more often. Melanie Klein, at least as represented by Ron Britton (1989) and John Steiner (1989), nominated the father as the one who introduces the shift, from our infantile belief that we are central, to a more mature acceptance of our occasionally peripheral position in the scheme of things. This is the Kleinian perspective on the Oedipal situation: in any threesome (such as constructed by father, mother, and child) each comes to feel excluded at some time or other. There is certainly an element of truth in this, though we may ask ourselves how much threesomeness there is in the average household during the new-baby phase of the family, let alone later, with three or four children, and there is also a question as to who actually feels most excluded—mother, father or baby. There may be a great deal of variation.

But there are at least some shreds of reality discernible here. Lacan (1966) also makes the position of the father crucial: a very stern third party, this Dad who, clothed in Authority and Duty and Reason, is to shift the toddler from his baby-phantasy of centrality. There is something risible about this theory of fatherhood, which must *inter alia* apply to Andy Capp, Mr Pooter, Lord Emsworth, the emperor Nero, and the Royal Georges of the nineteenth century. (For further discussion of the role of the father as seen in the history of psychoanalytic theory see J. Klein, 1995, Chapter 9).

Another recent theory, perhaps more acceptable-sounding but also presenting difficulties to more empirically-inclined minds, sees the internalized parental couple as the crucial element in the development of happy loving personalities.

The loving parental couple internalized

The history of psychoanalytic ideas on love between adults has had its vicissitude. The twentieth century opened with Freud's highly individualistic–mechanistic model—each person motivated by his or her biologically given instincts, other people being irrelevant except insofar as they allowed themselves to be objects for the cathexis of an instinctual drive that directed itself at them. Hence the preference, throughout that century, for the use of the word "object" rather than "person": the personality of the instinctual target did not matter in this model, since people were just objects for a cathexis. C. J. Jung was the great exception at that time, running with the notion of *coniunctio* from the start of analytic thinking: the *coniunctio* is not unlike what was to develop into the concept of the combined parental object. However, the main Freudian stream continued mechanistic and individualistic for many decades.

Melanie Klein, a follower of Freud's who emerged in the thirties of the twentieth century, made space for a more relational theoretical model than Freud's: the mother and the infant interacted and influenced one another, at least in the phantasy of the infant. Gradually more tolerance came to be given to the theory that the mother, as an actual person and not just a figment in the baby's phantasy, had an effect on the baby's psyche. The way mothers and infants behaved in the relationship came to be considered relevant: there was more to the relationship than instinctual gratification and terror. It became permissible to think that relationships can lead to gratifying states that involve more than simple object-cathexis. Bliss was no longer confined to delusional solitary fulfilment.

But Kleinians have always tended to be more captivated by the shadow side of relationships. Hence, the concept of the internalized parental loving couple was also first propounded in its negative form, as displayed in the pathology of people who cannot tolerate that two important people (father and mother) can be happy with each other with a happiness that has nothing to do with the excluded-feeling third party (Britton, 1989). It has to be admitted that it does not come easily to most of us to rejoice spontaneously that those who love us also love one another and, moreover, in ways we cannot participate in. But if we do manage to rejoice, the theory is that we have internalized a loving relationship that can act as an unfailing source of well-being.

The "loving couple" concept has unselfish love built into it, since the person who has internalized a loving parental couple is by definition happy in the love the other two have for each other, as well as in the love each has for him or her, the subject who, if all goes well, loves them back. But a shortcoming of the theory is that it depends so heavily on the assumption that we all had two parents who exemplified a loving couple—otherwise what is it that has been internalized? Moreover, inevitably but unfortunately, the phrase has come to refer not only to actual memories of actual parents, but also to any strands of loving feelings that originated from a range of other experiences—many strands from a wide range for fortunate people, and a small or even minuscule quantity for the less fortunate. This modification weakens the appeal of the idea but probably brings it more in line with how things actually happen. More acceptable somewhat similar theories, less uniquely dependent on the parents, are canvassed below, on pp. 181–184, 209–210 and 226–227.

Because what developed first was an interest in the terrifying possibilities of threesome relationships, it took about half a century for the majority of psychotherapists to come round to the idea of the benign potential of parental coupling. In the final quarter of the twentieth century, however, the more open acceptance of adult sexual affection has been gaining strength, validating what now appears obvious to those who, born later, were less entangled in the Victorian/Edwardian mores of what was then conventional psychoanalytic theory. What appears obvious now, was not so then: that there is bliss in adult interrelatedness, in sexual congress, in loving living, *intrinsically*, though naturally coloured and limited by earlier experiences *and that such love need not frighten the children*.

The more intricate aspects of Melanie Klein's theories are not easily summarized by those of a very different cast of mind, and it is probably best to rely on Hinshelwood's invaluable *Dictionary of Kleinian Thought* (1989). There we find, as the last sentence under the heading COITUS:

Klein also described an object which she termed "the combined parent figure", which is the infant's phantasy of the parents as locked together in mutual preoccupation with each other.

The next item is:

COMBINED PARENT FIGURE ... The phantasy of the combined parent figure is that the parents, or rather their sexual organs (see PART-OBJECTS), are locked together in permanent intercourse; it is the earliest and most primitive phantasy of the oedipal situation: "A special intensity is imparted to this dangerous situation by the fact that a union of the two parents is in question ... these united parents are extremely cruel and much dreaded assailants" (Klein, 1929, pp. 210 –218). "The combined parent figure is expressed as mother with the father inside her". (Klein, 1932, p. 69).

The infant's fury leads him or her to imbue this intercourse with as much violence between the parents as he or she is feeling towards them, writes Hinshelwood, and

> The intercourse the parents perform is dangerous to themselves, and there are horrendous hostilities between the child and this particularly menacing figure. The combined parent figure is one of the most terrifying persecutors in the *dramatis personae* of childhood.

The entry continues,

> Meltzer (1973) described the development of sexuality and creativity in the personality in terms of the struggle to move beyond this part-object figure to reconstruct it in whole object terms with more realistic versions of the mother and the father, a process inherent in the depressive position. Internally such a realistic parental intercourse forms an internal object that is the basis—or is felt to be the fount—of personal creativity: sexual, intellectual and aesthetic.

While Hinshelwood's language is on the dry side, Meltzer's is unselfconsciously florid and may strike some readers as ludicrous. Moreover, when we read his praise of the mother, we soon realize that he lauds only her reproductive processes, and those only when policed and nourished and redeemed by the father. To Meltzer's mind, for instance, the origin of the mother's milk is the father's semen (1973, p. 69). There is here no space and no need to reduce the supercharged metaphors of Meltzer's imagination to something calmer with fewer incidental infelicities but, to summarize drastically and with the more immediately acceptable elements brought to the fore: Meltzer considers the internalized parental couple to be benign and the source of creativity and worthwhile work. He almost incidentally sets a standard that enables us to distinguish between art and pornography, and between loving intercourse and perversion (1973, Chapter 24). But here are two characteristic examples from Chapters Nine and Eleven of *Sexual States of Mind*.

> In order, therefore, to understand the complex structure of affects, impulses, phantasies and anxieties which make up the adult sex life, we must turn our attention to the nature of the coital relation of internal parents, as we are able to construct it from psychoanalytical

data. The first principle that must be understood is that the coital relation of internal objects has an overwhelming relation to that dependence of infantile parts of the self on the internal mother which is the foundation of all stable and healthy psychic structure. This dependence we know to be of two sorts: in the first instance, on the mother's capacity to receive the projection of infantile states of mental and physical distress, experienced as persecution by bodily contents, especially the faeces and urine. In psychic reality all persecutions coming from outside the infant's body are experienced as secondary to the expulsion of those contents. The baby depends on the mother's capacity to return to it parts of the self, which have then been divested of all persecutory qualities, by means of the feeding relation to the breast. In connection with these two primal functions of the internal mother, her dependent relation, in turn, to the internal father and his penis and testicles is experienced as essential for her survival, and for the survival of the babies-inside-the-internal-mother, whose welfare is felt to be a prerequisite for her generosity and benevolence ...

. The inside of the mother's body is felt furthermore to acquire penis-like structures from coitus with the father ... These functions are of two types, keeping order and protecting. Thus the flow of milk is felt to be regulated by a nipple–penis. [Meltzer, 1973, p. 68]

... the definitive act of coition is serious ... It is work, not play, and has a sense of urgent and immediate relation to the stresses of the day, week, era, as the introjective identification, with its cosmic scope, takes hold of the mind-body ...

In its deepest, most basic, primal meaning the woman is in distress and in need and in danger; the man is her servant, her benefactor, her rescuer. She is in distress at the plight of her internal babies, in need of supplies to make the milk for her external babies and in danger from the persecutors her children have projected into her. She needs good penises, and good semen, and must be relieved of all the bad excreta. She will be content, satisfied, safe, while he will be admired, exhausted, exhilarated—triumphant. [*ibid.*, p. 84]

Disregarding, as far as one can, the language in which these phenomena are cast, one may recognize the processes as emblematic of a sense of fit, or right pattern, of discovery and recognition, of forms answering to our subjectivity, of creativity, generativity, new things growing out of what is already there, two entities combining that rightly belong together. Plato's metaphor in the *Symposium* comes to mind, where humankind is imagined to have started four-legged, four-armed, with a head twice the size, but now cloven into our present shapes because we misbehaved; the myth warns us to behave now, lest we be cloven again and condemned to hop on one foot, with half a head.

The myth is of things lost to one another, that should not have been sundered. Is this what happened to the Mariner? Was he too separated from his hate, which he was therefore powerless to control, and too separate from his love, which therefore could not exert control? The Mariner is overwhelmed by his own depths; his hate expresses itself in action and so he has to face his hate and its consequences. He now has to find a love he did not know he had. Fortunately it comes from the same depths, and surprises him. Now he has to live on, and integrate the two.

CHAPTER SIX

Love, some examples

T he present chapter comes at the question of love from a different angle, not theorizing but presenting a selection of writings by poets and mystics who at various times described their experiences of love, especially of loving God and feeling loved by God. What they say is interesting in itself and also because of what they say about God's response. Since they do not get this in a hundred-percent objectively unmistakable shared-reality e-mail sort of way, we can speculate more freely about different ways in which love can be understood. This understanding must depend at least in part on such factors as the personality of those reporting their experience and how this may have been shaped by idiosyncratic or cultural variations in the course of development.

It may be relevant to recapitulate the limits of our reach, as set out in Chapters Two and Three: when we consider reports on the love of God, we cannot know whether the love we are considering is the love of a constant and unchanging Object that may appear to show different aspects to different people, or whether we are looking at an entirely internal event subjectively generated by the speaker. In the latter case one hundred percent, but also in the former case though to a lesser extent, the nature of that love is determined by the local culture and by personal psychodynamics. If we ask whether the love that people express in their writings comes from their own need to love, or whether it is evoked by love from elsewhere, "out there", we cannot confidently assert the answer. Or, to put it the other way round, we cannot know whether, because of our pain or disappointment or ill will, we exclude intimations of an Other "out there" who loves us, or whether we do so because there really is nothing out there except our own projections.

Much of the writing of the mystics has come down to us in instructional-letter form, which was used either for convenience or as a literary device. The form lends itself to telling others how to do something—in the present case, how to climb a path, the mystics' ladder to love. These instructional communications have a tendency to dwell on the eradication of the self or of the sense of self, both often considered a hindrance to loving endeavour. Many are preoccupied with what precludes or occludes the love they seek, and with the struggle to be rid of whatever hampers a fuller experience of their love; Chapter Eleven considers these clinically very interesting issues of narcissism, its phenomena and how to get rid of them. The hatred of self which some of our writers express may appear unbalanced to our eyes; it is the hatred of a person struggling to get clear of the sticky habits of narcissistic feeling and thinking. Thomas à Kempis, the fifteenth-century author of *The Imitation of Christ*, writes, for instance: "Understand that you have made no progress until you have begun to feel yourself inferior to all" (Book 2, Chapter 2,2). Many writers advocate a way of abnegation, *via negativa*, which we may contrast with the positive *via affirmativa* recommended by those overcome by the experience of love, and filled with gratitude and a sometimes strange unself-consciousness.

Example: the sense of absence, of lack and of longing for love

Henry Suso, a Lowlander from the fourteenth century thought to have had an influence on Thomas à Kempis (vid. *Oxford Dictionary of the Christian Church*, 1957) wrote:

My mind has from the days of my childhood sought something with an earnest thirst of longing, Lord, and what that is I do not perfectly apprehend ... it is something that draws my heart and soul after it, and without it I can never attain perfect repose ... [Suso, Prologue to *The Little Book of Eternal Wisdom*]

Descriptions of longing for something we do not have, yet without which life seems hard to bear, are poignant to read, all the more because they so often awake in us feelings that might well carry resonances from a period in our lives when our needs could only be met by a mother or other carer who, with the best will in the world, cannot always be there at the exact moment she is needed. And all this, before we have the concepts in terms of which we might at least comprehend our misery. So there may be in these descriptions, a sense of desolation, at times of schizoid depression, of nothingness, abandonment and loss. A poem by St John of the Cross portrays this pain poignantly, each stanza ending with the despairing refrain that being alive is killing him. Using the brilliant Roy Campbell translations:

I live without inhabiting
Myself—In such a wise that I
Am dying that I do not die.

Within myself I do not dwell
Since without God I cannot live.
Reft of myself, and God as well,
What serves this life (I cannot tell)
Except a thousand deaths to give?
Since waiting here for life I lie
And die because I do not die ...

If in the hope I should delight,
Oh Lord, of seeing You appear,
The thought that I might lose Your sight
Doubles my sorrow and my fear.
Living as I do in such fright,
And yearning as I yearn, poor I
Must die because I do not die. [St John of the Cross, "The soul which suffers with impatience to see God", 1542–1591]

In one of Gerard Manley Hopkins' dark sonnets, the need for a caring motherly response flickers between the divine and the human.

No worst, there is none. Pitched past of grief,
More pangs will, schooled at forepangs, wilder wring.
Comforter, where, where is your comforting?
Mary, mother of us, where is your relief?
My cries heave, herds-long. ... [Hopkins, 1953, "No worst, there is
none. ..."]

The sense of something lacking, as a mode of experiencing love,
is also beautifully expressed by Ann Ridler, a twentieth-century
poet, in her verse-play *Cain*, at the end of which the chorus prays:

That the apple without core
The seedless briar
The house with no door
Love without longing
Here only a hopeless mystery
May find their heart and lackless love in thee. [Ridler, 1943]

Love and the life-cycle

Some writers convey an amazed sense that we can be known and
recognized by our loved one, while yet the loved one is
unknowable. In a similar vein, they often convey a sense of total
security in the loved one's love, accompanied by this amazed
disbelief that it should be so. And indeed there is perhaps a kind of
impertinence in believing that we can ever be totally known by
another person so that we can be loved without reserve,
unconditionally. Psychotherapists might attribute this ambivalent
feeling to memories of totally possessing, but in a part-object kind of
way, the breast of the mother, without any sense, at the time, that
there is more to be known—such knowledge comes later. Our
confidence in being loved, and our surprise at it, may echo from an
earlier era in our experiences of parents and siblings—preconcep-
tual experiences—of events that cannot be spoken of because the
words were not there at the time, experiences of love before the
advent of shame and guilt. Equally, our lack of confidence in love
may come from less happy early events.

There are many kinds of loving, many meanings to love. It
would be tedious to explicate, in each example of what follows, just

how a psychotherapist might comment. Provided we tread delicately, not too ploddingly, we may encounter some interesting two-way traffic, by means of which theories of psychodynamics illuminate some of our writers' experiences in new ways. Conversely, our writers' experiences, described before psychoanalysis was dreamt of, may throw light into corners that psychotherapists have not as yet looked into. If psychotherapists come to this literature with fewer professional preconceptions than we are in the habit of bringing to our case-histories, we may get quite an open-minded if still limited overview of love's great variety.

As we cannot undo our training, it may be as well to make explicit what, because of that training, psychotherapists are bound to have in mind as they read this material. It will be interesting, and conform to current psychotherapy habits, to notice the number of persons apparently present in the mind of the speaker or writer. As the next three chapters will illustrate, the incomplete development of object-constancy may be evident in descriptions of love and happiness that seem to refer to the writer's experience of togetherness or oneness in such a way that there is not a sense of an attachment between two, more a sense that there is only one person, one merged consciousness, one presence. From a different psychological source come descriptions of non-merging love and union or unity in which there is a sense of encounter. There are, of course, also more straightforward descriptions of love, more like the love we are currently used to, of one distinct person for another, or, sometimes, the love of one person for what is only a selected part of an other—part-object love. Also, we can sometimes distinguish when the direction of love is as from a parent to child and when it is more like that of a child for a parent.

Within descriptions of the more two-person kinds of love, we may distinguish the developmental stage to which the writer harks back. Are we hearing the baby-like love for the breast, or the toddler-like awareness either of grown-ups' frustrating ways or of their helpful expertise in providing what is wanted, or the child's trust that in its venturesome excursions it will be shielded from too much harm? Or are we hearing the excitement, adventure and discoveries of adolescence, perhaps accompanied by fear when going where grown-ups have indicated you should not go? And so on.

Thus psychotherapists might guess that seventeenth-century

Brother Lawrence had a parent who dealt tolerantly with childish misdemeanours, responding with a cuddle, perhaps.

> If sometimes my thoughts wander from God by necessity or infirmity, I am presently recalled by inward motions so charming and delicious that I am ashamed to mention them here. [Brother Lawrence, second letter]

Similarly we may surmise that it is from a stage of development when shame was a powerful emotion that George Herbert, Brother Lawrence's contemporary, derived his famous poem:

> Love bade me welcome; yet my soul drew back,
>   Guilty of dust and sin.
> But quick-eyed Love, observing me go slack
>   From my first entrance in,
> Drew nearer to me, sweetly questioning
>   If I lacked anything.
> "A guest", I answered, "Worthy to be here:"
>   Love said, "You shall be he".
> "I, the unkind, ungrateful? Ah, my dear,
>   I cannot look on Thee". [George Herbert, 1593–1632, "Love"]

In this poem the day is eventually won by the willingness to obey that marks fortunate children able to feel confident in their parents' judgement, and he does sit down and eat—after much argument. But it is a near thing.

These two quotations describe feelings involving two persons. We can find two-person accounts derived from infant experiences, from childhood, adolescence, and from maturity. Sometimes a kind of parent–child relation is involved; sometimes—though more rarely—the relation is as between adult lovers. Except in the context of the theology of the Trinity, there is not much on the model of three-person love such as would occur between three members of a family, though there is a good deal that may be seen as unconsciously Oedipal. In the world of Oedipal love there are by definition three persons, three corners to fight from. Usually there is the important *me*, the important *you*, and the third who should not be there. In the family this shows when the father, or the mother, or the child, feels painfully marginalized by the preoccupations of the other two. The feeling is then as between two persons, one of whom thinks that the relationship would be just fine if only that intrusive third person were not there, spoiling the bliss. In extreme versions of this, one person in the pair may be unwilling—or may think of the other as unwilling—to have any existence separate from the loved one. The next sub-section illustrates that this can become a relationship in which one partner is required to love nobody—or else everybody and everything indiscriminately—the lack of preference and the disregard of every quiddity proving the supremacy of the uniquely loved one.

Examples of exclusivity sometimes amounting to phobia

Fifteenth-century Thomas à Kempis writes, in *The Imitation of Christ*, Book Two, Chapter One:

> When a man values things as they really are, and not as the world says or thinks they are, he is truly wise, and has learned from God not men. He who knows how to live an inward life, and to give little heed to outward things, need not choose particular places or wait for the particular times for his works of piety. A spiritual man can recall his thoughts at once because he never gives all his mind to outward things. He that is inwardly well disposed and well ordered takes no notice of the strange and wicked doings of men. For the more one mixes in worldly business, the more hindrances and distractions one meets ...
>
> ... If you would deny yourself all comfort from without, you might enjoy heavenly meditations and be always glad within.
>
> And if all were well within your soul, and you were thoroughly clean of heart, everything would lead to your peace and profit. But because you are not yet thoroughly dead to yourself and detached of all earthly goods, you find that many things disgust you and rob you of your peace ... If you would deny yourself all comfort from without, you might enjoy heavenly meditation and be always glad within.
>
> We must not trust greatly in weak mortal man, however helpful to us and beloved. Neither should we take it too much to heart if we are sometimes thwarted and contradicted. He that is with you today may be against you tomorrow, for men are often as shifty as the

wind. Put all your trust in God; keep fear and love alike for Him
alone ...

... Why do you so much as look round you in this world, when it is
not to be your resting place?

A hundred and fifty years later, we find Brother Lawrence's first
letter expressing the same idea, a little more healthy-mindedly by
our standards, a little less intensely, but still with the idea that it is
alright for a jealous God, or any other jealous lover, not to want us to
find gratification anywhere else, and psychotherapists may be struck
by the oedipal flavour of this insistence on being a pair, the rejection
of the possibilities of three or more people loving one another.

... What I sought after ... was nothing but how to become wholly
God's ... I renounced for love of Him everything that was not He;
and I began to live as if there were none but He and I in the world.
[Brother Lawrence, *The Practice of the Presence of God*, first letter]

Example: a lack of claims secures a father's love

For centuries, spiritual advice seems to have emphasized the
importance of submission, to counteract any phantasies of self-
importance the child (or the ruler's subject) might entertain. You
must not assert your needs too forcefully to the person who loves
you. In modern psychotherapists' terms, the danger of punishment
from a jealous parent is averted by giving up what you want. This
may be seen in terms of oedipal fears, or as influenced by the child-
rearing practices of that day, which could tend toward this kind of
attitude, as we may guess from some of the chapter-headings in *The
Imitation of Christ, Book Three*.

8. On humbling oneself in the sight of God.
9. We must refer all things to God, as their last end.
11. The desires of the heart must be examined and controlled.
12. On acquiring patience, and striving against the flesh.

In more detail we find, in the text:

A great bar to God's visiting our souls is a certain false independence and great confidence in ourselves. [Book III, Chapter 9,2]

And,

> Study, my child, to do the will of others rather than your own.
> Always desire to have the least rather than the most. Always seek
> the lowest place. Always desire that the will of God may be wholly
> fulfilled in you. [Book III, Chapter 23,1]

Examples of childishness, eager obedience, and glad submission

Sometimes love brings humility, sometimes a very self-effacing
modesty, sometimes a conviction of ineradicable unworthiness. It
also, though more rarely, brings the thought that listening to the one
you love is more to the point than many protestations. But all these
attitudes are easily coloured by ideas that come from the culture's
child-rearing practices, ideas about how the good child should be.

George Herbert (1593–1633) wrote at a time when authority,
including parental authority, was thought of as legitimately
requiring obedience to an extent difficult for us to imagine, the
dominant culture taking it for granted that those in authority were
right, indeed appointed by God who was always right. Not
surprisingly, Herbert thought of God as a strict disciplinarian.
One of his poems, "Discipline", which used to be sung as a school
hymn, begins:

> Throw away Thy rod,
> Throw away Thy wrath;
>   O my God,
> Take the gentle path ...

and ends,

> Throw away Thy rod;
> Though man frailties hath,
>   Thou art God:
> Throw away Thy wrath. [George Herbert, "Discipline"]

In several other poems also, God is experienced as making Herbert
behave—for his own good, of course. "The Collar" begins:

I struck the board, and cry'd, "No more,
   I will abroad",
What, shall I ever sigh and pine?
My life and lines are free; free as the road ...

But after thirty more lines of this kind of tantrum, he ends:

But as I raved and grew more fierce and wild
   At every word,
Methought I heard one calling, "Child",
And I replied, "My Lord". [George Herbert, "The Collar"]

Was the toddler phase of Herbert's life perhaps of particular poignancy to him? Besides "Love bade me welcome" there is also an endearing hymn of his, about the joys of being safe with his loved one and being unable to express himself in words—again the age seems to be between two and five.

My joy, my life, my crown:
My heart was meaning all the day,
   Somewhat it fain would say,
And still it runneth muttering up and down
With only this, my Joy, my Life, my Crown. [George Herbert, "A true hymn"]

Nineteenth-century Teresa of Lisieux wrote explicitly that she studied to behave like a child, in a letter to the Reverend Mother Marie de Gonzague:

I looked in the Bible for some hint about the life I wanted and came across the passage where Eternal Wisdom says "Is anyone simple as a little child? Then let him come to me". To that Wisdom I went ... I read on and this is what I found: "I will console you like a mother consoling her son; you shall be like children carried at the breast, fondled on a mother's lap." Never were words so touching, never was such music to rejoice the heart. I could, after all, be lifted up to heaven, in the arms of Jesus. And if that was to happen, there was no need for me to grow bigger; on the contrary I must be as small as ever, smaller than ever. [Knox, 1958, p. 248]

St Teresa's mother died when Teresa was four years old, leaving her with her adoring and adored father and several sisters. Two of these took the veil before she did, and her younger sisters and a cousin did so after her. By the age of fourteen she was agitating in a formidable way—writing to the Bishop, writing to the Pope—to be allowed to enter the convent of her choice in spite of the rules that did not admit girls at this young age. Aware that her father was upset at the thought of losing her, she wrote of "this great sacrifice which is demanded of him" and also of the pride to be felt by her family at being related to this prodigy—herself. In keeping with nineteenth-century Romanticism about women, there are times when she sounds as though being a ninny were a form of holiness. In a letter to Sr. Marie, her sibling as well as her sister in religion, she writes, when she is a grown woman,

> "I'll try to put a few words together in a childish way, though always with the feeling that human speech itself is incapable of reproducing those experiences which the human heart only perceives confusedly.
>
> Don't think of me as buoyed up on a tide of spiritual consolation; my only consolation is to have none on this side of the grave. As for the instruction I get, our Lord bestows that on me in some hidden way, without ever making his voice heard. I don't get it from books, because I can't follow what I read nowadays ... The science of loving, yes, that phrase wakes a gracious echo in my soul; that's the only kind of science I want—I'd barter everything away, everything I possess to win it, and then, like the Bride in the Canticles, think nothing of my loss. It's only love that makes us what God wants us to be, and for that reason it's the only possession I covet. But how to come by it? Our Lord has seen fit to show me the only way which leads to it, and that is the unconcern with which a child goes to sleep in its father's arms." [*ibid.*, p. 227]

Example: love as a (well-intentioned) persecutor, the Hound of Heaven

I fled Him, down the nights and down the days;
I fled Him, down the arches of the years,
I fled Him, down the labyrinthine ways
  Of my own mind; and in the midst of tears
I hid from Him, and under running laughter.

Up vistaed hopes I sped;
And shot, precipitated,
Adown Titanic glooms of chasmed fears,
From those strong Feet that followed, followed after ...

... Still with unhurrying chase,
And unperturbed pace,
Deliberate speed, majestic instancy,
Came on the following Feet,
And a Voice above their beat—
"Naught shelters thee, who wilt not shelter Me. ...

... Strange piteous futile thing!
Wherefore should any set thee love apart?
Seeing none but I make much of naught" (He said),
"And human love needs human meritings ...

Alack, thou knowest not
How little worthy of any love thou art!
Whom wilt thou find to love ignoble thee,
Save Me, save only Me?
All which I took from thee I did but take,
Not for thy harms,
But just that thou mightst seek it in My arms. [Thompson (1859–
1907), "The Hound of Heaven"]

Examples of fearful and of trustful dependence

There are despairing, dramatic forms of dependence. Fourteenth-
century St. Catherine of Siena exclaimed that ...

... nothing except doing God's pleasure is of any value. The trouble
is that no opportunities occur to people as worthless as myself.

May it be your pleasure, O Lord, that the time may come when I
shall be able to pay you at least one farthing of the great sum I owe
you.

Be pleased to ordain that this servant of yours, O Lord, may serve
you in some way.

And Thomas à Kempis, gloomy as so often about people's capacity
to behave themselves, or God's ability to like them, writes

A great bar to God's visiting our souls is a certain false independence and great confidence in ourselves. [Book 2, Chapter 7,2]

But there are sunnier souls. Fourteenth-century Lady Julian of Norwich was one. Perhaps she too had toddler memories, but how different from George Herbert's or Francis Thompson's. She knows about the pleasures of supportive parents who enjoy children. No wonder she writes "All shall be well and all manner of thing shall be well". (Thirteenth Revelation, Chapter 27.) She writes of our self-disgust when we know we have done wrong, when "we know our sin" ...

... when we see ourselves so foul, we know that God is angry with us for our sin.

But since we then pray contritely, God forgives us.

It is then that our Lord in his courtesy shows himself to the soul, gaily and with cheerful countenance, giving it a friendly welcome as though it had been suffering in prison. My beloved, he says, I am glad you have come to me. In all your trouble I have been with you. Now you can see how I love you. We are made one in blessedness. [*Revelations of Divine Love*, Thirteenth Revelation, Chapter 40]

and

A constantly recurring feature of all the revelations which filled my soul with wonder as I diligently observed it, was that our Lord, as far as he himself is concerned, does not have to forgive, because it is impossible for him to be angry ...

The soul can see ... that we are eternally united to him in love, so it is absolutely impossible that God should be angry ... Where our Lord is, peace reigns. [*ibid.*, "About certain things in the previous fourteen revelations", Chapter 49]

Julian does not associate this kind of love directly with fathers, or with men. She has confidence in a God who is a loving mother. In her writings she repeatedly affirms that, much as she loves the Virgin Mary, the Blessed Mother of the Middle Ages, and much as Jesus loved his mother, Jesus is our true mother. Psychotherapists of our time could bet fairly confidently that Julian had warm reliable parents.

God is nearer to us than our own soul, for He is the ground in which it stands, and He is the means by which substance and sensuality are so held together that they can never separate. Our soul reposes in God its true rest, and stands in God its true strength, and is fundamentally rooted in God its eternal love. [*ibid.*, Chapter 59]

And seventeenth-century Brother Lawrence is reported to have told his interviewer that when he began his business "he said to God, with a filial trust in Him",

O my God, since Thou art with me and I must now, in obedience to Thy commands, apply my mind to these outward things, I beseech Thee to grant me the Grace to continue in Thy presence, and to this end, do Thou prosper me with Thy assistance, receive all my works, and possess all my affections. [*The Practice of the Presence of God*, Third Conversation]

Examples of happiness in the presence of the loved one

Naturally much is written about the love we feel when our loved one is actually there with us, both in the secular and in the religious sphere. Simone Weil (1950) had this delightful surprise. She was going over George Herbert's "Love bade me welcome ...", one of her favourite poems, when she experienced a direct contact with God.

It was during one of these recitations that Christ came down and took possession of me. In my arguments about the insolubility of the problem of God I had never foreseen the possibility of that, of a real contact, here below, person to person, between a human being and God ... I felt, in the midst of my suffering, the presence of a love like that which one can read in the smile of a beloved face. [Weil, 1950, p. 35]

Also when saying the Lord's Prayer

... or at other moments, Christ is present with me in person, but his presence is infinitely more real, more moving, more clear, than on that first occasion when he took possession of me. [*ibid.*, p. 38]

Even in the loved presence, a future time of absence may be

dreaded, and we may be haunted by some knowledge that, behind
the sense of a presence that comes occasionally and is in that sense
incompletely felt, there is a reality that is always there, is complete,
though not here and now. Like an infant's growing awareness that
behind the reliable comfort is a person who provides what is needed
but whose presence cannot be controlled or possessed. This
understanding is perfectly expressed by Charles Williams, some
of whose characters tend to remind themselves that "This is not
Thou but Thou art this also" (*War in Heaven*, 1930, p. 51 and p. 240,
Many Dimensions, 1931 p. 245 and *The Figure of Beatrice*, 1943, *passim*).

When the loved one appears, there is delighted recognition, as
when Dante hears Beatrice exclaiming

Ben sem, ben sem Beatrice.

and when Julian of Norwich had her revelations:

After this, our Lord showed Himself, in glory even greater than I
had seen before, so it seemed to me ... And he said again and again:
It is I, it is I who am most exalted, it is I whom you love. It is I whom
you delight in ... it is I whom you serve; it is I whom you long for,
whom you desire; it is I whom you mean; it is I who am all.
[*Revelations of Divine Love*, Twelfth Revelation, Chapter 26]

Sometimes this presence is experienced as a great stillness, or as
a union (of which more in the next chapter) that leaves nothing to be
desired or performed:

If you would ask, what is its essence—
This summit of all sense and knowing;
It comes from the Divinest Presence—
The sudden sense of Him outflowing,
In His great clemency bestowing
The gift that leaves men knowing naught,
Yet passing knowledge with their thought. [St John of the Cross,
"Verses written after an ecstasy of high exaltation"]

More sedately, eighteenth-century Gerhard Tersteegen wrote
very contentedly of

... the short rule of perfection, so to walk with God as we would
deal with our best friend, whom we love sincerely, whom we trust

without reserve or suspicion, to whom we reveal ourselves without shame, and in whose company we delight to be; who pleases us in everything, in what he is and what he does and whom we seek to please in all we do and have. [Tersteegen, letter VI]

Examples of the more mature forms of loving

The Lady Julian of Norwich combines the adult domestic and the adult festive in a way that has won her friends for six centuries. To her, love is like an unending party—she tactfully makes it clear it is not an orgy—with your loved one as the host, seeing

> ... our Lord as the head of his own house, who had invited all his dear servants and friends to a great feast. Utterly at home, and with perfect courtesy, himself as the eternal happiness and comfort of his beloved friends, the marvellous music of his unending love showing in the beauty of his blessed face. [The Sixth Revelation, Chapter 14]

More mature love requires what Melanie Klein named the depressive position, a deceptive name for a mental attitude that is depressing only when contrasted with hectic manic gaiety, but the term is in general use and so we use it. Those who have achieved the depressive position are able to acknowledge that their feelings sometimes pull them in opposite directions: to kill and to preserve, to act or speak, and also to sit still and listen, to feel at the same time amazingly privileged and quite undeserving. It takes maturity or, to put it operationally, the mature can be recognized by their ability to keep in mind two requirements that are not easily reconciled.

Whenever one tidies concepts, for the sake of theoretical consistency or for range of application, some interesting juxtapositions and contrasts get lost. Because we are still affected by the Victorians' and Edwardians' romantic reactions against their own domestic and sedate ways, we tend to lack respect for the kind of quiet piety that the Quakers, among others, were able to maintain for centuries, yet it is a form of loving quite as useful and beautiful as the more noisy effusions: married love may often be like this. This kind of love sits still and listens and can wait to respond, not impulsively but within an appropriate context.

We can see something like this in the literature. Walter Hilton, for example, from the fourteenth century, discusses the mystic dyad and how to achieve that good state of mind, and how to climb the "Ladder of Perfection". We need humility and love:

> Humility says "I am nothing. I have nothing". Love says "I only desire one thing, which is Jesus". [*The Ladder of Perfection*, Book 2, Chapter 21]

A soul conformed to the likeness of Jesus desires nothing but him, he writes.

> If only you could understand this, you would see that Jesus is everything and Jesus does everything. You yourself do nothing: You simply allow him to work within your soul, accepting sincerely and gladly whatever he deigns to do in you. [*ibid.*, Book 2, Chapter 24]

Is it impertinent to guess at the sort of childhood experiences that little Walter had? St John of the Cross, two centuries later, can strike an equally everyday note. You could just be lucky:

> For all the beauty life has got
> I'll never throw myself away
> Save for one thing I know not what
> Which lucky chance may bring my way …
>
> The man who strains for wealth and rank
> Employs more care, and wastes more health
> For riches that elude his stealth
> Than those he's hoarded in the bank;
> But I my fortune to advance
> The lowlier stoop my lowly lot
> Over some thing, I know not what,
> Which may be found by lucky chance,
>
> For that which by the sense down here
> Is comprehended as our good,
> And all that can be understood
> Although it soars sublime and sheer;
> For all that beauty can enhance—
> I'll never lose my happy lot.
> Only for that, I know not what,
> Which can be won by lucky chance. [St. John of the Cross, "With a divine intention"]

This sounds, typically for St. John of the Cross, like the attitude of a quite young adventurous man. Highly educated, intellectual, ultimately very influential even in his own time though twice confined to inactivity in a sort of imprisonment for expressing views the church authorities of his time did not like—just to remind ourselves that religion and goodness and good sense are only tenuously related, by lucky chance as he might well say—St. John of the Cross has an interestingly adult flavour. He certainly does not confine himself to the quiet holy life. He comes across as a person much aware of the *tremendum*, with an inner landscape as rugged as his native Spain. His metaphors of love and of encounters with the Holy are in terms of long tramps over the hills, being drunk, courting, and sexual enjoyment. But he is also the proponent of everyday experiences made holy, and of active enjoyment of unions human and divine. In "Songs between the soul and the bridegroom", the soul—the bride—sings:

> Where can your hiding be,
> Beloved, that you left me thus to moan?

And so on for forty-one stanzas, with much detail of the fun the lovers have, until in the end, the bridegroom finds her:

> Now, as she long aspired,
> Into the garden comes the bride, a guest:
> And in its shade retired
> Has leant her neck to rest
> Against the gentle arm of the Desired. ["Songs between the soul and the bridegroom"]

Even more explicitly sexual is the "Song of the Soul in intimate communication and union with the love of God":

> Oh flame of love so living,
> How tenderly you force
> To my soul's inmost core your fiery probe!
> Since now you've no misgiving,
> End it, pursue your course
> And for our sweet encounter tear the robe!

In the same century Brother Lawrence, in most ways a contrast to John, not learned in scholarship, amiably sedate, equally adult, with another kind of healthy-mindedness, comfortable with himself, displays a similar down-to-earth intimacy with the ineffable, and the conflict-free lack of alienation that John enjoyed when not afflicted with his dark night of the soul. Lawrence lived with his sense of the Holy by roundly declaring that everything is holy, and that the Other is here and now. He is reported as saying

> that it is a great delusion to believe that prayer ought to differ from other times, that we are as strictly obliged to adhere to God by action in the time of action as by prayer in its season. That his prayer was nothing but a sense of the presence of God, his soul being at that time insensible to everything but the divine love, and that when the appointed times of prayer were past he found no difference because he still continued with God, praising and blessing Him with all his might, so that he passed his life in continual joy. [*The Practice of the Presence of God*, Fourth conversation]

To direct his attention, he seems to have been able to hold in mind his sense of the incomprehensibility of God and at the same time God's loving-kindness and nearness. When he could not make sense of these apparent contradictions he seems to have just shrugged his shoulders: "Well, what can one expect, after all, God is mysterious". Of course, all of us must shrug before the ineffable eventually, but Lawrence does it so comfortably!

From this we move appropriately to Leigh Hunt, who, a century later (1784–1859), expressed what may still be thought a typically English pragmatic view of what love is.

> Abou Ben Adhem (may his tribe increase!)
> Awoke one night from a deep dream of peace,
> And saw, within the moonlight in his room,
> Making it rich, and like a lily in bloom,
> An angel writing in a book of gold:—
> Exceeding peace had made Ben Adhem bold,
> And to the presence in the room he said,
> "What writest thou?"—The vision rais'd its head,
> And with a look made of all sweet accord,
> Answer'd, "The names of those who love the Lord."
> "And is mine one?" said Abou. "Nay, not so,"
> Replied the angel. Abou spoke more low,

But cheerly still; and said, "I pray thee, then,
Write me as one that loves his fellow men."
 The angel wrote, and vanished. The next night
It came again with a great wakening light,
And show'd the names whom love of God had blest,
And lo! Ben Adhem's name led all the rest. [Hunt, "Abou Ben Adhem"]

Twentieth-century Simone Weil appears quintessentially French to English eyes. The austerely cerebral side of her nature is likely to have had an origin in her family-situation as well as in the French culture of her day, which tended to force the intellectual formation of its brighter children and perhaps still does. Very widely read, Jewish by birth, she was deeply responsive to Christianity at its best. Her "Spiritual Autobiography" gives an insight into the way her earlier life coloured her religious experiences, and accounts for the sense of painful striving—nothing is ever enough—that characterizes much of her all too short life.

At fourteen I fell into one of those fits of bottomless despair which come with adolescence, and I seriously thought of dying because of the mediocrity of my natural faculties. The exceptional gifts of my brother, who had a childhood and youth comparable to that of Pascal, brought my own inferiority home to me. I did not mind having no visible successes but what did grieve me was the idea of being excluded from that transcendent kingdom to which only the truly great have access and where truth abides. I preferred to die rather than live without that truth. [Weil, *Waiting on God*, 1950, p. 30]

After a while, she writes, she realized that anyone can get there who works hard enough. She became a stoic.

The duty of acceptance in all that concerns the will of God was ... impressed upon my mind as the first and most necessary of all duties, from the time I found it set down in Marcus Aurelius under the form of the *amor fati* of the Stoics. [*ibid.*, p. 32]

Attracted by stoicism, she goes beyond it, as Marcus Aurelius did before her. In "Last Thoughts" she writes:

Every existing thing is equally upheld in its existence by God's creative love. The friends of God should love him to the point of merging their love into his with regard to all things here below.

When a soul has attained a love which fills the whole universe indiscriminately, this love becomes the bird with the golden wings which pierces an opening in the egg of the world. After that, such a soul loves the universe, not from within but from without, from the dwelling-place of the Wisdom of God, our first-born brother. Such a love does not love beings and things in God, but from the abode of God. Being close to God it views all beings and things from there, and its gaze is merged in the gaze of God. [*ibid.*, p. 61]

Weil advocated a kind of holy inactivity she called *hypomene*, which might perhaps be freely translated as *Waiting on God*, the title of her book of letters and essays.

The attitude which brings about salvation is not any form of activity. The Greek word which expresses it is *hypomene*, and *patienta* is rather an inadequate translation of it. It is the waiting or attentive and faithful immobility which lasts indefinitely and which cannot be shaken. [*ibid.*, p. 149]

She derives the word from what the Roman door-slave was supposed to do, who sits all day by the door in order to open it at whatever time the master comes, so that the master does not have to trouble himself.

... Active searching is prejudicial ...

God tells us through his prophet what we must do. "Vacate et vedete quoniam ego sum Deo". [*ibid.*]

In English: be passive and empty, to know how I am God.

Simone Weil's life and thoughts are original and profoundly moving. She tried, almost entirely on her own, to live a spiritually pure and conscientiously moral life in a world much like our own, whose corruption, exploitation and callousness oppressed her constantly and so inescapably that she felt she must share the life of those most at the mercy of these malign processes. She did not want to live a life that would give her more material gratification than was afforded to the most unskilled labouring men or women, indeed to people even further down the socio–economic scale, and without their less holy compensations. Believing in the sacraments as they were thought of in the 1930s and 1940s, she yet stayed outside the church, feeling it inappropriate to share in the felicities which she believed the church to have available because, more urgently than this, she felt she had to share the deprivations of the most unfortunate.

Weil thought that some failures in love might be due to our immaturity. She had in mind only the most spiritual kinds of love, but some of it also applies to love between ordinary people, for our expectations of love are often so sublime as to be unrealistic and unachievable without huge effort, as many people discover when they guilelessly commit themselves to loving someone for ever, without any preparation for such an undertaking. Weil considered that we might be too unformed to dedicate ourselves in any meaningful way to the love of God; it might be best to practice easier forms of loving until we were ready for the love of God effectively and realistically, much as everyone might benefit if we had to take care of a puppy or a kitten before committing ourselves to a human baby. It may be presumptuous to assume that we are ready to take on *mysterium tremendum* the moment we first hear of it, when we are as yet making a great mess of human loving. Weil evolved a theory of "implicit" forms of the love of God which, if we engage in them, will enable us eventually to love God above all, in unencumbered happiness and union. Such a practice-run

> ... cannot have God as its object, since God is not present to the soul, and never yet has been so. It must then have another object. Yet it is destined to become the love of God. We can call it the indirect or implicit love of God. [*ibid.*, p. 90]

She identified three of these implicit forms, three loves in which God is present though hidden: religious ceremony and ritual, the beauty and order of nature, and our fellow human beings. These are three conduits through which we can come to a state of mind that enables us to love God more as God is, who by then may have become apparent to us behind all the transparencies.

Final examples: completion and repose

> O Godhead: You are a deep sea, into which the deeper I enter the more I find, and the more I find the more I seek. The soul revels in You. [Catherine of Siena, Eighth Letter]

Here is no sense of anything but enjoyment, without knowledge of what is being enjoyed. The soul realises that it is enjoying some good thing that contains all good things together, but it cannot comprehend this good thing. [Catherine of Siena, Twelfth Letter]

You are our resting-place. When we come to you we have nothing else to search for or to desire, or to disquiet ourselves at all; and then our soul perceives that it has reached the haven where it would be; it has found the place where it can rest. [Tersteegen, letter VIII]

CHAPTER SEVEN

Blurred boundaries and bliss, union, communion and projective processes

I n the chapters on love, the focus was on love. In this chapter the focus is on enjoyment, pleasure, happiness, and other such irenic feelings, not much mentioned at this time of writing except in connection with sex and other consumer goods. The *Shorter Oxford English Dictionary* defines bliss as "blitheness" and under blitheness we find "gladness, enjoyment, esp. the beatitude of heaven". In connection with the adjective blithe, the *Dictionary* offers "jocund, gay, sprightly, merry, joyous, cheerful, glad, happy, well", uncommon words, when we consider how frequently we encounter love-related words in print and speech. Is it just our convention not to allude to happiness, enjoyment and pleasure so much, or do we conceal these feelings from ourselves, or do we just not feel them so often? Certainly it is worth noting that, at the time of writing, at the turn of the millennium, psychotherapists are tending to ignore expressions of such positive feelings in the expectation that they cover other feelings, thought to be more genuine, of depression and anger. Are those psychotherapists always right about this, or are they projecting their own experiences of darkness on to a world that, whatever its appalling atrocities and occasional preference for dreariness, is yet at many moments cheerier than they can perceive? Is the only thoughtless fun we are allowed either in bed or under the influence of chemicals?

Because of their traditions and training, few psychotherapists just now take a serious interest in their patients' reports on the stirrings of joy, felicity or contentment, and we are perhaps less perturbed by the absence of these feelings than is in the best interests of our patients; such disregard may give them the impression that these feelings are irrelevant, unimportant, or displaced aspects of psychic life, or perhaps just by-products of more important events. But Heinz Kohut is among the exceptions. It is not irrelevant that he sees idealization (almost universally written off as neurotic) as capable of being a positive and benign process. Thus in his discussion of "Miss V" he takes trouble to understand the flattened affect and sense of strain in her life.

> Miss V., a forty-two-year-old single woman, a talented but unproductive artist, had sought analysis because of recurrent episodes of fairly severe but nonpsychotic, empty depression ...

> I have in recent years, after gathering a considerable amount of clinical experience in this area, analysed two other patients suffering from recurrent nonpsychotic empty depression—i.e. depressive episodes in which guilt feelings and/or self-accusations played no significant role—suffered by women whose personality make-up was not unlike Miss V.'s. [Kohut, 1977, p. 58]

Kohut refers to

> ... the primary defect in Miss V.'s personality structure—dynamically related to the periods of protracted enfeeblement of her self, when she was lethargic, unproductive, indeed lifeless. [ibid., p. 59]

And he comments:

> Whatever the exact diagnostic category may have been, into which her mother's disturbance fell, it is clear that as a small child the patient had been exposed to traumatic disappointments from the side of her mother, whose mirroring responses had not only been deficient much of the time (either altogether absent or flat), but also frequently defective (bizarre and capricious). ... [ibid., p. 60]

> The propensity toward the periodic enfeeblement of Miss V.'s self was thus established in early childhood in the pathogenic matrix of

her relation to the mirroring mother. Miss V. had, however, been a vigorous and well-endowed child who did not give up the struggle for emotional survival. Trying to extricate herself from the pathogenic relation with her mother, she had attached herself with great intensity to her father, a successful manufacturer with frustrated artistic talents and ambitions who, on the whole, responded to his daughter's needs. Her relation to the father thus became the matrix from which she developed those talents and interests—in the terms of clinical theory, those compensatory structures—which ultimately led to her career. And from it also grew the idealised aims that stimulated the creative potential of her self. [*ibid.*, p. 61]

Speaking generally, psychotherapists disregard or misprize the phenomena of joy, of rapture, of loving unreservedly. This is so whether the love is of art, of God, of swimming, horses, the clarinet, or whatever: joy is not given as much attention as, say, the lavatory. But there must be room in a healthy and happy life for something to which the heart is given unreservedly. That being so, it may be spoken of, and its absence remarked. On the other hand, are some people on the mystic path perhaps too complacent at times, too unregarding or too ignorant of the oppression in everyday life felt by those who carry taxing responsibilities of domestic or paid work?

Admittedly, people may take unrealistic manic flights from the stresses of life. Yet we should not sideline, by silence in the consulting-room, the knowledge that everyone, whether or not they have known good child-care, needs at times to love unreservedly and be happily absorbed by the enjoyment of love. If we ignore that need, though it may come in the form of a passion for Inuit culture or interplanetary travel, there will be a sense of lack and emptiness in the consulting-room. C. S. Lewis, in many ways as boisterously extravert and prosaic a nuncle as one could come across among educated early-twentieth-century men, was six years old when he had his first intimation of what he called Joy. Decades later he was to write:

As I stood beside a flowering currant bush on a summer's day, there suddenly arose in me without warning, and as if from a depth not of years but of centuries, the memory of that earlier morning at the Old House when my brother had brought his toy garden into the nursery. It is difficult for me to find words strong enough for the sensation which came over me; Milton's "enormous bliss" of Eden comes somewhere near it. It was a sensation, of course, of desire;

but desire for what? Not, certainly, for a biscuit-tin filled with moss, nor even (though that came into it) for my own past, ... and before I knew what I desired, the desire itself was gone, the whole glimpse withdrawn, the world turned commonplace again, or only stirred by a longing for the longing which had ceased. It had taken only a moment of time; and in a certain sense everything that had ever happened to me was insignificant in comparison. [Lewis, 1955, pp. 18–19]

Rebecca West, contemporary with C. S. Lewis though her book was not published until 1984, writes of a similar experience. Her heroine, with her sisters, her brother and her mother, is looking at the first flowers they had ever grown in their garden.

It was then, I remember, that my happiness became ecstatic, that I felt again impatience because one cannot live slowly as one can play music slowly. What was happening was the vaguest possible event, a matter of faint smiles and semi-tones of tenderness. A woman in late middle-age, four young girls and a schoolboy were looking at two common sorts of flowers and were not so much talking as handing amiable words from one to another, like children passing round a box of chocolates. I could not imagine why the blood should sing in my ears and I should feel that this was the sort of thing that music was about. But the moment passed before I could explain its importance to myself, for someone called from the house, and we looked around irritably, angry because our closed circle was broken. [West, 1991, pp. 11–12]

Both these incidents took place in gardens; gardens seem to have an affinity with bliss. Paradise is a garden, after all. But W. B. Yeats found rapture in a London café, as did Betjeman's lovers (*viz*. sup. p. 36)

My fiftieth year had come and gone,
And I sat, a solitary man,
In a crowded London shop,
An open book and empty cup
On the marble table-top.

While on the shop and street I gazed
My body of a sudden blazed;
And twenty minutes more or less
It seemed, so great my happiness,
That I was blessed and could bless. [Yeats, 1990, "Vacillation"]

A young Polish girl, Eva Hoffman, later in the twentieth century, remembers.

> It is a sunny fall afternoon and I'm engaged in one of my favourite pastimes—picking chestnuts. I'm playing alone under a spreading, leafy, protective tree. My mother is sitting on a bench nearby, rocking the buggy in which my sister is asleep ... I pick up a reddish brown chestnut, and suddenly, through its warm skin, I feel the beat as of a heart. But the beat is also in everything else around me, and everything pulsates and shimmers as if it were coursing with the blood of life. Stooping under the tree, I am holding life in my hand, and I am in the centre of a harmonious, vibrating transparency. For that moment I know everything there is to know. I have stumbled into the very centre of plenitude, and I hold myself still with fulfillment, before the knowledge of my knowledge escapes me. [Hoffman, 1989, *Lost in Translation*, pp. 41–42]

Ann Ashworth (1998, p. 9), a member of the Quaker Universalist Group, is impressed by

> Annie Dillard, a scientist with a religious sense of wonder [who] suggests that as infants we are most astonishingly set down here and begin at once upon our required function to explore the place. Scientists, artists, poets and mystics remain infants in this sense, always exploring, always astonished, always ready to behold the burning bush ... In *Pilgrim at Tinker Creek*, Dillard relates how a blind girl, after an operation in which she received her sight, saw what she described as a tree with lights in it—presumably flowers or fruit.

>> "It was for this tree I searched through the peach orchards of summer, in the forests of fall and down winter and spring for years. Then one day I was walking along Tinker Creek thinking of nothing at all and I saw the tree with the lights in it. I saw the backyard cedar ... charged and transfigured, each cell buzzing with flame. I stood on the grass with the lights in it, grass that was wholly fire ... It was less like seeing than like being for the first time seen, knocked breathless by a powerful glance. The flood of fire abated , but I'm still spending the power ... I was still ringing; I had been my whole life a bell, and never knew it until at that moment I was lifted and struck ...

>> The vision comes and, mostly, goes, but I live for it, for the moment when the mountains open and a new light roars in spate through the crack. [Dillard, 1975, p. 38 and p. 42]

Later in the book, Dillard speculates:

> The question for agnosticism is "Who turned on the lights?" The
> question from faith is "Whatever for?" [Ashworth, 1998, p. 9]

Representative of a more Christian and therefore more personal
perspective, St Teresa of Avila writes, of the fourth stage of prayer—

> Here there is no sense of anything but enjoyment, without any
> knowledge of what is being enjoyed. The soul realises that it is
> enjoying some good thing that contains all good things together, but
> it cannot comprehend this good thing. [*The Life of the Holy Mother
> Teresa*, Chapter XXI]

and in response to her question about what the soul does in prayer,

> The Lord said to me "It dissolves utterly, my daughter, to rest more
> and more in me. It is no longer itself that lives, it is I. As it cannot
> comprehend what it understands, it understands by not under-
> standing". [*ibid.*]

The *Shorter Oxford English Dictionary*'s first entry for "rapture" is
in terms of being seized and carried off. Lacking a sense of humour,
the *Dictionary* reminds us also to think of rapture as "the act of
conveying a person from one place to another, esp. to heaven" and
that hence rapture is "a transport of mind, ecstasy, now esp. ecstatic
joy or delight". In keeping with twentieth-century ways of thinking,
which fear to be mocked for imagining God as an old person with a
beard, nothing in these dictionary-definitions hints at anything
interpersonal: the definitions of rapture are divorced from loving a
person or being loved. So indeed are some earlier accounts, and at
least one twentieth-century description by a believing Christian:
Simone Weil describes for a priest-friend how she had started to say
the Lord's Prayer with concentrated attention and how this had
transported her to an object-less state of rapture:

> At times the very first words tear my thoughts from my body and
> transport it to a place outside space where there is neither
> perspective nor point of view. The infinity of the ordinary expanses
> of perception is replaced by an infinity to the second and sometimes
> to the third degree. At the same time, filling every part of this
> infinity of infinity, there is silence, a silence which is not an absence

of sound but which is the object of a positive sensation, more positive than that of sound. Noises, if there are any, only reach me after crossing this silence. [Weil, 1950, p. 38]

Teresa of Avila distinguishes between an experience of union, which she sees as eventless from onset to end, and rapture, which comes as a shock; against the former, resistance is possible, but not against rapture.

The Lord carries up the soul just as one might say the clouds gather up the mists of the earth, and carries it right out of itself. [*The Life of the Holy Mother Teresa*, Chapter XX]

The experience appears to be of being lifted up and carried about, and liking it but not liking the lack of control, maybe rather like the experience of an infant under indifferent child-care, say a professionally-minded wet-nurse. In the days of high infant-mortality, perhaps small babies, when picked up and carried about, were glad to be taken notice of, however roughly—at least they were not ignored. Brother Lawrence, we may speculate, had happier infant times.

Whenever Thou, O Lord God, all-holy lover of my soul, drawest near to me, my whole being is filled with joy. Thou art my glory and the joy of my heart. [Brother Lawrence, *The Practice of the Presence of God*, Second Letter]

and:

At other times when I apply myself to prayer I feel all my spirit and all my soul lift itself up without any care or effort of mine, and it continues as it were suspended and firmly fixed in God, as its centre and place of rest. [*ibid.*]

It is difficult to get a clear picture of what makes them all so happy. They write of rapture, bliss, peace, joy, but not psycho-analytically and, inconveniently for our purpose, they usually drift off into other topics, such as how to behave well. But the sense of union is certainly a recurrent source of happiness—again, some-times with a resonance from infancy—the writer having no consciousness of self but still aware of being blissfully at one with some greater being.

I want to explain the soul's feeling when it is in this divine unity. It is plain enough what union is: in union two separate things become one. [*The Life of the Holy Mother Teresa*, Chapter XX]

Fortunate infants may have experienced this boundless bliss and happiness uncontaminated by fears for the future or memories of past pain, at a time when life was not experienced in conceptualized mode, let alone in clear words. These moments could have an unbounded, ineffable quality, which can be alluded to but not described.

The gift that leaves men knowing nought,
Yet passing knowledge with their thought. [St John of the Cross, "Verses written after an ecstasy of high exaltation"]

Christopher Bollas (1987), centuries later, was to write of the "unthought known"; these accounts seem to have that element in them.

Love, and a sense of undeserved bounty gratuitously offered, commonly celebrated in religion, is available to many fortunate infants and fortunate adult lovers. Different writers seem to draw on different stages of the human life-cycle for the language in which to phrase these kinds of feelings. Perhaps because of the long celibate tradition of Christianity, there are relatively few resonances from sane mature sexual experience. St John of the Cross is an exception; he is the great poet of adult bliss analogous to the soul's happiness with God. There is a masculine sense of enterprise in his descriptions of seeking for a lover, in his quest for God. Both active and passive, he obviously enjoys the whole process, as in his "Song of the soul in rapture at having arrived at the height of perfection which is union with God by the road of spiritual negation".

Upon a gloomy night,
With all my cares to loving ardour flushed,
(O venture of delight!)
With nobody in sight
I went abroad when all my house was hushed.

In safety, in disguise,
In darkness up the secret stair I crept,
(O happy enterprise)
Concealed from other eyes
When all my house at length in silence slept ...

Oh night that was my guide:
Oh darkness dearer than the morning's pride,
Oh night that joined the lover
To the beloved bride
Transfiguring them each into the other.

Lost to myself I stayed
My face upon my lover having laid,
From all endeavour ceasing ...

In "The song between the soul and bridegroom", there is courtship:

Rejoice, my love, with me
And in your beauty see us both reflected:
By mountain-slope and lea,
Where purest rills run free,
We'll pass into the forest undetected.

There are references to adult genital love-making in the "Song of the soul in intimate communication and union with the love of God" (see p. 120). There are adult elements in other writers too, though not always so strikingly and not so genitally, among the sane ones, anyway.

The majesty and beauty remained so deeply imprinted on my soul that they are unforgettable ... The soul is itself no longer: it is intoxicated. [*The Life of the Holy Mother Teresa*, Chapter XV]

Julian of Norwich has an image of happiness as a grand endless party, a robust grown-up image (see p. 118). But focusing on the bliss-of-union aspect of some mystics' lives may confuse our understanding of them. Julian, John, Teresa of Avila, Lawrence and others led lives as busy as modern corporation executives, creating and managing organizations, writing, teaching, and training. After the peace and union that marks St Teresa's second stage of prayer, for instance, comes a third stage that shows that this kind of mystic experience combines well with normal practical activities.

This state of prayer seems to me a most definite union of the whole soul with God, complete but for the fact that His majesty appears to allow the faculties to be conscious of and to enjoy the great work that he is doing ... There is the will, alone and abiding in great peace, while the understanding and the memory are so free that they can attend to business or do works of charity. [*ibid.*]

And Brother Lawrence, busy kitchen-porter and later something like catering-manager as well as spiritual adviser, can nevertheless write that

There is not in the world a life more sweet and delightful than that of a continual conversation with God; those only can comprehend it who practise and experience it. [Brother Lawrence, *The Practice the Presence of God*, Fifth Letter]

The bliss of breakthrough and mended splits

There is a structural connection between instances of the more adult experience of bliss, and the instances of revelation, of parameter shift, alluded to in previous chapters as the joy of finding and recognizing a world that is more transparent than had been previously thought, when a greater congruence or fit is revealed than had been hoped for. Coleridge's Mariner had his moment of surprise, of transparency and breakthrough, when the horrendous snakes became messengers of beauty and grace; and overall his story is of a man who is overwhelmed by a knowledge of himself and his world that he had hitherto denied, and who is now integrating it—that is, effecting a union with it, and feeling at one with himself. Dante had this kind of revelation whenever he met Beatrice; that was when he knew who he was, and for what purpose he had these breakthroughs into new knowledge of himself and of his place in the world. It is what C. S. Lewis must have had in mind when he called his autobiography *Surprised by Joy* (1955), and Hopkins when he wrote

> let joy size
> At God knows when to God knows what; whose smile
> 's not wrung, see you; unforeseen times rather—as skies
> Betweenpie mountains—lights a lovely mile. [Hopkins, 1953,
> "My own heart let me more have pity on"]

A breakthrough may bring about an emergence into greater harmony, a growth into something more unified, with a better congruence and a more focused sense of fit. What had been thought one thing, separate from some other thing, now appears in a context not hitherto suspected. What had appeared separated by a boundary, with a thick pencil-line round it, is now seen as a necessary part of some more comprehensive complexity. These surprising shifts are not uncommon in adolescent development but they may occur at any time if we are lucky. Of course they are not necessarily experienced in a religious context. The sense of two parts that at one time belonged together, or that ought to belong together, is at least as old as Plato's *Symposium*, and has to an extent been revived in the Jungian concept of the *coniunctio*, and by the post-Kleinian notion that until people are reconciled to the idea that their parents also belong to each other in a relationship that excludes the child, people cannot be at ease with themselves, cannot have inner harmony and a feeling of oneness with others.

As ever in these discussions, the question we must not ask—for we cannot achieve a definitive answer—is whether we are here considering an integration in a person's inner world, or whether we are considering a more accurate and comprehensive encounter with what is not us but other—if indeed we can validly make such a distinction.

Nature mysticism

The experience of union and breakthrough may be cast in a religious idiom and be in that sense interpersonal, but it need not be so. As an example from the eighteenth century comes a poem by a considerable poet, of whom Samuel Johnson spoke as poor Kit Smart because he was not always in his right mind. His "Song to David" is a rapturous outpouring of bliss, without reference to anyone actually experiencing the bliss—the boundary line between himself and other blissful existence is not there. Three stanzas may stand for all thirty-eight, all overflowing with joy, like St. Francis' *Canticle*.

> For Adoration seasons change,
> And order, truth, and beauty range,
>   Adjust, attract, and fill:
> The grass the polyanthus cheques;

And polished porphyry reflects,
  By the descending rill.

Rich almonds colour to the prime
For Adoration; tendrils climb
  And fruit trees pledge their gems;
And Icis with her gorgeous vest,
Builds for her eggs her cunning nest,
  And bell-flowers blow their stems.

The spotted ounce and playsome cubs
Run rustling 'mongst the flowering shrubs,
  And lizards feed the moss;
For Adoration beasts embark,
While waves upholding halcyon's ark
  No longer roar and toss. [Christopher Smart, "A song to David"]

Wordsworth's poetry abounds in instances of this sense of unity with nature, though the rapture is more sedate, more philosophical, and a touch more interpersonal. Rather than adduce his familiar verses, however, here is a similar experience put into words by a twentieth-century psychoanalyst already quoted in more obviously professional contexts.

... as a child, I spent a lot of the time wandering about on my own. In some ways, the world was not as dangerous as now, and my mother gave me considerable freedom to wander as I pleased. So, for me, the fields, the woods, the trees, perhaps even the sky were like an extension of home. They were part of my territory—a kind of outreach of it—but one in which I could feel alive and nourished, rather than oppressed and hemmed in.

In this mode, then, I felt like lord of my own kingdom. Although I was alone, I found "soul food" everywhere—the shapes and sounds, the colours and smells of the natural world were all there to support me. *I was alone, but when I reached out, something responded.* You can imagine how readily I warmed to the poet Wordsworth when I discovered him years later! He was talking of *my* experience when he wrote of nature as a *presence* by which one feels in some way looked after.

Nature, of course, is not always experienced in this way; nor would I suggest that there is in fact a spirit in nature which some can sense and others cannot. I am merely saying that the natural world can lend *itself* to being experienced in this way when a person reaches out towards it from a particular state of need. [Wright, 1996, pp. 71–72]

Some pages of great subtlety and sympathy, in R. C. Zaehner's *Mysticism Sacred and Profane* (1961, pp. 45–49), explore the state of mind in which a person feels deeply and rewardingly involved with something other and greater, when this other is experienced *via* nature or in nature. He quotes Richard Jefferies, a nineteenth-century mystic who fiercely rejected organized religion and scorned other people's hopes of a benign Deity or a benevolent Nature, yet knew these raptures.

> I was utterly alone with the sun and the earth. Lying down on the grass, I spoke in my soul to the earth, the sun, the air … I thought of the earth's firmness—I felt it bear me up; through the grassy couch there came an influence as if I could feel the great earth speaking to me … I spoke to the sea … I desired to have its strength, its mystery and glory. Then I addressed the sun, desiring the soul equivalent of his light and brilliance …

> Touching the crumble of earth, the blade of grass, the thyme flower, breathing the earth-encircling air, thinking of the sea and the sky, holding my hand for the sun-beams to touch it, prone on the sward in token of deep reverence, thus I prayed that I might touch the unutterable existence infinitely higher than deity. [Jefferies, 1912 edition, p. 104]

How can this be, asks Zaehner, that a man who does not think personally of these things, yet feels in communion with them? He comes to the conclusion, well before the time when the concept was formally evolved, that there is a process very like what has come to be called projective identification. Zaehner considers that Jefferies attributes some of his own apprehension of beauty and infinity to the world of nature, and that when he then contemplates that world, he is moved to rapture. He writes of Jefferies that "it is not the physical object with which he communes, but its 'inner meaning', the idea or essence that a man projects into it, or draws out of it" (Zaehner, 1961, p. 47). Its inscape.

These phenomena certainly touch on what has come to be thought of as "projective identification", but that process, or its cognates, may appertain only to one aspect of an experience that has other qualities. In the late twentieth century several other apparently unrelated psychoanalytic writers took an interest in these experiences and wrote about them, but these flickers never joined into one blaze. Perhaps we are not yet ready to work on the matter, but Chapter Nine (pp. 178–184) devotes some more attention to it.

The mutual rapture of three united elements

In Western culture, at least, we keep encountering the assumption that, ideally, three elements are required for an operational definition of the processes of living and loving. There is the constellation of father, mother, and child, the "nuclear family". Changing the focus, there is Otto Kernberg's succinct paradigm in which the basic units—the bricks with which our inner world is built—are the three elements "I" (the *subject*), "you" or "it" (the *object*), and, thirdly, the *process* or *relationship* between them, between subject and object, that binds them and defines them reciprocally as subject and object (Kernberg, 1976). This process or relationship Kernberg thinks of as instinctually or affectively driven—it gives the other two elements their meaning and unites them. In this way Kernberg reconciles Freudian classical instinct-drive theory with the later objects-relations approach.

This is a very useful way of thinking for clinical purposes, for instance when trying to understand a dream or some other form of coded behaviour whose meaning escapes the conscious person: we can see that somebody or some agency is doing something to somebody else or something else. Thus my dream of locusts descending on a field and devouring it, might be thought of as somebody or something (the subject, here represented by locusts) descending and devouring something or somebody (here represented by the field). I may then ask "Have my thoughts recently been in terms that could be described as of somebody—perhaps me, perhaps someone else—descending on and devouring somebody— perhaps someone else, perhaps me?" The verb or activity or process links two elements, one of which is subject and the other object, though we may have to puzzle out which is which.

The idea that the very real has *three* elements, with a third existing as a result of two other parts, and as real as they, is also shown in the Trinitarian approach of much Christian theology. In the context of an authoritarian intellectual climate this presented no problems—you believed because you were told to believe even if it sounded odd. Thus the Athanasian Creed, formulated at some time in the late fourteenth century, translated for the Anglican *Book of Common Prayer*, and still recited in churches, proclaims

> For there is one Person of the Father, another of the Son,
> And another of the Holy Ghost ...
>
> The Father uncreate, the Son uncreate, and the Holy Ghost uncreate.
>
> The Father incomprehensible, the Son incomprehensible, and the Holy Ghost incomprehensible.
>
> The Father eternal, the Son eternal, and the Holy Ghost eternal.
>
> And yet they are not three eternals but one eternal.
>
> And also there are not three incomprehensible nor three uncreated, but one uncreated and one incomprehensible ...
>
> And yet there are not three lords but one Lord ...

It makes no sense and the people who formulated it knew it could not be made to sound logical, but nevertheless they warned that it was what "except a man believe faithfully, he cannot be saved". Authority stifles thought. But there is more to be thought about; there are mystics who describe these arcane mysteries in a poetic fashion to which the heart may respond more wholesomely.

It is axiomatic in Christian theology that God is loving, God is love. Late fourteenth-century Walter Hilton, forerunner of modern operationalism, could maintain that love is not an abstract state of mind but always an action, an operation that is active between people whose nature is determined by its activity, just as the nature of the action is determined by those who engage in it. Thus for Hilton (as for Kernberg though he had different elements and activities in mind) there are not two elements fundamental to the process of loving between man and woman or parent and child, but three. The third element, as real as the other two, is the *expression* of the love between the other two, as a child may be thought of as an expression of two people's love for each other. (Walter Hilton, *Scala Perfectionis*, or, *The Ladder of Perfection*, first printed in 1494.)

The next step in Hilton's argument is that if God's parenthood depended on the existence of people who had to be there so that God could love them, that would limit God's omnipotence: God could not be loving them if they were not there. From this it follows, for Hilton, since God was not to be thought of as needing people, God's parental nature was expressed not only in relation to created humanity, but also intrinsically within the Godhead: God the Father is a loving parent to the Second Person of the Trinity, the Son who, reciprocally, loves the Father. And this parental–filial bond is so intense and so real that it is in itself also a person, a Holy Spirit person who links parent and child and is also God. This is an idea best expressed in poetry, as St John of the Cross was to do some centuries later in an amazing set of verses called "Romances", brilliantly translated by Roy Campbell.

> In the beginning of all things
> The Word lived in the Lord at rest.
> And His felicity in Him
> Was from infinity possessed.
>
> That very Word was God Himself
> By which all being was begun
> For He lived in the beginning
> And beginning had He none.
>
> He Himself was the beginning,
> So He had none, being one.
> What was born in the beginning
> Was the Word we call the Son ...
>
> ... As the loved-one in the lover
> Each in the other's heart resided:
> And the love that makes them one
> Into one of them divided,
>
> Then with one and with the other
> Mated in such equality,
> Three Persons now and one Beloved
> They numbered, though they still were three ... [St John of the Cross, "Romance I"]

This is also what Hilton believed, though he did not put it so succinctly.

Hilton's understanding of this mode of relating is further developed into ideas that match late twentieth-century psychoanalytic theories of projection and projective identification. From the starting point that "uncreated love is God Himself, the Third Person, that is, the Holy Spirit" (Book 2, Chapter 34), Hilton proceeds to distinguish God's uncreated love from our created love:

> Created love is that implanted and aroused in the soul by the Holy Spirit when it sees and knows Truth, that is, God. This love is called created because it is brought into being by the Holy Spirit. It is not God Himself, since it is created, but it is the love felt by the soul when it beholds God and is moved to love Him alone. [Book 2, Chapter 34]

Hilton then goes on to consider that many people cannot love unless they have already had experience of love. Created love, human love, depends on uncreated love. Our ability to love depends on the love we have been given—no mean psychotherapist, this fourteenth-century cleric, although the processes by which human love is inspired in the human heart were not to be formulated for centuries. But it is clear that for Hilton there was no thick black pencilled line marking a barrier between God and the human heart—God could go in and create things there. That is mysticism.

Centuries later, psychotherapists came across phenomena difficult to manage intellectually, all bundled into words like "projection" and "projective identification", words that need to be carefully examined for the assumptions on which their usage rests. Chapters Eight and Nine look at some descriptions of what may be similar phenomena, and at the intellectual assumptions on which those descriptions are based. There is no point in anticipating those pages but, essentially, it does seem that we have to rethink the more unimaginatively materialistic hypotheses of the last three centuries, according to which visually separate objects are impermeable to one another.

Immanence, transcendence, union, communion, and projective processes

For some seven centuries at least, until the second half of the twentieth, since when the tradition seems to have been transforming itself into something scarcely mystical, the Christian understanding of love, of God, of bliss and union, was easily clothed in the language of the Eucharistic ritual, as in this moving and succinct hymn that Hieronymus Praetorius—a Lutheran, by the way—set to music in 1601, and Messiaen in the twentieth century.

> O sacrum convivium quo Christus sumitur. Recolitur memoria passionis suis; mens impletur gratia. Et futurae gloriae nobis pignus datur.

> O sacred banquet in which Christ is received, the memory of his passion recalled, the mind filled with grace, and the pledge of future glory given us.

The word "Eucharist" derives from the Greek for "thanksgiving". The "Lord's Supper" of the early Christian era developed during the first millennium from a ceremonial evening meal in thankful remembrance of Jesus' self-sacrifice and hence of God's sacrificial love, and became a ritual in which the Second Person of the Trinity exists in bread and wine dedicated to that purpose. (Bouyer, 1956, especially Chapter 4). Wars have been fought ostensibly over the words to be used to describe what was thought to happen when the strict boundaries between material and spiritual cease to hold firm. Having recourse to another *Oxford Dictionary*, this time of *Christian Thought* (1957 edition), we find

> *Consubstantiation.* In the doctrine of the Eucharist, the belief, esp. associated with the name of M. Luther, that, after the consecration, the substances both of the Body and the Blood of Christ and of the bread and wine coexist in union with each other. Luther illustrated it by the analogy of the iron put into the fire whereby both fire and iron are united in the red-hot iron and yet each continues unchanged. The doctrine was formulated in opposition to the medieval doctrine of transubstantiation, acc. to which the substances of the bread and wine were no longer present after consecration, but only their "accidents" persisted.

However that may be, by virtue of this ritual the faithful recognize, in the bread and wine, the actual operation, or the actual being and nature and presence, of a loving and self-sacrificing God, and they find thus a tangible and practical means of union with Christ. This belief is perhaps best exemplified and articulated by

Thomas à Kempis in Book Four of his *Imitation of Christ*, where the author's sense of bliss, bounty and union is inextricably entwined with the Eucharist.

> O sweetest Lord Jesus, how great is the delight of devout souls, feasting with thee in thy banquet, in which no other food is set before us, but thyself, our only beloved, more to be desired than all the desires of our hearts. [Book IV, Chapter 2, 2]

> From thee this love proceeded; thy mercy shines in this. What infinite praise and thanks are due to thee for thy goodness. Oh how salutary was thy counsel when thou didst institute this sacrament. [Book IV, Chapter 2, 4]

and St Catherine of Siena:

> Sometimes he comes with such majesty that none can doubt it is the Lord himself; this especially so after communion, since then we know that he is here, for the Faith says so. Then he shows himself so much the lord of the inn, the soul, that it seems to dissolve completely and to be consumed in Christ. [Chapter XXVIII]

In the worship that centres in the Holy Communion, two tendencies appear identifiable, representing respectively the immanent in-here and the transcendent out-there: the formally consecrated wafers of bread, now Christ, can be consumed straightaway, or they may be reverently reserved in a specially marked place. Some of the worshipful literature is in terms of adoration of God in the reserved and ever-available sacrament, of *contemplating* God in it, of looking at it and generally dwelling on the sight and/or thought of God's especial presence, with awe and love. These raptures are different from those we find in response to the *incorporating* of the consecrated elements in the Holy Communion, raptures that are more conscious of the indwelling of God. The rite itself celebrates both the out-there and the in-here simultaneously, with amazement and gratitude that the out-there Master-of-the-Universe should willingly consent to a human-scale incorporation. In practice our writers often use out-there and in-here language indiscriminately—this may not be so surprising to those psychotherapists accustomed to encounter, as a matter of routine, the projections, identifications, introjections and projective identifications that constantly shimmer between people, as also in Hopkins' *Kingfisher* poem quoted in Chapter One.

Simone Weil would agree that these good things go on between God and us—her letters often gratefully refer to the goodness and beauty of God. But she was sophisticated enough to understand that we may also be engaged in projective processes that are not good, and in fact hinder redemptive activity. She is unceasingly appalled by the terrible things that happen to people and that people do to one another. After all, she was living in France during an enemy occupation, though I think her agonized sympathies ranged well beyond the immediate nationalistic into the economic sphere and also into the sphere of personal instinct-driven havoc.

> Outside ourselves we see evil under two distinct forms, suffering and sin: But in our feelings about our own nature the distinction no longer appears ... We feel in ourselves something which is neither suffering nor sin but the two of them at once ... This is the presence of evil in us ... The soul rejects it in the same way as we vomit. [Weil, 1950, p. 143]

To rid ourselves of our sense of suffering and sin, we locate their cause outside ourselves. She calls this process "transference", a word that psychotherapists use for something else. We should use the word "projection" for what she is describing here, which is also a more appropriate word to go with Weil's "vomit".

> By a process of transference we pass it [*viz.* the evil] on to the things which surround us. These things, however, thus becoming blemished and ugly in our eyes, send us back the evil that we had put into them. They send it back after adding to it. It seems to us then that the very places where we are living and the things that surround us imprison us in evil, and that it becomes daily worse. This is a terrible anguish ... [*ibid.*, p. 143]

She proposes that the evil and anguish caused by these very damaging projections can however be transmuted by the benign processes of projection implicit in the Eucharist.

> ... when people turn their eyes and their attention to the Lamb of God present in the consecrated bread, a part of the evil which they bear within, is directed toward perfect purity, and there suffers destruction.

It is a transmutation rather than a destruction. The contact with perfect purity dissociates the suffering and sin which had been mixed together so indissolubly. The part of evil in the soul is burnt by the fire of this contact and becomes only suffering, and the suffering is impregnated with love. [*ibid.*, p 144]

CHAPTER EIGHT

Beyond between within above— spatial metaphors and the intersect

I n general, and also among many of the more psychologically-minded, our understanding is made more difficult by the fact that we tend to think in terms of things, of discrete objects, when this is inappropriate. It can be counter-productive to try to understand something in terms of what it is rather than in terms of our experience of what it does or seems to do. Better than thinking in terms of what things are, is thinking in terms of processes. All this was considered at some length in Chapter Two.

But what if there are ineffable experiences, that is, experiences we cannot describe in terms of processes either—not in terms of what happened first, what happened then, what happened when factor x was introduced, what happens when factor x is not introduced, and so on? What if there are ineffable experiences that we cannot find even well-arranged words for? It was noted in Chapter Two that sometimes we can reduce the area of ineffability by creating new concepts, like the concept of "vitality affects"; music and the visual arts, and poetry, are also means by which we can communicate what would otherwise be inexpressible.

Metaphor, from which poetry benefits as much as it benefits from the use of vitality affects in sentence structure and from the sound of words, is another means by which we can communicate what would otherwise be ineffable. Indeed our language depends on metaphors to an extent that is not usually recognized.

Similes expressly state that something is *like* something else, as in "he had a smile like a sunbeam". Words such as "like" and "as" warn us that a simile is coming—the actual sun is not involved in the smile; the smile is not a sunbeam. Descriptions of "what it is like" are not descriptions of "what it is". Chapter Nine will give a selection of accounts of "what it is like". Those accounts are not to be relied on for information about "what it is", but they will at least give us some ideas of how ineffable experiences have affected a variety of people. All those accounts employ similes or metaphors.

Metaphors are trickier than similes, since there are no linguistic signs such as "like" or "as" to warn us that a description will only tell us "what it was like". The present chapter, which serves as an introduction to Chapter Nine, looks with a particularly anxious eye at the use of spatial metaphors when describing the ineffable: beyond, behind, inner, deeper, transcendental peak experiences in the fourth dimension, in the fifth, between, in potential space or transitional. ... For more than a hundred years we have raised eyebrows at ways of thinking that put God, the old man with the beard, in some space like "the highest", above the clouds, but still we think spatially. The spatial metaphors that came to be preferred later, of God within us, do not seem to me to have added clarity to the endeavour to find a space for God to be in.

That is for theologians to worry about. But the theories of psychotherapists are also infested with ideas that are heavily dependent on metaphors of space. We have invented a thing, called "the mind", "my mind", "your mind", and then engaged in controversy about the relative positions of minds, brains, spirits, souls and how to locate them in relation to one another. These words, which are used as if they were words for things like bricks or cabbages, are metaphors for processes. We cannot communicate without metaphors, but they are dangerous, and spatial metaphors in particular can be more a hindrance than a help to clear thinking: if we use our familiar experiences of space as a guide to situations in which space is only a metaphor, we are bound to reach unwarrantable conclusions.

Spatial metaphors when talking of people

As a rule, we talk as though there are clear boundaries between people: "I am Jo, you are Jim". Winnicott writes of a "limiting membrane" (1958, p. 239; 1965, p. 148), but while "limiting membrane" is a striking and useful metaphor for a process, it is not a thing. There is no membrane separating my mind from Jim's; there is nothing very analogous to skin that maintains our separate identity. At the start of life, the actual physical skin around the body, with its myriad separate sense-receptors for warmth, cold, pressure, touch and pain, is undoubtedly vital in establishing awareness of identity; all this is described movingly and with erudition by Biven (1982) in his paper on "The role of skin in normal and abnormal development, with a note on the poet Sylvia Plath". The sense of identity is undoubtedly initially mediated by an enveloping skin, but does the matter rest there? Just as there is a condition called "concrete thinking" which constricts imaginative and abstract thought, so there may be another condition, "concrete identity-awareness", which hinders even legitimate identification with anything that happens outside the skin's envelope.

> The boundaries of the self are quite different from the boundaries around physical objects. Even my body-self has boundaries which are different from the boundaries to cups and saucers and postage stamps. When I drive in my customary car and am getting through a gap, I think "I" am this wide. In someone else's car it takes a while for me to learn that "I" am a different width. When I use a mallet and chisel, "I" cut the wood. This is how I think of the work. I have to feel that it is I . . .

> We must not think of ourselves as having boundaries as definite as the shell around an egg. It is like believing that psychological objects are separated from each other by black pencil lines, the way objects are in drawings. Physically we are all separate. My eye is mine, not yours. Your digestion is yours, not mine. His measles are his, not ours. Psychologically this simply is not so. "My" mother is more mine than "my" teacher is; "my" apple is even more under my control but it is less reciprocal. I am my mother's daughter, my teacher's pupil, but hardly my apple's eater. Then again, my mother is also my sister's mother; and interestingly, "my mother" may be more mine than "our mother" is—or less, it depends on the facts of the situation. But what is not in dispute is that, when I say "my

mother and I", the boundaries between and around us are different
from when I say "our mother and I".

Again, I can think of "I" in a very narrow sense as in "I am thinking
of going to Australia"—the boundaries round my person and my
plans sounds clear. But what if I say, "We are thinking of going to
Australia"? Does this present a picture of me thinking, and my two
friends each also thinking? Or does it represent the result of our
discussion in which each of us has contributed? How are we to
think of "us" and "we"? Our digestive processes happen in a
place—the stomach—which has a distinct skin around it but *we do
not have skins around our minds*. [Klein, J., 1987, pp. 252–253]

Not only personal pronouns like "I" and "you" and "we", but
also prepositions like "between", adjectives like "deep", adverbs,
and other parts of speech, nudge us into thinking about ourselves
and our experiences as though they had clearly-pencilled boundary-
lines round them. With equally misplaced concreteness we think of
our "inner world" as "in" us, and of our "internalized objects" as
contained "in" our "inner" world. We think of some unconscious
processes as "deeper" in our inner world, meaning we are more
unconscious of them. We speak of "the" unconscious as though
"unconscious" were a place, whereas it is a set of processes. We use
words like "space" as in "inner space", "transitional space",
"potential space" when "realm" might lead to less misplaced
concreteness.

I and you and we and us

Even "you" and "I" can present conceptual problems when used
carelessly. These problems multiply with concepts like "us" and
"we" and the plural "you", and unconfusing language for what
goes on between us has not yet been found. "We" and "us" become
more mysterious concepts the more one looks at them, referring not
exactly to me or to you in entirety, but to something in which we
both participate, something we share, something that links us.

the great advantage of being alive
(instead of undying) is not so much
that heart no more can disprove than prove

what heart may feel and soul may touch
—the great (my darling) happens to be
that love are in we, that love are in we. [cummings, selected poems,
1960, 1923–1958]

"Us", an intersect

Venn diagrams, like the ones below, allow us to draw lines around a
set of items that shares a particular something (Allwein & Barwise,
1996). Thus one can draw lines around, for instance, everything I
think of as "I", which excludes everything I think of as "not I", and
one can draw lines around everything I think of as "you", which
excludes everything I think of as "not you". These boundary lines
are conventionally represented by circles.

I can draw a circle that encloses all that "I" am, and another
circle that encloses all that "you" are, floating in a universe "not I
and not you".

You and I may meet each other and find we share certain things.

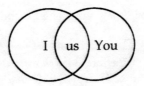

We now see a crescent shaped area:

enclosing what I am but not you, and another area:

enclosing what you are but not I, and an area like an olive pip:

an intersect, which we share.

We get, it will be noted, two kinds of "we" or "us".

Minimal:

and maximal:

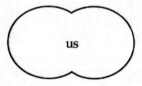

The maximal "we" or "us" represents a notion supported by an ancient joke:

Little Johnny: "My father and I know everything".
Sceptic: "What is the capital of China?"
Little Johnny: "That is one of the things my father knows".

The intersect can contain whatever you and I share—it is the word for a process both parties recognise when they say "we". It may even be one-sided. I may feel at one with my horse, a mountainside, a symphony, or something ineffable whose nature I cannot fathom but with whom or with which I have experienced an encounter, an at-one-ness, a relatedness; the horse or the mountain may not feel at one with me.

"Intersect" is, of course, a metaphor. Intersects may not exist in the sense in which Oxford Street exists—or it may—but I take the view that some intersects are realms to which "Highest", "Deepest", "Beyond", "Within" and other such spatial terms may apply. Hence one person's "Highest" may be another's "Within". "Beyond" may be "Between" in Winnicott's sense, seen from one of the points that anchor "Between".

In a theological context, the concept of intersect might help to make it possible to write, as St. Paul did often enough, that he was in Christ, and, on other occasions, that Christ was in him. The way we usually think of "in" does not really permit this, but the intersect does. These apparently spatial terms are words for psychological processes. The words indicate experiences that are felt to involve something outside the pencil lines of our normally experienced selves (which tend, at least to begin with, to be based on body experiences). The next chapter takes further our understanding of the varied ways in which the intersect may be experienced.

Pencil marks within "I"

While it can be agreed that "us", describing something about you and me, is obvious in meaning, yet it has something ineffable when one tries to describe or explain the process which turns you and me into "us". Within the self (note the preposition "within") similar problems are encountered; R. D. Laing calls these *Knots* (1970):

> You can never find what you are looking for because you are what you are looking for and since you are the self you have lost—who else—the self you are trying to find is the you that is trying to find the self that is trying to find you. So since you have never been lost you can never be found. [Laing, 1970, p. 122]

and

> The self you are trying to find is the you that is trying to find the self you are trying to find so you will never find yourself since you have never lost yourself since the self you have lost is the you that has lost it. [*ibid.*]

We have difficulty in communicating even when we want to say something simple like "I ate the chocolate pudding although I did not really want it". We have as yet no convenient way of describing what it is in us (oh dear! "in") that makes it possible for us to go "yes-pudding" and "no-pudding" simultaneously, though we have names for the phenomenon. We can call it "ambivalence" or "splitting". After a hundred years of silence on the subject, we are again taking an interest in the phenomenon called "dissociation"— but we still have no solid theory about how it works, only picture-language, and metaphors, and case-stories. (Of course, we also do not know as yet whether we are here making a puzzle out of what is actually a peculiarity of our grammar, or whether we have got hold of a valid problem in describing mental processes.)

Moreover, just as our experience may tell us that the boundaries between one psyche and another are less sharply defined than the boundaries between a cup and a saucer, we also know that our conscious processes are different from our unconscious processes, and separate in ways it might also be possible to represent by a pencil line, just as a pencil line was used in the diagram to distinguish between "I" and "I-as-part-of-us", as in "I am a logician, we are logicians, but I am not a boring logician like you". That is, "being boring" does not belong in the intersect "we"—it belongs to the segment "you". How I define myself on a particular occasion depends on whether I want to own as mine, those things that are not exclusively mine but shared with someone else (or something else).

Similarly, how I define myself on a particular occasion depends on whether at that moment I acknowledge those things I believe to be mine though I am unconscious of them just now. Experience tells us that we have mental processes that can feel very separate from us, not us at all, so that we find special words for these experiences —"Inspiration" or "the Muse" or "Holy Spirit" or, indeed, "the devil". Problems arising from this kind of thing are considered in Chapter Nine, which follows.

One language has become accepted in the last one hundred years, that attempts to differentiate between what a person is conscious of and what a person is less conscious of. Conscious and less conscious states of mind have been represented, or rather pictured, as something that looks on paper rather like a cloud, or a potato. Again, we rely on pictures with pencil lines to convey meaning, and then the meaning that we grasp is inevitably affected by the logic of pencil lines.

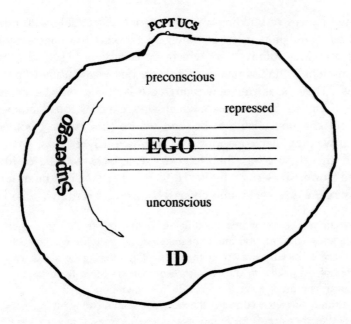

This picture is combined from p. 29 of Freud (1923) *The Ego and the Id*, and p. 105 of the *New Introductory Lectures* (1933).

In this picture, this spatial metaphor, we see the bodily urges, collectively called the Id, contained and filtered by more rational processes, the containment being represented by the pencil lines that are a barrier to the id, the bodily urges; the pencil lines represent the rational processes collectively called the ego. The urges are further constrained by moral considerations collectively called the superego, and represented by a thickening of another pencil line. PCPT UCS stands for the unconscious perceptual system, which contains everything we could in principle be aware of, consciously or not.

For the first fifty years of psychoanalytic history, such pictures were found helpful in conveying original and unfamiliar ideas. But no sooner had they begun to be drawn than the human (or perhaps only Western) preference for thinking concretely in terms of spaces and containers misled us into thinking of "the unconscious" as a space, "in" which resided "the instincts" and "drives". Unacceptable phantasies were also thought of as being in and coming from "the unconscious". But neither neurology nor logic nor indeed experience will allow this. There is a continuous flow and interchange between conscious and less conscious processes. Much damage has been done to our chances of building a useful theory, compatible with other theories about human functioning, by thinking too concretely of "the conscious mind", "in" which are conscious ideas, and "the unconscious", "in" which are "unconscious ideas" called "phantasies". There is, as we know though our language may be loose, a state of flux so that notions of which we were conscious a moment ago become unavailable to us, and we become aware of others, which we may then consciously or unconsciously dismiss.

In the description that follows, sensitively translated from Freud's original German by W. H. S. Sprott (1937), it is interesting to notice Freud's own doubts about relying on pencil-drawn theories.

> When you think of this dividing up of the personality into ego, super-ego and id, you must not imagine sharp dividing lines such as are artificially drawn in the field of political geography. We cannot do justice to the characteristics of the mind by means of linear contours, such as occur in a drawing or in a primitive painting, but we need rather the areas of colour shading off into one another that are to be found in modern pictures. After we have made our separations, we must allow what we have separated to merge again. Do not judge too harshly of a first attempt at picturing a thing so elusive as the human mind. [Freud, 1993, p. 105]

It is difficult to resist the impulse to quote from what Freud goes on to say, on the next page.

> ... it can be easily imagined that certain practices of mystics may succeed in upsetting the normal relations between the different regions of the mind, so that, for example, the perceptual system becomes able to grasp relations in the deeper layers of the ego and in the id which would otherwise be inaccessible to it. Whether such a procedure can put one in possession of ultimate truths, from which all good will flow, may be safely doubted. All the same, we must admit that the therapeutic efforts of psychoanalysts have chosen much the same method of approach. For their object is to strengthen the ego, to make it more independent of the super-ego, to widen its field of vision, and so to extend its organisation that it can take over new portions of the id. Where id was, there shall ego be. It is reclamation work, like the draining of the Zuyder Zee. [ibid., p. 106]

CHAPTER NINE

Processes in the intersect

"I knew a metaphor when I heard one, and I liked metaphor better than reason. I have known many atheists since Sam, and they all fall down on metaphor"

Robertson Davies, 1973, *Fifth Business*, pp. 58–59

T he end of Chapter Five looked briefly at theories about internalized parental couples, theories that promised more positive and creative life-experiences to those whose internalized objects could be experienced as harmoniously related. Chapter Seven made reference to a kind of inner breakthrough and re-integration that could prove crucially benign in a person's life, and also noted a related kind of ineffable experience, in which the boundaries of the self were felt to blur. Chapter Eight considered some of the language and logic used in descriptions of such experiences; the concept of "intersect" was introduced as an aid to understanding them. This present chapter simply displays, without too much analysis, some of the great variety of ways in which such experiences can be described.

Faced with that great variety, one is almost bound to ask if these accounts could possibly all be accurate descriptions. How is one to react to such diversity? On the one hand we can follow mankind's madder tradition, argue about who is right, and end up defending one possibility as the fittest to survive. Force is sometimes used to do so. Alternatively, we might adopt what Michael Jacobs (2000) commends in a very interesting chapter called "Polymathic Thinking", which requires

> the willingness to enter fully into the experience of other forms of discourse and different belief systems, and into wider aspects of the internal and external world—not necessarily to embrace them all, and certainly not to become a narcissistic know-all, but to extend the discovery of one's own identity. [Jacobs, 2000, p. 97]

We may find some descriptions sympathetic, others unfamiliar, even weird, some challenging, some enriching, yet others irrelevant or boring and unimaginative. The diversity is dazzling and so is the diversity of "explanations" implied in the accounts.

> The gods did not reveal, from the beginning,
> All things to us; but in the course of time,
> Through seeking we may learn, and know things better.

> But as for *certain* truth, no one has known it,
> Nor will we know it; neither of the gods,
> Nor yet of the things of which I speak.

> And even if by chance we were to utter
> The final truth, we would, ourselves, not know it;
> For all is but a web of guesses. [Xenophanes 500 B.C.E.; quoted by Rowe, 1993]

For the sake of order and tidiness, the material for the present chapter has been organized into categories. These are of course inevitably somewhat arbitrary, even gross, but one has to start somewhere.

- Common ground for Jungian, Freudian, and Kleinian traditions
- Hinshelwood on projective identification
- The contribution of mathematical set-theory
- Jung's Archetypes; Charles Williams' Images
- Williams on indwelling, co-inherence, exchange and substitution

- Later Jungian examples of a sense of contact with something greater
- Experiences of contact with something greater, accompanied by disagreeable loss of identity: Grotstein, Grotstein's Bion, and Eigen
- Bollas, Krieger and Meltzer on aesthetic moments and the apprehension of beauty—worship
- Bootstrap theories of the apprehension of beauty; Likierman and Mendoza,
- Inspiration and creativity
- Martin Buber on you-and-me, I-and-whatever-else
- Relatedness: a form answering to our subjectivity—Harold Searles and Kenneth Wright
- With Winnicott in the intersect
- Ogden's intersubjective space

Jungian, Freudian, and Kleinian traditions on common ground

The concept of a common ground of unconscious mental processes keeps appearing and disappearing in various forms in the history of psychotherapy. Many writers have speculated about an overlap— i.e. an intersect of one person's mental processes and those of another. Some have speculated that all the mental processes of some people—or perhaps of all people—are naturally though unconsciously in communication. In the language of Analytical Psychology (the Jungians, so called for convenience), this overlap area is "the Collective Unconscious". The history of the concept may be left to the historian of ideas, but the modern version owes some of its origins to the attempt, at the turn of the nineteenth/twentieth centuries, to follow through some ideas then prevalent about "the Id".

"The Id" may be thought of as a collective noun for the biological drives, but from the beginning it was endowed with very marked spatial connotations, as though the Id were a place, an area, a repository, consciousness of which was repressed. "The Unconscious" also came to be a thought of not as an adjectival phrase appertaining to unconscious mental processes, but as referring to a container of repressed impulses and drives. Later "the Unconscious" also came to be thought of as containing phantasies of which a person might at one time have been conscious but which were now repressed. We may leave the historian of ideas to trace the times when "the Unconscious" and "the Id" were thought of either as the same thing or as distinct, and how various other functions and structures came to be attributed to one or the other. Of importance to the present discussion is the idea that "the Unconscious" of one person might be in touch with or merged with or identical with "the Unconscious" of other people, and the idea that there may be a realm where individual minds meet or mingle with one another, and perhaps also with other entities in a "Collective Unconscious". In this realm, at least some of our motivations are thought to originate.

Different assumptions are made by different writers as to whether a realm of this kind resides in each person individually, or whether it is a part of a person that is in union with other people— or with all creatures, a view that is maintained by many Creation Spiritualists.

It is a realm thought by many to be the source of the shared symbols in terms of which we express ourselves. Jung's Archetypes are psychological counterparts to the sociologically oriented "collective representations" posited by Emile Durkheim, more or less Jung's contemporary (see also pp. 54–55). And students of classical philosophy may see the resemblance to Plato's realm of Ideas, an important way of viewing the world much debated by Christian theologians. The influence of Plato is strong on all writers educated in the classical nineteenth-century mode. Here may therefore be the place to quote Harold Searles, for whom Platonic Idealism had practical implications examined in more detail below. He concurs with William James' opinion that "the whole universe of concrete objects ...

... swims ... for all of us, in a wider and higher universe of abstract ideas" ... But I disagree with his view that it is this state of affairs which gives significance to what we perceive—which gives significance to, for example, our nonhuman environment. I believe, on the contrary, that the *less* marked is this state of affairs, the *more* significance do we find the nonhuman environment to possess for us. The more we are able to relate ourselves to this environment as it really is—the more our perception of it becomes freed from seeing it to be bathed in Evil or Good or what not—the more satisfying and rich is our relatedness to it.

My conviction in this regard is based upon my own personal experience and upon my experience with psychiatric patients. ... I shall describe many instances in which patients' relatedness to their nonhuman environment, and to themselves, is extremely distorted because these patients react to abstract ideas, figurative concepts, as though they possessed concrete reality, a reality far more tangible to the patient than that possessed by all sorts of objects which are most concrete, most "real", to the non-psychotic and relatively speaking non-neurotic person. I feel that the more completely man can penetrate any such veils of reified abstract ideas, veils which are at their most blinding in the case of the psychotic person, the more satisfyingly alive will be his relatedness to the nonhuman environment. [Searles, 1960, p. 116]

The writer Charles Williams is unusual in imagining this realm of symbols to be not only one where minds can meet, but also one where minds and symbols (often markedly resembling Plato's Ideas) and bodily people engage in important transactions of a mutually helpful or damaging kind. Williams is almost entirely original and not well-known, and is accordingly given what some may feel to be a disproportionate number of pages below. In quite other ways, this common-ground realm is thought by some psychotherapists to be where the processes of "projective identification" take place.

Hinshelwood on projective identification

It may be noted, however, that Hinshelwood explicitly denies that this is the way Melanie Klein regarded projective identification. Hinshelwood's invaluable *Dictionary of Kleinian Thought* (1989) scrupulously distinguishes and defines the many uses to which the term has been put since it came to the fore in the nineteen forties and fifties. Excluding the bibliography, Hinshelwood devotes twenty-four pages to a consideration of the uses made of the term "projective identification". Near the end of his examination he comes to a sub-heading, "The interpersonal process". In those last pages he tries to impress on the reader that Klein and the mainstream of Kleinians did not entertain the notion that there is a condition in which the mental processes of patient and psychotherapist, or of any two people, meet and interact interpersonally in another sense than can be accounted for by perceptions of and deductions from subtle behavioural indications of the other's phantasy life. There is no intersect of the kind that would be created by a mental space equally occupied by two people, in which important transactions are handled on a plane removed from what can be photographed. He cites Ogden 1979 and 1982 as presenting the contrary view—Ogden is give space at the close of the present chapter.

Hinshelwood is careful in his formulations, and his citations never allow the process to be thought of as an interpersonal one: it is always one person's phantasy, conscious or unconscious, happening in that person's mind. Other people can be affected, of course, by someone's phantasy that he or she can manipulate them by the power of thought alone, but it is a phantasy not a fact. Hinshelwood returns several times to the distinction, exemplified by Betty Joseph's work (1975 and later) that people may become aware of a thought or a phantasy that seems to be their own but that they then realize is one that the other person has been entertaining about them: this thought had not arisen from their own cogitations but had sprung from the impact of the other person's hints and behaviour. This happens in common life, and also in the psychotherapists' consulting-room, where it has to be examined in order to help patients to understand their mental processes better. But we do not, according to Hinshelwood, have to believe in an interpersonal process such as direct thought-transfer would be. There will have been no transaction, no sharing, no mutually stocked intersect of that kind. Hinshelwood insists that Joseph is describing what the experience was like for her, subjectively, in the consulting room; she is not asserting objectively that this is how the process works.

The contribution of mathematical set-theory

An interesting and useful contribution comes from Bomford (1999), whom Polonius might have called a clerical-mathematical-Jungian. His *Symmetry of God* takes up some of the logic of the mathematics of set-theory (whence the Venn diagram also derives) first introduced to psychotherapists by Matte Blanco in 1975. Psychotherapists may find Matte Blanco's kind of mathematical structuring useful in keeping their own thoughts tidy when in the presence of patients with major thought-disorders. Bomford uses it to good effect in keeping our thoughts steadily focused while trying for a deeper understanding of mystical experiences. Aristotelian logic, which we tend to think of as the only rational kind, does not govern our unconscious processes. We have known this explicitly ever since Freud looked at slips of the tongue, of dreams, and other ways of defending ourselves against things we do not want to know. According to Matte Blanco, the operations that mathematicians use in set-theory are identical with the ways in which our unconscious processes operate, where "yes" can mean "no" as well, "here" can mean "there" as well, "I love" can mean "I hate", and so on. "Then" can mean "now" and can mean "forever". Admitting this kind of logic does allow us to reconsider some of the tenets of theology and some of the descriptions of mystics more calmly: it lessens our sense that the whole area is unpredictably irrational. In his book, Bomford is scrupulously neutral on the question whether there is a God independent of our thinking processes; he belongs to the Jungian camp by reason of the respect he has for the power of unconscious processes in contributing to our sense of the ineffable.

Jung's Archetypes; Charles William's Images

In the second half of the twentieth century, many Jungians appeared to turn away from the consideration of a concept that seemed in the first half to be a most characteristic feature of Analytical Psychology: the Archetypes, defined by that rather determinedly nineteenth-century-positivistic psychoanalyst Charles Rycroft as

> a Jungian term for the contents of the collective unconscious, i.e. for innate ideas or for the tendency to organise experience in innately predetermined patterns. [Rycroft, 1968, p. 9]

According to this way of thinking, some people, though they seem unaware of the operation of Archetypes in their lives, are nevertheless thought to be attuned to them. Others are unaware and not in tune; they attempt to construe their experiences in purely personal terms and are to that extent handicapped in their understanding of how it is with them and their world. In this context, Archetypes are not thought of as benign or malign; how they operate in people's lives depends on how people relate to them when they express themselves in everyday life, consciously or unconsciously. For an interesting fictional account of how the concept is used in psychotherapy, one may refer to *The Manticore* (1972) by Robertson Davies, the middle novel of *The Deptford Trilogy* (1983). But the concept receded into the background, at least for a while. It may be enjoying a minor revival *via* Donald Meltzer (1973) who, in some ways following Bion, tends to write in rather devout-sounding terms of his patients' phantasies or images of their parents' body-parts and of their sexual intercourse as though we are born with these phantasies, of which we may make constructive or destructive use in our lives—the resemblance to Jung's Archetypes is unmistakable.

For Jung there was no great separation between people's minds and the Archetypes; there was constant if mostly unconscious interaction between them. In a rather parallel way, Charles Williams entertained the idea that there is no impermeable boundary that puts our selves with our separate identities in one strictly defined realm, and puts symbols, or Images, in a strictly separate universe elsewhere. Williams depicts a world in which Images and people interact with each other continually, at our initiative *or theirs* for, in Williams' imagination at least, the Symbols are motivated by their own nature and inner logic in their commerce with us. In the introductory chapter to *The Figure of Beatrice* (1943)—the word "figure" plays on the different meanings that can be attributed to that word—Williams cites with approval the three characteristics that defined symbols for Coleridge:

i.   a symbol must exist in itself
ii. a symbol must derive from something greater than itself, and
iii. a symbol must represent in itself that greatness from which it derives.

Williams prefers the word "Image" to the word "Symbol", "because it seems to me doubtful if the word symbol nowadays sufficiently expresses the vivid individual existence of the lesser thing".

Beatrice was, in her degree, an Image of nobility, of virtue, of the Redeemed Life, and in some sense of Almighty God Himself ...

Just as there is no point in Dante's thought at which the image of Beatrice in his mind was supposed to exclude the actual objective Beatrice, so *there is no point at which the objective Beatrice is to exclude the Power which is expressed through her* ... she herself is [for Dante] the only way by which that other Power can be known ... The maxim of his study, as regards this final Power was: "This also is Thou, neither is this Thou". [Williams, 1943, pp. 7–8; my italics]

In commenting on Dante's meeting with the poet Folco in Paradise, Williams draws on Dante's words to explain what he means here: Dante says to Folco,

Già non attendere: io tua domanda,
S'io m'intuassi, come tu t'inmii. [Canto IX, vv 80,81]

translated by Dorothy Sayers (1962) as:

I would not wait for thee to make demand
Could I in-thee me as thou in-meëst thee.

In more everyday language:

I would not have had to wait for you to voice your wish
If I could have made myself yours as totally as you have made yourself mine.

Williams continues:

This is one of Dante's most concise and most intense sayings, and one of the most significant. He uses the prefix a number of times— by accident or design. The life of the Blessed Virgin "in-heavens" her—"inciela" (III, 97). Each seraph "in-Gods" himself—"india" (IV, 28); the ladies, often enough, have been "inamorata". [Williams, 1943, p. 205]

Williams on indwelling and co-inherence

Williams seems to have seen people both ordinarily, as we all do, more or less, but also in terms of their capacity to ally themselves with or allow themselves to be possessed by powerful Images, whose dynamic nature is separately located. In his eyes, people are people, each person with a personal nature, but people are also capable of being taken over by a powerful Image whose nature is independent of them. Williams wrote a number of novels around this notion: his good characters, whom Williams endows with his own view of the good person's place in the universe, at appropriate moments recollect themselves and say, "This is not Thou but Thou art this also".

In these novels, the plot is always bound up with our relation to the world of symbols: Images. What Williams has in mind is a universe in which symbols have rather more power than we usually assume them to have. In *The Place of the Lion* (1933b), the everyday visible world and the world of the Images interpenetrate so that Images are visible to the characters in the novel as huge Lions and Snakes and such, and they have effects like earthquakes and fires, as well as taking over the minds of people who let them. In *All Hallows' Eve* (1941), Images have dealings with the dead, and with those living who meddle with the dead. In *War in Heaven* (1930), Images participate with more ordinary mortals in a struggle over the possession of the Philosophers' Stone, itself an Image.

The images, of course, are themselves transparent: they are symbols of a reality they represent. Conversely, those characters in the novels are themselves, as well as "the only way in which those other Powers can be known". (Williams, 1943, p. 8). The person, the character, is not the symbol, but the symbol, "in-dwelling", is also the person. "This is not Thou", one might say, "but Thou art this also". One might say just that about, for instance, Sibelius' *Finlandia* symphony: "This is not Finland, but Finland is this also", and about a Finnish landscape one might say, "This is not *Finlandia* but *Finlandia* is this also". Or about Botticelli's *Primavera* in London's National Gallery, we might say "This is not Spring, but Spring is this also". We may say that there is an intersect in which there is something of Botticelli and something of Spring and something that comes from the dynamic of our own minds. Similarly there can be an intersect of something of Sibelius, something of Finland, and something of ourselves.

"Co-inherence" is Williams' word for such processes. In *The Descent of the Dove* (1939) Williams makes this process, or perception, central to all Christians' experience. "Co-inherence" has dozens of entries in the index of *The Descent of the Dove, a short History of the Holy Spirit in the Church* (1939), and it forms the background to all Williams' novels. It is also basic to his understanding of Dante. The figure of Beatrice represents not only the woman she is; she is also the divine principle operating in Dante's life, and this not in what we might think of as a symbolic way, but because God is in her for this purpose. But then, God could not be in her for this purpose if she were not willing to be in God: co-inherence.

Williams on exchange and substitution

The notion of co-inherence, daring as it is, leads Williams to yet more daring concepts, of "exchange" and "substitution"—these are what he believed people can do for each other in a world that features co-inherence. What Williams means by these terms may be best understood if they are approached step by step.

1. At the simplest level, A does something for B under a commonly understood convention that takes it for granted that then, or at some other time, B will do something for A. We could call this *Individual Exchange.*
2. In the next case, C does something for D under a commonly understood convention that C and D belong in a social context where everyone occasionally does things for other people and that this evens out in the long run with all better off and no one worse off. We could call this *Communal Exchange.*
3. Next along the scale, E might do something for F without expectation of repayment, because E's sense of well-being, or love of people, or other altruistic motive, leads E to do so. That is *Generosity.*
4. At a yet more complex level, we get *substitution and exchange: co-inherence.* G is let off whatever G would normally expect to do because, gratuitously, H will do it. It is different from Generosity because of the element of intersect: G-in-H, or H-in-G.

For our purpose, *Descent into Hell* (1937) usefully presents these ideas of Williams' on how the realm of Images intersects with our everyday world, and on substitution and co-inherence in particular.

The illustrative passage which follows cannot do these ideas justice, in spite of its length: the whole novel is needed as a context, plus *The Figure of Beatrice*, plus *The Descent of the Dove*, and even then some readers may feel repelled by what Williams has to say or how he says it. The passage comes from his Chapter Six, "The doctrine of substituted love" and gives an account of a conversation during the rehearsal of an amateur dramatic production. Peter Stanhope, a poet and playwright, is chatting to a young woman who has a small part in the play. The passage has had to be severely reduced from its admirable original, and not all the punctuation indicative of omission (...) is shown, to make the reading easier on the eye.

> "Tell me why you always look so about you and what you are looking for ... There's nothing worth quite so much vigilance or anxiety".

> "I have a trick", she said steadily, "of meeting an exact likeness of myself in the street ... It comes from a long way off, and it comes up towards me, and I'm terrified—terrified—one day it'll come up and meet me ... and then I shall go mad or die".

> "But", he said, "that I don't quite understand. You have friends; haven't you asked one of them to carry your fear?"

> "Carry my fear!" she said ... "How can anyone else carry your fear? Can anyone else see it and have to meet it?"

There are, however, many psychotherapists who know what it is to carry a patient's fear.

> "You're mixing up two things ... The meeting it—that's one thing, and we can leave it till you're rid of the other. It's the fear we're talking about. Has no one ever relieved you of that? Haven't you ever asked them to? ... And if not, will you let me do it for you? ... Then you needn't fear it, at least, and then again, for the meeting— that might be a very different business if you weren't distressed ...

> "When you leave here you'll think of yourself, that I've taken this particular trouble over instead of you. You'd do as much for me if I needed it, or for anyone. And I will give myself to it, and imagine it, and know it, and be afraid of it. And then you won't".

> She said, very doubtfully: "It isn't yours—you haven't seen it. How can you—"

"Come", he said. "It needs only the act. For what can be simpler than for you to think to yourself that since I am there to be troubled instead of you, therefore you needn't be troubled—And what can be easier than for me to carry for a little while a burden that isn't mine? ..."

Here, again, is a process at least some psychotherapists know about.

"When you are alone", he said, "remember that I am afraid instead of you, and that I have taken over every kind of worry. Think merely that; say to yourself—'he is being worried', and go on ..."

"I am to remember", she said ... "that you are being worried and terrified instead of me?"

"That I have taken it all over", he said, "so there is nothing left for you".

"And if I see it after all?" she asked.

"But not 'after all'", he said. "The fact remains—but see how different a fact, if it can't be dreaded!"

...

Stanhope, turning his eyes from her parting figure, settled himself more comfortably in his chair ... He recollected Pauline; he visualized her going along a road, any road; he visualized another Pauline coming to meet her. And as he did so his mind contemplated not the first but the second Pauline; he took trouble to apprehend the vision, he summoned through all his sensations an approaching fear. Deliberately he opened himself to that fear, laying aside for a while every thought of why he was doing it, forgetting every principle and law, absorbing only the strangeness and the terror of that separate spiritual identity ...

... His goodwill went to its utmost, and utmost goodwill can go very far. It went to all but actual vision, and it excluded his intellectual judgment of that vision. Had he been asked, at that moment, for his judgment, he would have answered that he believed sincerely that Pauline believed sincerely that she saw, but whether the sight was actual or not he could not tell. He would have admitted that it might be but a fantastic obsession of her brain. That made no difference to his action. If a man seems to himself to endure the horrors of shipwreck, though he walks on dry land and breathes clean air, the business of his friend is more likely to be to accept those horrors as he feels them, carrying the burden, than to explain that the burden cannot, as a matter of fact, exist. [Williams, 1937, *Descent into Hell*, Chapter 6]

Psychotherapists cannot fail to notice some resemblances between the processes Charles Williams is describing, and what goes on in the consulting-room, where the distresses that are as yet unmanageable by patients on their own, may be transformed by the therapist's containing and metabolising responses. (See also Chapter Eleven pp. 254–257.) Though coming from an unusually exotic region, it would be a pity to ignore what Williams' imagination suggests to us, for there are resonances with processes many psychotherapists practise.

Later Jungian examples of a sense of contact with something greater

It is one of the distinguishing marks of the Jungian school of Analytical Psychology, that they allow for a common realm in which all may share, in which all are rooted though we may be unconscious of it. This is one of its attractions for those who do not want a psychotherapy that disregards the ineffable. An eminent Jungian writes:

> I tend to regard religious experiences, in the first instance at least, as part of the "non-I" part of the Self entering or becoming known to the "I" part. They therefore connote for me a potential for further self-realisation, further restoration of an original unity and in-touch-ness with oneself and with Reality. This entering may take the form of an implosion, a revelation, a break-through from the non-I into the I, or a personal, quasi-sexual mystical impregnation or union. [Redfearn, 1985, p. 48]

This is a Jungian's description of an intersect. Redfearn must mean here that he has a Self, part of which is not-Redfearn. This not-Redfearn is not just a side of Redfearn of which he is unconscious; it is Redfearn in an intersect that also holds something Other. Redfearn, typically of this school of thought, credits this Other with a kind of Reality that warrants a capital initial. This Reality is Redfearn's (or he is Its) but it is also other people's.

Nathan Field (1996), another eminent Jungian, posits a rather similar realm where people may encounter one another, similarly an intersect invested with reality or at least with an other, though not an other that merits Redfearn's capital initial. Field identifies a range of states of consciousness. At one extreme is an animal *one-dimensionality* in which events are experienced but there is no awareness of time, and no perspective on time, so no pattern of meaning can form, life being just one thing after another. In *two-dimensional consciousness* there are only the extremes of nice/not-nice, here/absent, love/hate, but no gradations—if ego-processes exist at all here, they are very primitive (p. 60). *Three-dimensionality* is the "familiar territory of so-called normal experience, which Freud called secondary process" (p. 67). "The three-dimensional holds all that civilized society holds dear: rationality, balanced adulthood, fairness, flexibility, restraint, the ability to listen and respect the integrity of the other" (p. 68). In his Chapter Eight, Field considers the *"Fourth Dimension"*:

> One of the ways in which the four-dimensional states can be experienced is the simultaneous union and separation of self and other. I have in mind those moments when two people feel profoundly united with one another yet each retains an enriched sense of his or her own identity. We are not lost in each other, as in fusion, but found. [1966, p. 71]

According to Field, this is where we may find Maslow's "Peak Experiences" (1968) and Bollas' "aesthetic experience", "when a person feels uncannily embraced by an object" (Bollas, 1987, p. 4). Field gives many examples of sharing such experiences with patients in his consulting room, and he considers them essential for patients' recovery and well-being. He refers to other writers' experience of states of mind he considers similar, and to Jung's scheme, in which the Self is not a discrete individual's possession but rather partakes, at an unconscious level, of a more universally shared life. In this "fourth dimension" of existence we can meet our patients to our common benefit. Field believes that without this dimension we are handicapped in our therapeutic endeavour. Writing that the Freudian positivistic approach "cannot reach the cold split-off schizoid parts of us", Field continues:

> The surgical probe of insight cannot melt this frozen core; it can be

reached only by the therapist's own heart and soul, which is what Jung (1954) meant by "coniunctio" and Bion called "at-one-ment". [Field, 1996, p. 142]

Jung seemed able to induce the dissociative capacity in himself by "lowering his consciousness"; this gave him greater access to the patient's unconsciousness and a direct sense of what it felt like to be the other person. When this state of mutual fusion takes place, the patient too must have a sense of profound connection, bringing the healing awareness that, for a little while, the unbearable isolation has ceased. [ibid., p. 89]

Experiences of contact with something greater, accompanied by disagreeable loss of the sense of identity: Grotstein, Grotstein's Bion, and Eigen

For many Jungians the intersect is a friendly experience "melting the cold schizoid elements". Clearly, some people can lose themselves in the experience and are very happy about it. But others feel it to be a desolating nothingness or emptiness where the customary sense of self is lost, as are the everyday assumptions by which we live. They experience depression and terror. The blurring of boundaries may have very different meanings for people of different predispositions and may be differently experienced by them. Marcus West, in an unfortunately as-yet unpublished lecture, considers the intersect to be a state that is incompatible with what he calls the ego, by which he means the everyday self and the everyday assumptions by which we live. West is acutely sensitive to the pain such loss of ego may cause. He, and others like him, usefully counteract the unthinking sentimental assumption that everything in the universe would be fine if only we saw it in the right way. This was not the experience of the Old Testament writers, nor of the hell-fire threatened people of the Middle Ages, nor of Luther and Calvin.

It appears that different people have different, apparently equally genuine, experiences in the intersect—an odd fact, leading to the perhaps facile guess that there may not be so great a difference between what some describe as desolate emptiness and others as blessed fullness. Perhaps it depends on what people bring to the experience from their inner world. Zaehner (1957, Chapter Five and *passim*) has many references to the collective unconscious, positively and/or negatively experienced. So has William James.

Grotstein (1997) and Eigen (1998), psychoanalysts on the margin of the conventional, have written with respectful terror about ineffable experiences, in a style that suggests that they have personal knowledge of what they write about, a style that goes back to Isaiah and Ezekiel. They know the overwhelming power of the phenomena they describe; they feel an awe that transcends the usual facile assumptions that what is greater than us must also be kinder, more moral, and describable in terms that we can effortlessly understand. Both equate the great ineffable experiences with the powerful forces that erupt from some people's unconscious processes, and thus with what is rather comfortably diagnosed by more sedate minds as a psychotic breakthrough. Certainly some of the examples would find an acceptable place in William James' great work.

Grotstein and Eigen feel supported in their views by their reading of W. R. Bion's writings, how justly, only an expert could determine. Bion, a highly original and respected psychoanalyst, entertained mystical hypotheses some of which have a Jungian flavour. He postulated an ineffable mental process, "O". Briefly, analyst and analysand endeavour to understand the operation of "L" (Love), "H" (Hate) and "K" (Knowledge), and their opposites, in the analysand's mind. Somewhat apart from that, beyond "K", stands "O", Absolute Truth, Ultimate Reality. Bion's ideas are difficult, as is his language, but there do seem to be resemblances to ideas held by many Jungians. Thus "O" is, among other things, what Bion ultimately strives for in his work. Is not this "O" like what Field works toward? We may add, in a timid footnote, that "K" seems to relate to quiddity and that there is something other than "K", beyond "K", that is transparent and can reveal "O".

Grotstein (1997), in a detailed paper, elaborates on his understanding of the mystical elements in Bion's thoughts. He quotes from Bion:

> In the first stage [of group development] there is no real
> confrontation between the god and the man because there is really
> no such distinction ... In the second stage the infinite and

transcendent god is confronted by finite man ... In the third stage the individual—the mystic—needs to reassert a direct experience of the god ... The individuals show signs of their divine origins ... [just as the gods of the previous stage show signs of human origin]. The individuals may be regarded as being incarnations of the deity; each individual retains an inalienable element which is part of the deity himself that resides in the individual. [Bion, 1970, p. 77]

This quotation conveys the Jungian element in Bion's thinking well, but this is not what catches Grotstein's attention. Rather, it is

what Bion hints but fails to say—but I feel constrained to state it for him ... what Freud could not have stated—that ... "God" and the unconscious are the same phenomenon seen from different vertices. [Grotstein, 1997, p. 83]

Freud could not have stated this, *inter alia* because he was committed to a positivist view of his subject-matter, but Bion, according to Grotstein, was not positivist: he finds elements in Bion's writings to show that Bion's "O" is not only awe-inspiring but, if not a-moral, at least beyond our notions of morality and kindness. In this, Bion would then be in the tradition of Luther and Calvin:

"O" overreaches Heaven and Hell in its ultra-majestic, paradoxical sweep ... the experience of "O" may be dreadful like the sight of Sodom and Gomorrah, the Medusa, or Hades—or beatific and serene, depending on the vertex of emotional maturity and preparedness from which one approaches it ...

... I believe that we are born into "O" (or the "Real" in Lacan's 1966 terminology) and are hopefully rescued under the beneficent canopy of the organising and mediating "filters" of the paranoid–schizoid and depressive positions ... which mediate and give cosmogonic meaning to the randomness that we would otherwise experience. [Grotstein, 1997, pp. 85–86]

If Grotstein is to be thought of as on the margin of the psychoanalytic canon, Eigen may be thought of as rather further out. But the useful contribution of these two is that they are writing with respect about phenomena shunned by more pin-striped psychoanalysts. Eigen, in *The Psychoanalytic Mystic* (1998), equates manic high spirits and depressions with mystical encounters.

... I can think back at when I was in my 20s, on a bus, being in extreme agony. I just suddenly lost consciousness and dipped into this sense of agony that seemed to be located in my chest. It was a terrible psychological pain, that I imagined and felt in my chest area. I went further and further into it, and I doubled over on the bus, and then all of a sudden, quite surprisingly, not having any mental frame for what was happening, the pain opened up and became a radiant light. Where before there was just agony and horrendous pain, without my knowing what had happened, suddenly there was bliss ... It turned into a terrific light that left me wishing it would never end. Of course, the pain didn't go away, but the bliss never left me either. [Eigen, 1998, p. 181]

These kinds of experiences cause Eigen to view with some reserve any assumptions as to the uniqueness and the boundaries of the self:

My use of the word *self*, at this time in my life isn't quite the same as it was when I was 20. I think our capacities generally involve some mixture of how we experience ourselves: on the one hand, there's a personal, warm and immediate experience; on the other hand, there's an awareness of being given to ourselves as pretty anonymous, as pretty impersonal.

What we do, then, with what's personal at one moment and what freaks us out as anonymous, or as standing against us from within ourselves in another moment, can vary ... It's a matter, I think, of informal use and what mileage one gets from a term like *self* at a given point in one's life ... [*ibid.*]

Eigen provides generous examples of his professional work with people visited by extraordinary experiences. Of necessity he works mainly not with the joyous manic but with the ones whose experiences are terrifying, who tell of encounters with thunderstorms, unshielded Jehovah, and other soul-shaking events. It is difficult to determine whether Eigen sees these tremendous experiences as encounters with an Other, or as Jungian experiences of the Collective Unconscious, or more as an individual's personal reality experienced with either felicity or agony in unconsciously processed ways, or, as the old theologians thought, as encounters with a God or a devil distinctly out there. And are psychotherapists able to decide? Eigen clearly relates to his patients with admirable respect, and sustains them in their ordeals. He certainly seems of use to them, more use than I or other blander souls could be. He keeps them for years, and keeps validating for them that their experiences are worth respect. Less confident psychotherapists, ministers of religion and other professionals, using the techniques they are trained in, would not be able to hold such patients.

But as so often, on the fringes of the professionally respectable, there are those who are finding respectful ways of working with these kinds of people, or these kinds of moods, and they are beginning to venture some theoretical formulations. Instances may be found in the 2001 *Proceedings of the Second Multidisciplinary Conference on Mental Anguish and Religion* (Conference Convener: Canon Ian Ainsworth Smith, Hospital Chaplain at St George's N.H.S. Health Care Trust). Included are papers by psychiatrist Andrew Powell and by counsellors Nigel Hamilton and Alistair Ross (Director of the Bridge Pastoral Foundation). There are ample bibliographical references to other papers also.

Bollas, Murray Krieger, and Donald Meltzer on aesthetic moments and the apprehension of beauty—worship

I do not intend to write about shared beliefs in this chapter, but rather about that occasion when a person is shaken by an experience into absolute certainty that he has been cradled by, and dwelled with, the spirit of the object, a rendez-vous of mute recognition that defies representation. [Bollas, 1987, p. 30]

These are the words of a poet who wants us to know about an ineffable event. Bollas' "aesthetic experience", "when a person feels uncannily embraced by an object" (1987, p. 4) is in a straight line of descent from the orthodox positivistic "oceanic feelings" that Freud attributed to early infant memories of being with mother (Freud, 1930).

In the aesthetic moment the subject briefly re-experiences, through ego-fusion with the aesthetic object, a sense of the subject attitude towards the transformational object, although such experiences are re-enacted memories, not recreations. [Bollas, 1987, p. 17]

The "subject attitude" is reminiscent of Schleiermacher's "dependence" and Otto's "creature-feeling" (see p. 62). The element of worship is unmistakeable.

Bollas is considering re-enacted memories here, not new perceptions. His concern is "the aesthetic moment, when a person engages in deep subjective rapport with an object" (1987, p. 28).

> The aesthetic moment is a caesura in time, when the subject feels held in symmetry and solitude by the spirit of the object. "What would characterise experience as aesthetic rather than either cognitive or moral", writes Murray Krieger, "would be its self sufficiency, its capacity to trap us within itself, to keep us from moving beyond it to further knowledge or to practical effort". Whether this moment occurs in a Christian's conversion experience, a poet's reverie with his landscape, a listener's rapture in a symphony, or a reader's spell with his poem, such experiences crystallise time into a space where subject and object appear to achieve an intimate rendez-vous. [*ibid.*, p. 31]

Krieger's book, *The Theory of Criticism*, to which Bollas refers here, was published in 1976. One may speculate that Bollas may have been in the States when these ideas were circulating and may have taken part and indeed have contributed to their development. Donald Meltzer, also originally from the United States, uses much the same terminology though to rather different effect and he may also have been around at that time. In his very distinctive fashion, Meltzer, in collaboration with Meg Harris Williams and gratefully acknowledging his debt to Klein and Bion, extols a consequence of the love between mother and infant that takes them both to a state of mind Meltzer calls aesthetic—each lost in love and wonder at the loveability and wonder manifest in the other's face, indeed so absorbed that the love and wonder become part of a new object of contemplation, an object called Beauty. Meltzer appropriately calls the book of essays in which he explores these possibilities *The Apprehension of Beauty* (1988).

Meanwhile Meira Likierman (1989) was constructing her scholarly and humane review of similar apprehensions and experiences, which she, like the other psychoanalysts, attributed to memories of happy early moments with the mother. She gives some moving clinical examples of the association between the perception of sources of light and the apprehension of what she called the *sublime*. She considers and reshapes Freud's view of creativity as a sublimation of unacceptable impulses, and also Klein's view that art is compelled by—or even originates in—the need for reparation. Likierman's understanding of early infant life is one in which each event is experienced as an eternity, limitless in time, for ever, everywhere, though it is in due course replaced by another limitless event. There is not a before or an after or a context—there are no pencil lines around anything. This makes an experience ecstatic, sublime. Such experiences of light are to be found in accounts of revelations in many cultures, and also in accounts of the experiences of artists such as van Gogh.

Likierman (1989) considers supremely good experiences to be *sublime* rather than *ideal*, the important difference being that the sublime is experienced in the nerves and sinews whereas the ideal is a phantasy. Winnicott had the idea that huge anxieties arise from repressed memories of an unbearable event that has already happened, which is experienced as yet to come. He writes "the unbearable has already happened". In something like the same way, Likierman postulates that for fortunate people, the sublime has already happened—and may, of course, happen again.

Bootstrap theories of the apprehension of beauty: Likierman and Mendoza

Likierman encourages us to imagine the ecstasy of taking in milk, as experienced by an infant just ready for it. She notes that the infant is not passive: it suckles; effort is required.

> What I wish to stress is that appreciation and the experiencing of beauty are not passive experiences in which the individual's role is just to adore. "Taking in" goodness is impossible without an active investment of "psychical quality" in what is being incorporated. This active nature of early pleasure is the prototype of adult creativity. [Likierman, 1989, p. 146]

Likierman insists that "the experiencing self continually impregnates sensory 'data' with meaning that is personal" (1989 p. 136). The effort never stops.

Our sensory knowledge of natural forms, which makes possible an understanding of them, and an ability to represent and re-create them in the mind, ... constitutes the more primitive aspect of aesthetic experience, which gradually develops into a taste and an ability to judge and appreciate beauty. In maturity we do not regard sensory processes and sensations as a full experience of beauty. While these remain a dimension of it, the aesthetic experience would be impoverished without a much deeper investment of our own selves in it. [Likierman, 1989, p. 136]

We have here the beginnings of a bootstrap theory—a theory of development in which something that starts at a primitive level can take in whatever helps it to elaborate on that state and develop to a next one, and then do it again. Each elaboration makes the next state of sophistication possible, modifying the original capacities until their primitive origins become less relevant to the current ways of responding. An attractive model of the bootstrap is put forward by Steven Mendoza in "The emerging religious dimension of knowing in psychoanalysis" (2003), which can be used to bring out the implications of this kind of theory for phenomena which will be discussed under the heading of "Will" and "Volition" in Chapter Ten. Mendoza takes as one of his starting points a quotation from Meltzer to the effect that

the most evolved part of an individual's mind lies beyond the experience of self, and is apprehended as object. [Meltzer, 1973, p. 78]

This object is "O", is beauty. In a personal correspondence about an earlier version of his paper and of these pages, Mendoza amplifies:

To paraphrase: "the most evolved part of my mind lies beyond my experience of self, and I apprehend the most evolved part of my mind not as self but as Object". [Mendoza, personal communication]

and later:

The object which I think Meltzer refers to here is the object we call God. I think that he believes that what we experience as God is actually the most evolved part of an individual's mind which lies beyond the experience of self and is apprehended as object. This is the divine in man and may be experienced as a presence of God or as immanent in the external world. It is quite proper that it should not be sensed as self since the narcissistic or egotistical is not divine. Nor is this sense of God the sense of deity having existence in itself and being omnipotent and omniscient and therefore being an object of intercession such as Christian theology might treat of. But it might be not very different from the God of Martin Buber. [*ibid.*]

In Mendoza's view,

even to call "O" a mental process is not ineffable enough. I think "O" is that ineffable from which everything comes and of which we know nothing. It is not psychological, it is transpersonal, it is not external reality. It lies beyond the arbitrary distinction between the physical and the psychological, physical and psychological being merely cognitive constructs by which the mind organizes the world. [*ibid.*]

Mendoza argues that, with our attention directed to what is good and beautiful we develop an ever finer understanding of, and admiration and indeed longing for, the excellence to which we aspire, but to which we could not aspire if we did not already to an extent possess it. This good internal object is ours and yet not ours since we derive it from what we introjected. What may have started on mother's lap can become internalized and identified as the supreme good object, if we make the effort.

Mendoza goes further, again modestly using Meltzer's thoughts as a point of departure.

Although the title, *The Apprehension of Beauty*, suggests that beauty is an object which is apprehended, I think Meltzer intends more a beauty that is a quality of object-relating rather than an object itself. Hence, as I understand it, the aesthetic experience, if allowed to us, may be a basis upon which we can "bootstrap" towards religious experience ... Thus, apprehending the beauty of the mother on the basis of primary love ... we apprehend the possibility of beauty itself and, by bootstrapping, the possibility of the apprehension of the divine, beauty pervaded by love leading to wisdom and the direct evolution of "O". Of course, not all of this may happen in infancy. Often the potential of infant and latency experiences is realized in adolescence and on into the second half of life. [*ibid.*]

Mendoza's admiration and gratitude toward Donald Meltzer led him, in my view, to attribute to Meltzer his own lucid understanding. But conscientious scholarly readers may judge for themselves. The same question arises when Mendoza writes:

> Where Meltzer writes of the evolution of the self through dependence in relation to internal objects, I do not think he is talking about development sustained by the care of the external parents but about psychic evolution through the ministry of internal objects whose not-me quality takes the self beyond the egotistical consciousness of the narcissistic organization. [*ibid.*]

In passing, we may notice Mendoza's hostility towards his "egotistical" self-consciousness, a hostility he shares with many who condemn such awareness as narcissistic. Chapter Eleven, on Narcissism, looks in more detail at this self-contempt. Mendoza goes on to refer to his and perhaps Meltzer's belief that there is a "spiritual sense of the evolution of the individual to a psychic organization which transcends the personal".

> The transcendent is sometimes given a manic quality of ecstatic transport and Divine Visitation, as in Freud's discussion of the oceanic. It also means transcendence of self, a sense of the existence of others, an objectivity of consciousness, a sense of being a custodian of a common consciousness. Many of us have known this occasionally as an emotional experience of joy and seriousness. Perhaps Freud, for all his creativity, was never vouchsafed a sense of the wonder of his own discovery and any understanding of the valid religious experience this comprises. [*ibid.*]

About his own approach Mendoza writes, in generous response to my enquiries:

> I have tried to write a psychoanalytical paper and to avoid a mystical one. I have tried to write in such a way that those who choose to may read into what I say more that is implied than is explicit. If they want to understand they will; if you try to exhort them to apprehend something greater than the self which reveals the beauty of the world and the moment of consciousness, then they may treat that exhortation as a manic effusion or feel to themselves to be spectres at the feast. My purpose is not to show how much further than psychoanalysis our capacity or experience goes but to show how much further psychoanalysis can go. [*ibid.*]

A Freudian post-scriptum on the bootstrap theory

An odd precursor of the bootstrap may be found in an essay by Freud on "The economic problem in moral masochism", in the course of which Freud speculates on a possible proof from history of the persistence of the Oedipus complex, which he regards as "the origin of morality in each one of us".

> In the course of development through childhood which brings about an ever-increasing severance from the parents, their personal significance for the super-ego recedes. To the imagos they leave behind are then linked on the influences of teachers, authorities, of self-chosen models and heroes venerated by society; these persons need no longer be introjected by the ego, which has now become much more resistant. The last figure in the series beginning with the parents is that dark supremacy of Fate, which only the fewest among us are able to conceive of impersonally. Little can be said against the Dutch writer, Multatuli, when he substitutes the divine pair LOGOS KAI ANANKE for the MOIRA of the Greeks; but all those who transfer the guidance of the world to Providence, to God, or to God and Nature, rouse a suspicion that they still look about these farthest and remotest powers as a parent-couple—mythologically—and imagine themselves linked to them by libidinal bonds. [Freud, 1924a, p. 24]*

Inspiration and creativity

Creativity is a complex activity that requires frequent shifts between conscious and less conscious processes. It has long been recognized that creativity arises from an intersect of conscious and unconscious processes in the mind of an artist, often a conflicted artist. The psychoanalyst Anton Ehrenzweig needed no further postulates to explain inspiration. For him, it came from usually split-off or repressed unconscious phantasies that can become conscious when suitably disguised, as in dreams, stories, visual shapes, metaphors or patterned sounds. This is the soundly orthodox Freudian background to *The Hidden Order of Art* (1967), in which Ehrenzweig explores a wonderful range of artistic productions in a continually exciting way.

Meg Harris Williams also writes about the sense of unfamiliarity

---

*Logos, ananke and moira are perhaps best rendered as rationality, causality and fate.

and surprise that the creative mind can feel when the product of unconscious forces is made manifest. She defines inspiration as a "process by which the mind is fed by its internal objects" (1997, p. 35) and one might not need thumb-screws to get Ehrenzweig to agree with this, though he conceptualises the process rather differently. Closely associated as Harris Williams is with Meltzer, the internal objects to which she refers appear to act like those posited by Meltzer in *Sexual States of Mind* (1973) (*q.v.* also pp. 100–102, and 175) and perhaps also, in a different language, like Mendoza's internal objects. Harris Williams' objects, like Likierman's, Meltzer's, and Mendoza's, are objects that have been internalized by the artists, and are thus the artists' objects. But her quotations from Dante appear to show that Dante did not think of himself as the source of inspiration. Dante personifies the process in the language of his day but he indicates clearly that, in his view, the intersect from which creativity springs contains elements of Amor, who is not Dante, as well as elements of Dante himself. In many places, Dante declares that he is not the source of what he is saying, as in the very verses quoted by Harris Williams.

> I'mi son che, quando
> Amor mi spira, noto, e a quel modo
> ch'e ditta dentro, vo significando. [Purgatorio, xxiv, 52–54]

> When Love moves me
> I take note
> And as Love dictates
> I tell you exactly.

This sense that the provenance of inspirations cannot be confidently claimed as coming from oneself, is a common experience of creative people. Thus Martin Buber writes,

> Again and again I am reminded of the strange confession of Nietzsche when he described the event of "inspiration" as taking but not asking who gives. [1923, p. 162]

Buber adds that "even if we do not ask, we should thank", and he ends this discussion with the words:

> He who knows the breath of the Spirit, trespasses if he desires to get power over the Spirit to ascertain its nature and qualities. But he is also disloyal when he ascribes the gift to himself. [*ibid.*]

Martin Buber on the intersects you-and-me and
I and-whatever-else

Buber appears to have enjoyed his experiences in the intersect without any loss of his sense of self. In many ways he understands his experiences as a Jungian would:

> Now from my own unforgettable experience I know well that there is a state in which the bonds of the personal nature of life seem to have fallen away from us and we experience an undivided unity. But I do not know—what the soul willingly imagines ...—that in this I had attained to a union with the primal being or the godhead. That is an exaggeration no longer permitted to the responsible understanding. Responsibly—that is, as a man holding his ground before reality—I can elicit from those experiences only that in them I reached an undifferentiable unity of myself without form or content. I may call this an original pre-autobiographical unity and suppose that it is hidden unchanged beneath all biographical change, all development and complication of the soul. Nevertheless, in the honest and sober account of the responsible understanding this unity is nothing but the unity of this soul of mine, whose "ground" I have reached, so much so, beneath all formations and contents, that my spirit has no choice but to understand it as the groundless. [*Dialogue*, 1947, p. 43]

It was in the spirit of a Jewish mystical tradition that reveres words and the Word, that Buber wrote, in the opening pages of *I and Thou* (written in 1923 and published in English in 1937) that there are two Primary Words.

Primary words do not signify things, they intimate relationships.

Primary words do not describe something that might exist independently of them but, being spoken, they bring about existence.

Primary words are spoken from the being. [1923, p. 1]

As so often, our understanding is hampered by grammatical and syntactical differences between English and German, the language in which Buber wrote simply and stylishly. It is unfortunate that "Du", actually the German intimate personal form of address we would normally translate as "you", was rendered "Thou" in 1937, just as Strachey had earlier translated Freud's simple "Ich" as "ego", presumably because simple personal pronouns were thought too vulgarly common. Such translations are misleading. Buber is not singling out the relation between a person and God, who would in English tend to be addressed as "Thou". He is writing about "you" and "me", and if that includes God as well, Buber may not object. But the English translation "I–Thou" which, to the English ear, inevitably suggests a relationship with God, now has such wide currency that it would just create further confusion to exclude it from use altogether in the present chapter.

One Primary Word expresses a relationship that is characterised by the rather stately Edwardian translator as "I-and-Thou" or even "I–Thou" but is perhaps best thought of as "you-and-me". In contrast to this is the relationship between a person and a thing: "I–it", or perhaps the meaning is best rendered by "I-and-whatever-else". The locution "I–it" or "I-and-whatever-else" recognizes that there are things in the world not affected by me, though they may affect me:

> It is said that man experiences his world. What does this mean? Man travels on the surface of things and experiences them. ... The world has no part in the experience. It permits itself to be experienced but it has no concern in the matter.
>
> Every "it" has boundaries shared with other things. But when people say "you" they are not talking to a thing, they are not "talking to" at all; they are relating to a person. [*ibid.*, p. 3]

That is my translation. Another way to translate that last sentence might be:

> When people say "you", they are not talking to a thing, a possession—they are not saying something about their possessions but about their relationships.

The original stately translation goes:

> When Thou is said, the speaker has no thing; he stands in a relationship.

Once people are in this relationship, Buber maintains, there are drastic alterations at the boundaries of their personalities. A new creation comes into being—a you-and-me like Dr Doolittle's pushmepullyou.

> When "Thou" is said, the "I" of the combination "I–Thou" is said along with it.
> *or* When I say "you", the "I" of the combination "you-and-I" is in there.

> The Primary Word "I–Thou" can only be spoken with the whole being.
> *or* When I talk to you as I should, I am quite open. In psychotherapists' language this would mean that there is a whole-object relation, a relation between persons.

> The Primary Word "I–it" can never be spoken with the whole being.
> *or* When I refer to something, anything whatever, I am not talking as a person, with my whole being—part of myself is not engaged.

When you and I meet as persons, we are both changed. The only changes in an "I–it" encounter—if encounter it can be called—happens in the head of the person who is talking, that narcissistic place.

It is worth just noting that some psychotherapists think and talk about their own and their patients' unconscious processes as though these are part-objects, important or unimportant bits of personality, while other psychotherapists address their patients more consistently as personal beings who may just now not be conscious of some relevant aspects of themselves—this is a more whole-object way of relating, more I-and-Thou, more you-and-I.

Buber also wrestles to put into words that sense of affinity with nature that he shares with many, with Harold Searles among others, who acknowledges his debt to him in the next sub-section.

> It is part of our concept of a plant that it cannot respond. Yet this does not mean that there we are given simply no reciprocity at all … there is a reciprocity of the being itself, a reciprocity which is nothing but being in its course. [*I and Thou*, 1923 (1937), p. 158]

The translator comments in a footnote that "being in its course" was the best translation he could find for the German "*Seiend*". Students of Winnicott's writings, which of course came later, might offer his "going on being" (Winnicott, 1965, Chapter 4) as a possible version. Buber is writing here of a sense of kinship with nature that is generated by one's sense that nature keeps on being itself—sometimes a harsh fact but also sometimes a comfort, as when

> that living wholeness and unity of the tree, which denies itself to the sharpest glance of the mere investigator ... discloses itself to the glance of one who says *Thou* ... [*ibid.*]

Buber goes further!

> Our habits of thought make it difficult for us to see that here, awakened by our attitude, something lights up and approaches us from the source of being ... and ... we have to do justice to the reality which discloses itself to us. [*ibid.*]

Almost, we can say hello to a tree and the tree will respond and greet us! In highly intellectual language, Buber appears to be describing here something very like what psychotherapists at present imagine a small child's universe to be like. The child's sense of contact and relationship may be in place and working before the development of the child's intellectual knowledge of the world as a realm "out there" and, in my view, before the development of symbolization and conceptualization in general. In a very poetic passage that foreshadows Winnicott, Buber writes with a father's tenderness of the infant's experience at that stage, as he imagines it.

> The most primal nature of the effort to establish relation is already to be seen in the earliest and most confined stage. Before anything isolated can be perceived, timid glances move out into indistinct space, towards something indefinite; and in times when there seems to be no desire for nourishment, hands sketch delicately and dimly in the empty air, apparently aimlessly seeking and reaching out to meet something indefinite. You may, if you wish, call this animal action, but it is not thereby comprehended. For these very glances will, after protracted attempts, settle on the red carpet-pattern and not be moved until the soul of the red has opened itself to them; and this very movement of the hands will win from a woolly Teddy-bear its precise form, apparent to the senses, and become lovingly and unforgettably aware of a complete body. [*ibid.*, p. 42]

and then Buber describes, as it were in slow motion, the creative act by which the baby calls an object into being.

Neither of these acts is experience of an object, but it is the correspondence of the child—to be sure only "fanciful"—with what is alive and effective over against him. This "fancy" does not in the least involve, however, a "giving of life to the universe"; it is the instinct to make everything into a *Thou*, to give relation to the universe. Little, disjointed, meaningless sounds still go out persistingly into the void. But one day, unforeseen, they will have become conversation—does it matter that it is perhaps with the simmering kettle?

It is simply not the case that the child first perceives an object, then, as it were, puts himself in relation to it. But the effort to establish relation comes first—the hand of the child arches out so that what is over against him may nestle under it; second is the actual relation, a saying of *Thou* without words, in the state preceding word-form; the thing, like the *I*, is produced later, arising after the original experiences have been split and the connected partners separated. In the beginning is relation—as category of being, readiness, grasping form, mould for the soul; it is the *a priori* of relation, *the inborn Thou* ...

The inborn Thou is realised in the lived relations with that which meets it. [*I and Thou*, pp. 42–43]

Buber is describing recognition, relatedness.

Relatedness, a form answering to our subjectivity: Harold Searles and Kenneth Wright

... some process exists by which we can reach out from ourselves towards what is outside ourselves and ... if we are lucky, or if we are blessed, this may lead us to find a form answering to our subjectivity. [Wright, 1996, p. 72]

Towards the end of the nineteen-forties Harold Searles, recently out of the army and later to become one of the great innovators of psychoanalytic psychotherapy, began to write on *The Non-Human Environment in Normal Development and in Schizophrenia*. It was so counter to the spirit of the time that no one could be found to publish it until 1960. The opening sentences of his preface celebrate what the Catskill region of the U.S. meant to him: "a beauty and an affirmation of life's goodness" and "moments of deeply felt kinship with one's non-human environment ... to be counted among those moments when one has drunk deepest of the whole of life's meaning". Kinship and relatedness are keywords for this innovator in the treatment of schizophrenic distress.

> I believe that there is indeed one basic attitude which is of general validity, one central emotional orientation to which the mature human being returns *vis-à-vis* his non-human environment ...: relatedness.

> By relatedness I mean, on the one hand, a sense of intimate kinship ..., on the other hand, a maintenance of our own sense of individuality ... [Searles, 1960, pp. 101–102]

Searles acknowledged his debt to Martin Buber (1957), agreeing for instance, that entering into a relationship presupposes "a primal setting at a distance"—there is no merging. However close our kinship to the nonhuman world, we are not *at one* with it (p. 102). Searles (1960, p. 117 ff.) quotes amply from Buber, and also from a study by Maurice Friedman entitled *Martin Buber—The Life of Dialogue* (1955).

> Thus I–Thou and I–it cut across the lines of our ordinary distinctions, to focus our attention not on individual objects and their casual connections but upon the relations between things, the "dazwishen" (the "in-between").

> I–It is the primary word of experiencing and using. It takes place within a man and not between him and the world. Hence it is entirely subjective and lacking in mutuality.

> I–Thou is the primary word of relation. It is characterised by mutuality, directness, presentness, intensity and ineffability. Although it is only within this relation that personality and the personal really exist, the Thou of I–Thou is not limited to men but may include animals, trees, objects of nature and God. [Friedman, 1955, p. 57]

In his turn, Kenneth Wright was to acknowledge his debt to Searles, especially as regards the idea that, in nature as in art, we find ourselves moved by what Wright was to clarify as "forms answering to our subjectivity", a relation Buber might characterize as I–Thou.

... Some process exists by which we can reach out from ourselves
towards what is outside ourselves and ... if we are lucky, or if we
are blessed, this may lead us to find a form answering to our own
subjectivity. [Wright, 1996, p. 72]

A form answering to our subjectivity is what Beatrice was to
Dante. That form, out there and in the heart, is to be found in another
person, another face, an embrace. Nothing new in that. But it can also
be found in a mountain, a fountain, a symphony, a tree, a horse, in
anything that is just then transparent and represents the ineffable
beyond quiddity, in a Beatricean moment full of significance. For
Buber, Searles and Wright, this experience is not to be equated with a
process of projection or projective identification: there is something
out there that fits in form, there is recognition as well as discovery.

Wright points to differences between his views and other
notions entertained at that time in the psychoanalytic world. He
postulates "something out there" resonating or responding to
something "in here", and "one can see that this is different from
something being merely projected into the object" (Wright, 1996,
p. 62). Projective processes are different from "a sense of fit" or
"equivalence", and they are not Searles' kind of relatedness.

The thing "out there" seems in fact to *respond* to the thing "in
here"—it does not merely act as a receptacle. [Wright, 1996, p. 92]

But note the word "seems". Wright does not quite commit himself,
as Buber and Searles do, to a mutuality of response.

How does it come about that we see what we see? We must have
had it in us at least potentially, to see those things in others.
Recognition is sometimes more like a growth than a flash. It may
require work, honesty, humility, proper pride and self-esteem, a
sense of perspective, to see ourselves in others and get this sense of
relatedness more into consciousness and into actions. (We know
about this process because it is how we work at becoming better
psychotherapists.) It is a dynamic process even when we are
relating to a hillside or a piece of music—more so, of course, when
we are relating to a person. No wonder that therapists have to have
a sound therapy before they can begin working therapeutically with
others. They must be able to recognize themselves *in* others. It is one
of Searles' principal therapeutic ingredients.

Searles' revolutionary contribution to working with people afflicted with schizophrenic symptoms was his theory that he, the therapist, by being so familiar with his own madness, his own wish to destroy, burn down, swallow, merge, chew up, whatever, and by being *comfortable* with it, enabled his patients, who were mad in much the same way if not to the same degree, to recognize that he and they were alike but that he was not terrified by what he was, nor driven into action by it. This recognition calmed the patients, made them more able to contain themselves because they could see that he contained much the same material. If he could contain himself, perhaps they could; he was the form answering to their subjectivity (Searles, 1979, Chapter 22, see also J. Klein, 1995 pp. 254–255).

The more we know ourselves, the more we are able to recognize (ourselves in) others, declared Searles. There are schools of thought that teach only the reverse of this process: that what we see in others we then make our own—we see it in others first and only thereupon in ourselves. It is likely that both these processes operate at one time or another. Why not? Sometimes introjection, sometimes projective identification, sometimes introjective identification, sometimes discovery, sometimes extractive identification (Bollas, 1987, Chapter Nine). The phrase "to see ourselves in others" covers all these possibilities and, indeed, the early psychoanalysts' "identification" did not distinguish between them.

Searles also points out that when patients perceive, in the transference, something in us therapists to love or hate or fear, it is always something that is not totally implausible. They have in fact detected in us a form answering to their subjectivity, which they may have magnified or coloured with their subjectivity but which is there in us, and we do our patients a disservice if we cannot acknowledge to ourselves the objective grain of truth around which the transference is built (1979, Chapter 22). So we carry on with our self-analysis alongside our patients.

When Searles wrote about our sense of kinship with non-human objects—hillsides, landscapes, the world around us—he thought in terms of our relating on two levels. We relate to them by what he called "displacement" from what we felt at some previous time about some other object—he called this "regression" later in the book—but also, he insists in italics, we relate to the cat as *being a cat, this cat*, and to the tree as *being a tree, this tree*. The cat is still this tabby, the tree still this oak, and the beholder remains Harold (1979, pp. 19–20). This is what Searles saw as *mature relatedness*; there is a deep sense of relatedness here but there is no merging, no loss of ego-boundaries (1979, p. 19 ff.). People are *more* themselves in Dante's heaven, not less; it is in hell that the loss of boundaries is felt, the punishing consequences of a person's stance in life. We are more ourselves before a painting we like, a cloudscape that holds us entranced, a loved person. It may also be remarked that this recognition has not so very much to do with words, with consciousness. As when in love, we cannot define so very clearly exactly what it is in the other that gives our love the quality it has. But in this process of recognition, there is always the knowledge that the other in some way fits in form.

In this chapter on the mature person's attitude toward his non-human environment, Searles insists that loss of the sense of self, while highly prized by many, is very different from the experience of relatedness he values. He does not consider regression to be a mature state of being. He writes that people are afraid to regress, which he quite understands and sympathizes with; because they fear regression, they fear relatedness although that is an entirely different mental process, and a very mature and constructive one. "Loneliness is assuaged, creativity freed, self-realisation fostered" (Searles, 1960, p. 127).

> I am inclined to believe that it is essential to the creative process that one becomes open to feelings of intense relatedness, and even oneness, with the totality of one's environment ... [*ibid.*, p. 125]

Using delightful illustrations from a wide variety of writers, Searles devotes the whole of Chapter Five to the psychological benefits to be derived from a mature relationship to one's non-human environment:

> the assuagement of painful and anxiety-laden states of feeling
>
> the fostering of self-realisation
>
> a deepening of the sense of one's own reality and of one's difference from the non-human environment
>
> a fostering of one's appreciation and acceptance of other people.

With Winnicott in the intersect

It was Winnicott who gave us non-Jungian psychotherapists in Britain the permission to look more freely at events in the intersect. He provided a way of thinking that felt legitimate, about experiences that the psychoanalytic tradition had until then declared illusory, sentimental, unscientific. With some justification, for psychotherapists, like other people, can write a great deal of sloppy nonsense in their endeavours to bring hitherto neglected mental processes under scrutiny. Be that as it may, Winnicott offered a more systematic way of considering the difference between the unreliable fanciful and what might be relied upon in professional discussion. English and pragmatic, but not positivistic, Winnicott built on what people said about what they felt. Tentatively, but with growing confidence he helped us accept our ability to have and not-have, be and not-be, know and not-know, as children do in pretend-play (cf. Steiner, 1985 and Fonagy, 1995). We could start to think about experiences where the generally accepted distinction between inner and outer, self and not-self, here and not-here, might not apply very strictly. Winnicott wrote bravely about

> a part which we cannot ignore, an intermediate area of experiences to which inner reality and external life both contribute. [1951, also in *Playing and Reality*, 1974, p. 4]

He made it possible for us to think systematically about a universe where, by virtue of a toddler's creativity, a teddy-bear and a toddler could talk to each other, and support and control one another, in ways quite understood by readers of A. A. Milne's Pooh stories, which psychotherapists had as yet little to say about. This realm, this state of being, where Christopher Robin and his bear have fun, Winnicott named an intermediate area of experiences, a transitional space. It is created by the toddler's imagination, and the toddler constructs it so that the teddy-bear is neither wholly at the toddler's command, nor wholly bear-as-seen-by-the-observer. In this realm both are, in Kohut's words, "independent centres of initiative and perception" (Kohut, 1977, p. 177): alive, active, and engaged with one another. Winnicott uses the term "transitional object" for bears and comfort-blankets and other such creations of the child's; the term "transitional space" is used for the realm of imagination in which such contact with toy bears is possible.

Winnicott confined his remarks to the world of babies and young children, and the meaning of thumbs, comfort blankets and teddy-bears. By 1960, conveniently re-published in 1965 (p. 50), it was possible to be a little more confident. In "Ego distortion in terms of true and false self" Winnicott wrote also about adults, and indeed about society.

> In the healthy individual ... who is a creative and spontaneous being, there is a capacity for the use of symbols ... Health is here closely bound up with the capacity of the individual to live in an area that is intermediate between the dream and the reality, which is called the cultural life. [Winnicott, 1965]

The word *area*, here used in the sense of "realm" or "universe of discourse", soon gained that unfortunately solidly concrete visual connotation already remarked upon in Chapter Eight, and became *space*.

Ten years later still, Winnicott (1969) offered a pragmatic means of distinguishing between inner life and external reality that cannot, for most purposes, be bettered; this was later to become Chapter Six in *Playing and Reality* (1974). In brief, he suggested that the infant mind operates in such a way that anything that appears to be strong, loving, and protective, and that can be relied upon to survive without retaliating even when attacked in an angry and destructive moment, may be declared to be really there, really other, not just something we dreamt up. So people and things, and whatever else there may be, are experienced as only potentially there (in potential space) until they have survived our angry greedy unreasonably demanding ways.

This is a pleasant operational test of what is really real, but it is here only mentioned by the way, in gratitude, before we turn to consider much that still needs to be sorted out, for Winnicott left us some knotty problems. We, the reading public of that time, had been gratefully plodding after him, thinking of teddy-bears, thumbs, and comfort blankets and, in more elevated moments, of Art and Culture and the Imagination. In fact, what Winnicott was discovering for us was a way of thinking about something elusive and ineffable at that time, so that we could have more precise conversations about experiences in which phenomena are not quite one thing or another, not quite "me" and not quite "not-me", in which people may share what is "between" them but does not belong entirely to one person or another.

This was very useful and enabled us to extend our thinking about the nature and role of transactions that involve symbols. The bear, that woolly thing on the floor, had meanings not dreamt of by the manufacturers. Winnicott had shown us that toddlers can create meaning; it is what human beings do. Once we could accept the idea of the toddler's creativity, we could extend its focus backwards in time from the bear at age one, to the comfort blanket or sucky or favourite woolly toy a little earlier, and then to the breast, earlier still. The absent but imagined breast (this passage continues a line of argument begun in Chapter Three) is now thought to be the first product of the child's creativity, and the first symbol.

The argument relies on two successive hypotheses. According to the first hypothesis, in the interval between the baby wanting the breast and the baby using the breast, something like the idea of the breast eventually arises within the infant, something that might be called a proto-concept of a breast, not yet a symbol of a breast. This proto-concept of a breast is created by the baby, the first product of the baby's creativity. The second hypothesis posits an "area", a "space", a "universe of discourse" where creativity takes place, a "transitional space" neither wholly mother nor wholly baby, to which both contribute or where both meet—an intersect. It is also called a potential space, because it is potentially full of symbols that may be created there.

Historically, Winnicott moved, from understanding something about the teddy-bear in a baby's life, to understanding something similar about the breast in the baby's life. But, perhaps because the baby relates to the breast or bottle before it is old enough to take an interest in teddy-bears, a confusion became established in discussions about creativity, among those who were influenced by Winnicott. They failed to give sufficient attention to an important distinction: what the baby does creatively with the breast is different from what the baby does creatively with the bear. The bear in the baby's life is almost entirely a creation, a creation limited by the continuous presence of what we may call the manufacturer's bear in its "bearness", though of course the imagination can play around it to an amazing extent. However, whatever the toddler may imagine, the bear never contradicts from its own initiative or perception. There is no creative bear, except derivatively if the child imagines the bear to be so. Now the breast is a different kind of creation, not only limited by what the baby imagines but also limited by the initiative and perception of the mother whose breast it is. One might say that the baby meets not only the breast it created, but also the mother as she is and as she feels herself to be, and the meaning, to her, of her breasts and her baby. Maybe this does no more for the breast that the baby creates than the baby's encounter with the bear is affected by the bear's consciousness of itself, but it is likely that the encounter between two consciousnesses is different in kind.

Certain things happen between the baby and the mother's breast that are vitally different from what happens between baby and bear, and it is important to be clear that what the mother does profoundly affects how the baby relates to the breast, and that this in turn is a cause of how the baby will in a little while relate to bears and other objects capable of symbolic meaning—the baby's capacity for later creativity depends to an extent on how the mother behaves. From day one, the baby encounters a breast (or perhaps a bottle, but for the present argument it does not matter which) that it can only control with the consent of someone else, and this makes a difference not always appreciated by all Winnicottians.

Moreover, it can be argued that the word "space" came to be used too generously. Too many phenomena were referred to Transitional Space or to Potential Space. The various ways in which these labels were used was not conducive to clarity of thought. All those "spaces" are not identical. All those phenomena—the thumbs, the comfort blankets, the teddy-bears, as well as kinship with nature and being able to paint and aesthetic experiences generally—may have a metaphor in common, that of a space in which we experience them, but they are not the same; they do not have similar positions in the psyche or in the rest of the world. Just as, though blackbirds and larks and thrushes are all legitimately called birds, it is not the case that they are all the same bird, it is not the case that all those "spaces" are the same space, or the same universe of discourse. Transitional phenomena occur in transitional space; potential phenomena in potential space, and so on. It may be as well at least to distinguish

a) OUR SPACE or TRANSITIONAL SPACE—a space where encounters between ourselves and (perhaps imaginary) others are experienced. When Winnicott gave the toy bear a space to be, he called that space "transitional" because he thought of the bear as a transitional object: he was thinking of some kind of intersect of three realms: (mother and her comfort, safe but not totally in control), (bear safe and not totally in control), (self safe and in control).

b) POTENTIAL SPACE—the space of creativity and inspiration, the playground of the artistic/psychotherapeutic/empathic/intuitive imagination. Here creative processes, id-processes, are one essential element, but ego-processes are inevitably also involved since we have to be proficient in our use of paint, violin bows, limbs, or language. What goes on in this sort of space is very different from what goes on in OUR SPACE. Control is exercised by ego-processes and by the nature of the materials—paint, strings, and so on, which set us limits we are free to explore.

c) CULTURAL SPACE—the space of Durkheim's collective representations (see p. 54–55), the realm of shared symbols. This space is not for any small number of people to control, or for any individual. It is created by collectivities of people large enough to have a shared culture; it is created by people using symbols whose meaning is recognised by others, and assented to.

Ogden's intersubjectivity

The concept of an intersect, where minds can meet and combine to create further thoughts, had a benign influence on psychotherapists' practice. We began to feel justified in our belief that it is not usually wise to say "You are avoiding the truth" or "What you are really saying is ..." from the Olympian heights of our specially trained wisdom. It was usually more accurate, more tactful and more likely to lead to understanding, if we spoke of possibilities whose origin was not definitely either in our own or in our patient's mind but rather somewhere in between in which we shared. We could say constructively, "I wonder if ..." and "Does it feel like ...?" and "Do you think that ...?" and "Are we constructing a picture of someone who ...?" Thomas Ogden elaborates this way of thinking in his own fashion, not in Winnicott's admittedly somewhat deceptively plain domestic style usually derived from the Anglo-Saxon, but in the more often schizoid Greco–Latinate style of American academe. One of his starting-points is a famous dictum of Winnicott's, (1965, p. 39 fn) that there is no such thing as a baby (only a mother-and-baby), which Ogden re-tailors as:

> I believe that, in an analytic context, there is no such thing as an analysand apart from the relationship with the analyst, and no such thing as an analyst apart from the relationship with the analysand. [Ogden, 1994, p. 4]

and on the same page of the same paper he writes of

> the experience of being simultaneously within and outside of the intersubjectivity of the analyst-analysand, which I will refer to as "the analytic third".

In a later paper he amplifies what he means by the analytic third: it is another pushmepullyou, another intersect phenomenon.

> ... the analytic third is not a single event experienced identically by two people; rather it is a jointly but asymmetrically constructed and experienced set of conscious and unconscious subjective experiences in which analyst and analysand participate. [1996, p. 584]

To take a common illustration, tennis is an intersubjective-third experience. Unless two or four people are playing, there is no such thing as tennis: when one participant walks off, tennis vanishes. Tennis is thus a "jointly constructed set of experiences" of the kind to which Ogden refers; it is created by people who participate in an activity in a particular way. And so in psychotherapy, and other kinds of encounter between people.

Ogden goes rather alarmingly far in his claims. He maintains that what is created by analyst and analysand is so much a thing in itself that "there is no such thing as an analysand apart from the relationship with the analyst", but fortunately he does not mean it rigorously, for he allows both parties to remember and ponder on their own, between encounters. More worrying is the rather extreme idea that all that needs to be done to help at least some sufferers (presumably those that can take the full treatment à la Kernberg as on pp. 258–259) is to analyse the intersubjective third, i.e. what goes on between analysand and analyst when they are doing analysis. This does sound rather like maintaining that tennis is all that matters in the life of the tennis-player. Of course, that may be true for some people, perhaps especially for those training to be world champions or professional psychoanalysts. But how do we know that it is true for Mr A with his psychosomatic allergies or Mr D with his inability to meet deadlines? His daughter refuses to sit her exams; it rained for the third year in succession during his annual holiday; his lady-friend has left him; he has arthritis, and all those things have meaning for him. If we give supremacy to those events in the intersect that are most obvious to the carefully trained analyst of the more traditional kind, we may fall into a sad misreading of the patient's total situation. And we may bring a useful way of thinking into disrepute with those who will not follow a potentially good idea to its extreme, admirable though Ogden's practice is shown to be by his illustrative case material. Perhaps all that is in dispute here is a style of presentation, but it has happened before that good new ideas were misunderstood, abused and popularized by the unimaginative, lazy or carelessly trained.

In conclusion

What do these descriptions of people's experiences of the intersect add up to? The development of theory never stops, and it has not stopped at the point we have now come to. Much work is needed before we can safely settle down with conclusions.

> But I shall say no more of this at this time; for this is to be felt and not talked of; and they who never touched it with their fingers may secretly perhaps laugh at it in their hearts and be never the wiser. [George Eliot's epigraph to Chapter LX of *Daniel Deronda*]

CHAPTER TEN

Will and attention

U ntil fairly recently, it was taken for granted that if people knew what they should do, they would do it and that if they were negligent in their duties, they should make an effort and mend their ways. Will-power and duty were part of the natural order as, of course, were "weakness" and "disobedience". There were simple alternatives: either what you should do was attractive so that you did it quite naturally effortlessly, or you had to make an effort, which you might do gladly or not. These ways of thinking were still very much alive a hundred years ago: it is interesting how much reference is made to them in the novels and essays of that time, and how little as the century wore on. Few case-descriptions in the *International Journal of Psychoanalysis*, or the *British Journal of Psychotherapy* or the counselling journals, make reference to will-power, self-command, self-control—control by means of ego-processes—exertions that had previously been thought to enable us to do the right things and avoid what is pointless or counter-productive or damaging to happiness or just plain wrong. In the ten years 1987–1997 there was no reference to WILL in the index of the *International Journal* and only one to ATTENTION, under "divided attention" (a concept used by Freud to explain how we can, for instance, concentrate so on *how* we are reading a passage aloud that we can loos the sense of *what* we are reading—Rizzuto, 1990, p. 264, referring to Freud, 1891).

Not so in the nineteenth century. Elinor in Jane Austen's *Sense and Sensibility* (1811) "had a mind awakened to reasonable exertion". She had

> an excellent heart, her disposition was affectionate, and her feelings were strong, but she knew how to govern them.

In Jane Austen's time it was taken for granted that feelings could, and at times should, be governed: indeed, the need for endeavour and effort was generally well thought of. These ideas have lost status until now they hardly figure in educated consciousness, and we have to remind ourselves of what is involved.

In the course of *Sense and Sensibility*, Marianne, "whose abilities were in many respects quite equal to Elinor's", her elder sister's, "learned to govern herself". Marianne

> was sensible and clever, but eager in everything; her sorrows, her joys, could have no moderation.

"Moderation" is here used in the sense the *Shorter Oxford Dictionary* calls now rare, as deriving from the root *moderare* "to reduce, abate, control ... to render less violent or intense". We are now coming to call this process "regulation" as in the phrase "affect-regulation" used later in this chapter.

Unlike Elinor, Marianne and her mother Mrs Dashwood "encouraged each other in the violence of their affliction" when they were asked to leave the house in which they had lived for many years and which, after Mr Dashwood's death, was found to have been inherited not by them but by other relatives.

> The agony of grief which overpowered them at first, was voluntarily renewed, was sought after, was created again and again. They gave themselves up wholly to their sorrow, seeking increase of wretchedness in every reflection that could afford it, and resolved against ever admitting consolation in the future.

> Elinor, too, was deeply afflicted; but still she could struggle, could exert herself ...

This struggle is about feeling something keenly and yet resisting the impulse to action. Elinor would exert herself; in contrast to those who "had neither the courage to speak nor the fortitude to conceal, ... she had a mind awakened to reasonable exertion" and said "my feelings shall be governed". This way of being is not much spoken of at present, perhaps because we feel it to be tainted by the often hostility-laden moralism of previous ages.

William James, Shand, McDougall, Stout: contemporaries of the young Freud

The psychologists from what we think of the pre-Freudian era—though they were contemporaries of the young Freud—were interested in the traditional moral elements of human nature as they understood them, and tried to formulate the mental processes that would "moderate" the expression of feelings and impulses that might otherwise be "immoderate". They were not far astray, although they used language we have since abandoned; their ideas are less sophisticated versions of current speculations still not quite solidly planted in a general theory. There is not space to summarize all they have to offer though, in spite of their obsession with the speculative detail, their prose often makes them a pleasure to read.

William James (1891), Stout (1899), William McDougall (1908) and Shand (1914) all had chapters on "Will" or "Volition", and "Intention" and "Attention", and these books would go into twenty or more editions. McDougall's *Social Psychology*, first published in 1908, went to 60,000 copies according to the preface in his next most popular book *Outline of Psychology* (1923). These writers had, each in his own way, a theory of personality structure and dynamics in which impulses or desires or feelings, and thoughts or ideas or memories, combined in complex organizations which they called "sentiments" and "attitudes". These were very like what Freud called "complexes", a term now also abandoned. Attitudes and sentiments combined in turn to form the total personality structure. No impulse or instinct, or idea or whatever, had power on its own: each operated only in concert with other processes that together formed the controlling context.

Inevitably there is something about these words and ways of

thinking that appears unsophisticated to us now. There was too much naming of parts, too much listing of emotions and too much verbal differentiating between them, long lists of what were thought the main sentiments. The language sounds old-fashioned—as does that of the Freudians who were their contemporaries—but the reader may well conclude, at the end of the arguments presented in this chapter, that they had the right intuitions about how the processes were likely to work. As William James wrote more than a century ago, in his *Principles of Psychology,*

> The first point to start from in understanding voluntary action, and the possible occurrence of it with no fiat or express resolve, is the fact that consciousness is *in its very nature impulsive*. We do not have a sensation or a thought and then have to *add* something dynamic to it to get a movement. Every pulse of feeling which we have is the correlate of some neural activity that is already on its way to instigate a movement. [James, 1891, p. 526]

McDougall (1908) writes that

> Some attempt must therefore be made to show that the effort of volition is not the mysterious and utterly incomprehensible process the extreme libertarians would have it to be; but that it is to be accounted for by the same principles as other modes of human activity; that it involves no new principles of activity or energy, but only a more subtle and complex interplay of those impulses which activate all animal behaviour and in which the ultimate mystery of mind and life resides. [McDougall, 1908, p. 231]

Could anything be more up-to-date than this in 2002?

Fallacies about "The Will" and the function of self-regard

At that time, it was a great step forward to abandon the idea that "the Will" was a separate organ of "the mind".

> It may be reasonably urged that the will is not an independent force ... it is an expression of the tendencies of emotions and sentiments; in them its innate qualities are manifested and its acquired qualities developed ... *In the sentiments alone* are resolutions formed, and choice manifested between their sometimes conflicting ends; they

only give the will to control emotion, and to be steadfast to the end. [Shand, 1914, p. 65]

And the science of character will deal with the Intellect as with the Will. It will regard the one no more than the other as an independent existence; but as organised in and subserving the system of some impulse, emotion or sentiment. The powers of the intellect, like those of the will ... will only be elicited in one or other of these systems. [*ibid.*, p. 67]

In 1945, M. C. D'Arcy was to propose that interest in "The Will" may have been a confusing outcome of the nineteenth-century Romantic Movement on the Continent, of Wagner and Nietzsche and other tragic-hero-oriented literary notables.

In this movement are to be found ... strange traits, the love for death, the refusal to accept life as it is, the longing for what is absent ... the lure of the strange and the ecstatic. [D'Arcy, 1945, p. 167]

and

Just as Bernard Shaw invents a Life Force, so too with equal imaginative certainty Schopenhauer posits a Will. Their creation, however, is coloured by their temperament; the same monster is advertised by one as a gospel of joy and by the other as a sentence of death. [*ibid.*, p. 168]

D'Arcy writes amusingly in terms that make a preoccupation with The Will appear a schizoid affliction. With intellectual fun, his chapter on "Reason and Will", from which these quotations come, examines the personalities of those who elevate the operation of will-power into pre-eminence. According to D'Arcy, they think of the will as operating independently from the rest of the personality, distinct from affection, respect, and other relationships. Quoting from *The Influence of Baudelaire* (Turquet Milnes, 1926), D'Arcy provides ample instances of moods with which psychotherapists are professionally familiar. From De l'Isle Adam, for instance, comes:

Si nous n'aimions plus rien, pas meme nos jeunesses,
Si nos coeurs sont remplis d'inutiles tristesses,
S'il ne nous reste rien ni des Dieus ni des Rois ... [D'Arcy, 1945, p. 178]

and on the same page we find some verses by Louis Bertrand that, translated, read

> Desert that no longer hears the voice of John the Baptist, Desert where no longer dwell the hermit and the dove. Even so my soul is a waste, where on the brink of the abyss, one hand stretched out toward life and the other toward death, I utter a despairing thought ...

and, on the next page, some lines from Massis' *Defense de l'Occident*, also unfortunately without any further reference:

> All the characters presented to us by the young writers are recognisable by one trait—they have no centre ... and this produces a strange similarity amongst them which serves to differentiate them from all human types which have existed in French literature down to the present day ...
>
> Not only have their minds and wills no distinct object, but it seems as if the subject writing were in search of some undiscoverable ego; as though modern subjectivism were bent on ending finally in a complete disintegration, a total resorption into the original chaos. So one might say that these characters arose out of the dissociation of a morbid psychology, and were no longer in quest of a personal identity in which they believed. [D'Arcy, 1945, p. 179]

This comes from the field of French literary criticism but we may note that it describes a kind of person we do at times see in our consulting-rooms. These are the people who, looking for ways to feel happier and better, and lacking the resources available to more fortunate minds, turn either to more rule-governed or more willpower-driven techniques for attaining peace of mind or a feeling of being in tune with the universe. The next chapter, which is on narcissism, looks at these in more detail.

British and American psychologists of the early twentieth century postulated a self-regarding sentiment—very like what was later thought of as ego or a sense of self or identity, such that

> the conations, the desires and aversions, arising within this self-regarding sentiment, are the motive forces which, adding themselves to the weaker ideal motive in the case of moral effort, enable it to win mastery over some stronger, coarser desire of primitive animal nature and to banish from consciousness the idea of the end of this desire. [McDougall, 1908, p. 213]

These writers postulated not more Will, but more self-regard, a set of processes whose descriptions quite resemble what came later to be thought of by some as a sense of self or of identity, and by others, as ego-processes, and by yet others as self-respect. Self-regard shall control what we do. I shall not do what I feel is "not me" or not worthy of me. The idea is, that we have evolved a sense of how we want to be, or at least of how we want to be regarded, and reference to this sense steers us. This idea re-appears in some form in all the later formulations canvassed in this chapter.

Will experienced as somehow independent of other aspects of the self

The subjective sense of something "in" us yet separate from us in some other sense, something that makes us feel under pressure to go in one direction rather than another, is still often part of our experience. We still say, though perhaps rather less frequently than in Jane Austen's time "I know I ought to go and see my aunt" with the implication that we do not want to but that something is nevertheless moving us to go and pay that visit. The knowledge of what we ought to do is often experienced as coming from a separate mental agency in our mind, called conscience or will. The place from which that knowledge comes is currently given less prominence in our notions of how we are constructed, but to the extent that we still feel the compulsion, we still feel it as somewhat external from the main body of our desires, much as we sometimes feel a wish for chocolates or alcohol as compelling us "in spite of our (main) self".

Steven Mendoza (2003; see also pp. 181–184 in the present volume) takes as one of his starting points a quotation from Meltzer to the effect that, "the most evolved part of an individual's mind lies beyond the experience of the self and is apprehended as object" (Meltzer, 1973). This (good internal) object is ours and yet not ours, since we derive it from what we introjected. Initially it came from our relationship with our parents and later from what, guided by these earlier introjects, we accreted as fitting and appealing, building on what we already had, which however we may only have been able to use because of the foundation on which we are building. And this foundation was not entirely ours to begin with and never can be, because of the role played by our admiration for other people's excellence which we may work to possess but which can never be entirely our own possession. Hence the sense of alienation as well as admiration.

At this point we pick up the discussion begun in Chapter Nine about the internalization of what is admired and how admiration can work as a bootstrap process, encouraging and enabling ever more admirable ambitions as the person becomes able to understand and admire ever more strenuous prowess in aesthetic and moral fields. The marriages we make, or the friends we seek out, encourage us to make more of some traits or interests, less of others. Our nearest and/or dearest may be interested in the refinements of classical music or walking along hilltops or anything else of importance to them—we need only not to be put off by such predilections or only mildly intrigued to start with but, through continued contact, this side of our potential is cultivated and expanded in ways that might not have been if those nearest had not been dear. Our attention is directed partly by what we already are, and partly by where we have—at the very least—not resisted directing it.

Voice from the back of the hall: "What about the soul?"

No precise teaching about the soul received general acceptance in the Christian Church until the Middle Ages. The Scriptures are explicit only on the facts of the distinction between soul and body, the creation of the soul of the first man by the Divine Breath (ruach), and its immortality ... St Paul's ... language is not entirely consistent, and spirit (ruach) sometimes denotes the principle of supernatural life in contrast to the natural life of the soul, and on other occasions signifies the higher powers (intellect and will) as opposed to the lower faculties (emotions etc.) [*The Oxford Dictionary of the Christian Church*, entry on "soul"]

The *Dictionary* shows the soul to be a pretty loose concept. Yet even today the word appears in fairly common parlance. Though theologians tend now to avoid it, it deserves a space in this chapter because it is so often used in connection with willpower and choice. Words are kept in common parlance when the concept is needed to describe something that keeps happening. What keeps happening is that people know from repeated experience that they have to draw on some effort to do something they do not want to do—visit auntie, refuse the third drink. Because of our unfortunate habits of thought, which are in terms of entities and nouns rather than processes and verbs—habits that have created confusion since Aristotle at least—whenever we do something that puzzles us we ask "What made me do it?" and we expect the question "What?" to be answered in terms of a thing, an entity—say "soul"—rather than in terms of a process that each of us evolved in our own life-time.

It is at least partly our unfortunate habit of thinking in nouns and entities, when verbs or processes or functions would serve us better, that makes "the soul" so difficult to think about. People sometimes experience themselves as concentrating on something in particular and, wanting to describe this experience, they fall back on assuming that there is some distinct part of themselves that is doing the concentrating, the soul part. That is what lands us with having to describe the soul: what is it? what else can we say *about* it? Such non-issues can be avoided by describing clearly what we were doing: we were focusing our attention; we can describe how that felt, what else happened at the time, how we thought about it afterwards ... Or, if we absolutely need a noun, we could use a verb-based noun like "attention", and make that into an adjective we can think about. We might describe a lazy soul as a not very attentive soul, a passionate soul could be described as a passionately attentive soul, and so on.

Early Freudians and the moderation (regulation) of feelings: ego-strength and ego-weakness

In the early days of the Freudian twentieth century, mental suffering was considered to derive from overstrong and misapplied superego controls. Many cases from that time suggest that the patients treated at that time were able to lead more comfortable and more productive lives once they had been helped to understand how their superego processes had operated to repress needs, impulses and desires that are actually quite acceptable. Irrational guilt seemed a major cause of inner conflict and thus of neurosis. In those early decades of great intellectual excitement, one may speculate, an assumption grew that the techniques of analysis that enabled people to undo their repressions and free them from too much superego control and guilt, would be sufficient therapy to counter most of the ills we might suffer from.

The early Freudians were very consistent. Neurosis was caused by unconscious conflict between impulses, or between impulses and common sense or conscience. If you made such a conflict conscious, you would free it of its irrational components. Then one impulse would prove stronger than the other, being more practical or more acceptable in the circumstances, and would win. End of conflict. End of neurotic symptom. Peace of mind restored: a purely mechanical consequence of freeing the impulse from the mistaken unconscious associations that had caused conflict. No need for the concepts of willpower or strength of mind. But patients did not always behave as they ought according to this theory, a fact that could not be disregarded indefinitely. So the theory had to include these exceptions, and analysts found themselves saying, in effect, "You are persisting in your neurotic behaviour because of your unconscious resistance to my explanation, but now that I have made you conscious of it by telling you about it, you do not need to defend yourself against it, so stop your resistance". In other words, the patient was to use his or her willpower.

That was a hundred years ago but, alas, just what the precise mechanism is by which we help our patients is still an avoided topic. We still do not sufficiently scrutinize the logic and the efficacy of our techniques and their outcomes. Though some headway is being made.

Undeniably, people have in varying degrees an ability to assent to and act on an impulse, or to refuse assent and inhibit—in a sense refuse to believe in—an impulse. What is that agency, that process that assents? We need not look for something other than was already suspected by McDougall's generation. The answer to "what is the agency that assents to an impulse or inhibits it?" is "the processes that assent to or inhibit it".

These processes are called "ego" and "superego" by psycho-analysts and others. Freud calls the ego the part of the id which has been modified by the direct influence of the external world ... The ego represents what may be called reason and common sense, in contrast to the id, which contains the passions ... In its relation to the id, it is like a man on horseback who has to hold in check the superior strength of the horse ... [1923]

And here lies the confusion. When we think of the ego as a rider on a horse, we think of an agent, a self-in-charge, yes, a Romantic Hero exercising Will, a person within us that rides the person we are. There is no such thing.

Strictly speaking, Freud described the ego as a set of processes that develop through contact with the external world on a cause-and-effect basis, giving and withholding assent to action according to the promptings of pleasure-seeking pain-avoiding id impulses (Freud, 1933). The ego, thus regarded, is a set of processes among other processes that contribute to the way we steer our way through the opportunities and dangers of life around us.

The concepts of ego-strength and ego-weakness have been appearing in psychoanalytic thinking since the nineteen-twenties but their meaning seems to have been taken for granted and I have come across no early definitions of them. Fenichel (1948) takes variations in ego-strength for granted, and the terms, "ego strength" and "ego weakness", appear in the index of his great work, but the passages cited contain no definition—their meaning has to be gathered from the context, as on p. 117, the page cited in his index:

The ego may be regarded as having been developed for the purpose of avoiding traumatic states ... This capacity depends on constitutional factors as well as on all of the individual's previous experiences. There are stimuli of such overwhelming intensity that they have a traumatic effect on anyone; other stimuli are harmless for most persons ... [Fenichel, 1948, p. 117]

If we look at another major pundit, twenty years later, we find exactly the same thing. Greenson (1967) discussed differences in the therapy of people with weak and with stronger ego-processes but he does not offer a definition either, only that

anti-analytic procedures are those which block or lessen the capacity for insight and understanding. The use of any measure or course of action which diminishes the ego functions of observing, thinking, remembering, and judging belongs to this category. [Greenson, 1967, p. 37]

and

People who suffer from a severe lack or impairment in ego functions may well be able to experience regressive transference reactions, but will have difficulty in maintaining a working alliance. [*ibid.*, p. 307]

In my view Greenson is still one of the clearest and most practical guides on how to analyse patients without damaging the strengths they have already. A very different intelligence, Otto Kernberg also takes such differences seriously and recommends supportive counselling techniques as the best procedures for helping people with very weak ego functioning (see also p. 260).

The other moderating or regulating process formulated by Freud was the superego, which adds a moral aspect to the rational cause-and-effect regulations of the ego-processes. The superego is "that part of the ego in which self-observation, self-criticism, and other reflective activities develop" (Rycroft, 1968, p. 160). And self-observation, if we look it up in Rycroft's *Dictionary*, is "observation of oneself, listed by Freud as a superego function on the ground that it arises by introjection of the experience of being observed by others, and that it is, in the first instance, moralistic" (*ibid.*, p. 149). Introjection is defined by Rycroft as "the process by which the functions of an external object are taken over by its mental representation, by which the relationship with an object 'out there' is replaced by one with an imagined object 'inside'. The resulting mental structure is variously called an introject, an introjected object, or an internal object" (p. 79).

This "mental representation", this imaginary object "inside", performs the same functions as, and may therefore be regarded as, the self-regarding sentiment of McDougall and his colleagues. The present chapter considers how dependence on a good (internal) object may be seen as solving conceptual problems concerning the exertion of the will, while the next chapter considers how such dependence may solve the practical problem of rescuing someone from too much narcissism.

Theories from the field of learning: maps and models

Contemporaneously with psychoanalytic developments, there came developments in the field of the psychology of perception and learning, increasingly important from the nineteenth-thirties on. Less verbal–philosophical, more experimental–physiological, learning-theories had initially been inspired by interest in the phenomenon of the reflex arc, whose sequence of stimulus-and-response can be modified by association with other sensory inputs occurring at much the same time. In particular circumstances, objectively separate events, once registered as "together" can in future evoke one another. Connections become established, perhaps as cause-and-effect, perhaps as one signalling the advent of the other, perhaps as either one carrying the meaning of both, depending on a whole set of conditions (see Klein, J., 1987, Chapter One, for a brief summary). The exact neurological sequences of events are still being investigated, but the gross outlines, rather woolly at the edges, have been spoken of for decades. They led Freud, long ago, to the useful technique of "free association".

Allan Schore (see pp. 95–96 and 223–226) has currently the most complete account of how these processes, enormously complicated of course, can form the basis of goal-directed, intentional behaviour, but to deal with his contribution here would be to jump the gun. His work validates the models constructed by necessarily more tentative precursors who did not have access to the information that has become available in the last half-century, precursors such as Hebb (1949), Hayek (1952), Bowlby (1969, 1973—consult his index on "working models"), and the conflation of their work in the first chapters of J. Klein (1987). In the language of those precursors, in the background of Schore's work is an assumption that there is something analogous to a store of more or less roughly organized inborn and acquired knowledge that includes everything individuals ever perceived or thought in the course of their life. This complex store of organized knowledge provides the basis for the construction of "maps", as it were, organized in terms of how things connect with each other in a person's present circumstances or, to put it the other way round, people experience what is around and within them at any moment in terms of their "maps". In this context, what a person wants at a particular moment is to be represented by a "model" of the desired situation. The "map" represents all the available possibilities just now, and the "model" represents the most desired state. The model is active in sending signals or messages: "This way! This way!", or "No! No!" when we move towards or away from a good match between map and model. It is as though on a walk from Maidenhead to Reading, whenever we take a path that will not get us there, a warning sounds in the mind (See Klein, J., 1987, pp. 54–55). To this we return on pp. 221–223 below, where perception is discussed in connection with attention and preference.

That is one aspect of purposive behaviour: goal orientation. Another aspect concerns the kind of help we needed in our development from childhood on, in order to acquire a really serviceable varied and detailed stock of maps. For we need help to develop clear strong signals "This way!", and unmistakeable bells ringing "No! No!" and, finally, we need help in developing an ability to resist distraction until the task is done. All this, the old psychologists took into account, in their language of drives and emotions and sentiments, willpower and volition and attention. From Drever's Penguin Reference *Dictionary of Psychology* (1963):

> *Attitude*: a more or less stable state or disposition of opinion, interest or purpose, involving expectancy of a certain kind of experience, and readiness with an appropriate response.

> *Sentiment*: an emotional disposition centring round the idea of an object ... sometimes expressed schematically as an idea + affect.

Instruction versus introjection or internalization

Learning that relies on association can be facilitated by good instruction: we do what we are told to do in circumstances we have been taught to look out for. In the training of psychotherapists, for instance, this kind of learning takes place through lectures, reading, discussions; as students we learn to recognize the signs we have been taught to look for in particular circumstances—signs of anger, attachment, transference, etc. Having been taught to look for them, they attract our attention. Those signs act as models giving direction to our use of our maps—we are reminded of what we learnt the signs might mean and that reminds us to respond in ways we were taught to hope might get us to the next part on our map, nearer to where we hope to get to. This way of thinking is quite compatible with early Freudian thinking, which focused on the regulation of our impulses by means of ego and superego processes, the former often created by parental instruction and the latter by parental rewards and punishment for behaviour that appears good or bad in the parents' eyes. Teachers are often *in loco parentis* and get results by similar means.

To the extent that there are differences in power between adults and children, or between other instructors and their students, the behaviour learnt in the relationship is not built on rational but on authoritarian foundations, and so there is necessarily an unconscious non-rational component in what in learnt, as regards ego-functioning and, more especially, as regards superego-functioning. Action governed by the more authoritarian superego-based form of learning is less flexible, less easily conscious and less easily modified than the more cognitive kind. In superego-based learning, aspects of the parent are taken over and made one's own—"introjected", or maybe the whole parent–child relationship is taken over so that it is as though the whole parental personality ruled from within the child—"internalization" (see Laplanche & Pontalis, 1988—not that the difference between these two processes matters for the present argument, and the two terms are here used as convenient.)

Introjection (or internalization)

Introjection is not the bit-by-bit associative learning that derives from instruction as just described, but is a wholesale swallowing of a complex chunk of experience, a configuration or *Gestalt* of experiences, a "taking-in" of an "object". Most of us cannot remember much about introjecting parts of our parents' personalities—we had not the consciousness or the self-consciousness to know we were doing it, but it is a process easily verified in the course of psychoanalysis. Though we cannot remember all our benign introjects, we are quite likely to have memories of ourselves being charmed and captivated by a teacher, or by an idol in the world of entertainment, or by a character in a book, and finding that we have changed the way we talk or move (and, less obviously, think or feel or see). In respects we could not spell out item by item verbally, we have swallowed an entire chunk, not in an itemized way but as a meaningful whole. It is a kind of learning, surely. It was the essence of apprenticeship as it used to be practised. In the course of their apprenticeship, the aspirant plumbers, or carpenters, or painters or dancers, were not only instructed about what to do, but soaked it up by being there when experienced practitioners did it, unconsciously absorbing a whole lot of elements in the pattern that was being presented to them. Even today, dancers learn mainly by introjection. Artists in general absorb configurations by introjection; so do many psychotherapists.

In current psychoanalytic terms, these configurations are called internal objects or introjects. Through introjection, we find ourselves feeling warmer towards some ideas or ways of being, while others leave us cold or antagonistic. From whomever we introjected— father, mother, brother or sister, as well as later figures like teachers or friends, psychotherapists, supervisors, or people we read about in great classics or in cheap novels—we derived our internal objects, through which we then feel drawn toward certain courses of action or belief, and adverse or indifferent to others. And this, of course, is cumulative: as our interests and habits are shaped by what we prefer, by what we value and aim at and are interested in, so our interests and habits are sharpened, honed, made more precise or more skilled.

In these ways the hundred-year-old notions of the superego, and will and volition, get a new coat of paint to help us understand how those two young women Elinor and Marianne came to develop, progressively allying themselves to those elements with which their environment presented them, which increasingly appealed to their nature as that nature refined itself.

(Not) thinking about a rhinoceros

I will now think of a rhinoceros.

One can say this, and one can successfully do it. Problems arise when we say

I will not think of a rhinoceros.

Problems also arise when we say

I will think of nothing but a rhinoceros for the next hour.

In practice, problems of will are problems of attention. Psychotherapists know of the importance of attention, since they endeavour to listen to patients not just attentively but with "free-floating" attention so that their own associations, while useful, do not come between them and what their patients are talking about. As a rule psychotherapists do not need to think about the "how", the nuts and bolts, of this attention, but McDougall and his contemporaries tried to; they "paid attention" to the role of attention in the exercise of will and intentional behaviour. When McDougall wrote

The essential mark of volition ... is that the personality as a whole, or the central feature or nucleus of the personality, the man himself, or all that is regarded by himself and others as the most essential part of himself, is thrown on the side of the weaker motive. [McDougall, 1908, p. 209]

he was writing about attention and, still on the same page, he concludes that

We may therefore follow Professor James when he asserts that "the essential achievement of the will is to attend to a difficult subject and hold it fast before the mind" and again that "the effort of attention is thus the essential phenomenon of the will".

and, finally, that

Effort of attention is, then, the essential form of all volition.

Mendoza (2003) considers that the internal good object "commands our obedience" first of all by virtue of its having originally been a powerful parental introject and later, if all has gone well, by virtue of its excellence. Obedience implies, among other things, that one has to watch for instructions about what is required. Whether by the route of introjection or by the route of learning, attention is required to keep us close to the good object.

As teachers know, people differ in the ability to focus their attention and to continue to focus for some time. Depending on the behaviour of the original introjects, and on the opportunity for appropriate introjections later, some people find this easier than others, having as one might say stronger wills than other people. There is also a relationship between the nature of the introjects and what can hold a person's attention: most people have wills that can particularly address themselves more to some area of concern and less to others.

Paying attention. How and why we do it

Attention became of major interest to experimental psychologists working on eye-movement and on what happens at less obvious levels of mental activity in the course of observable eye-movement. Such things are relatively easy to measure and the findings throw light on how the attention may be trained, (Hebb, 1949). Apparently when we (and indeed all animals with eyes) focus on a point—we might say "when we pay attention to a point"—we also see, though more vaguely, an area around that point, in such a way that if the point is on a line, the focus of the eye will travel along that line.

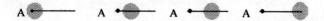

This becomes more interesting if point A lies between points B and C (Hebb, 1949, Chapter five).

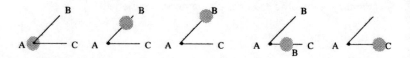

Focusing first on point A, the eye will repeatedly also travel A–B B–A A–C C–A A–B B–A A–C C–A, on and on, until a schema is formed in the brain, of BAC and CAB as well as AB and AC. If repeated often enough, this induces a kind of *expectation* that an angle BAC exists even when the eye is still focused on A, having not yet done the actual eye movements that outline AB and AC. One thing has led to another, and by focusing on A in this situation we have learned to expect an angle BAC.

One day we may have a surprise and focus on A expecting BAC but it does not happen. We blink and look again: we *attend*. The story does not tell whether we then see BAC or not; that is irrelevant—the fact that we *attended* to something is the point of the story. BAC has become a model on our map, an expectation to which we pay attention. But the story need not end there. The concept of *expectation*, now backed by neurological hypotheses, is only as small distance away from the concept of *intention*. Suppose we expect BAC and it does not happen. Our attention widens and we look around. We may try the same thing again, or we may try something a little different. What can be said about that? J. Klein (1987, Chapter 4) quotes Hayek (1952) to set this process in a wider context.

> The representation or model of the environment will thus constantly tend to run ahead of the actual situation. This representation of the possible results following from the existing position will of course be constantly checked and corrected by the newly arriving sensory signals which record actual developments in the environment ...

> The representations of the external environment which will guide behaviour will thus be not only representations of the actually existing environment, but also representations of the changes to be expected in that environment. We must therefore conceive of the model as constantly trying out possible developments and determining action in the light of the consequences which, from the representations of such actions, would appear to follow from it. [Hayek, 1952, p. 121]

Klein then considers how this can be further elaborated.

> Miller, Galanter, and Pribram offer some useful thoughts on this self-correcting gyroscopic process. They postulate an equivalent of Hayek's map, using the metaphor of imagery:

>> The Image is all the accumulated organised knowledge that the organism has about itself and its world ... It includes everything that the organism has learned—values as well as facts— organised by whatever concepts, images, or relations it has been able to master. [Miller, Galanter and Pribram, 1969, p. 17]

> Images can be organised into structures they call "plans". A plan is any hierarchical process that can control the order in which a sequence of actions is to be performed. At its simplest a plan is just a kind of elaborate concept. It is an idea of the steps needed to get from one situation to another—from London to Liverpool, for instance. More elaborately, the steps in the plan might be: if hungry,

you can get food by going to the kitchen, to the fridge, opening the door, getting out some cold chicken, and so on. The nature of such a plan comes partly from experience (Hayek's map) and partly from current information (Hayek's model).

What can be said about the processes involved in the selection, evaluation, and correction of plans of action? Miller, Galanter, and Pribram are interesting in that they construct a practical version of this process, which they call the "TOTE"—nothing to do with the racetrack, the word is an acronym for the sequence TEST–OPERATE–TEST–EXIT. A TOTE is a looped sequence, a feedback organisation such that when an action (an operation) is undertaken which is not right when tested, another action (operation) is undertaken, after which there is another test, and if things are still not right, there is another action, and so on, round and round in a loop.

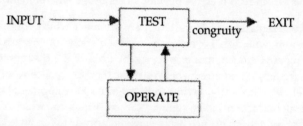

In words, reading from left to right, this says: a message comes in that something is happening peripherally (*input*). This message is TESTED centrally and may feel *congruous* with the map of how things should be, and that is the end of that (*exit*).

But if the message does not feel congruous with the map of how things should be, something is done: an OPERATION, which when TESTED, is then *congruous* with how things should be and that is the end of it (*exit*).

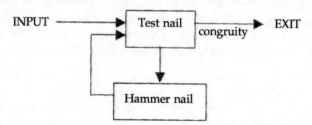

It can be seen that there may be several turns round the loop. Something is happening which, when tested, feels incongruous with how things should be. So something is done, which, when tested, is incongruous with how things should be. So something is done which, when tested, is incongruous with how things should be. So something is done which, when tested, is (at last) congruous with how things should be and that's the end of it—exit. [Klein, J., 1987, pp. 54–56]

"The interpretation toward which the argument moves is one that has been called the 'cybernetics hypothesis', namely that the fundamental building-block of the nervous system is the feedback loop ... Action is initiated by an incongruity between the state of the organism and the state that it is being tested for, and the action persists until the incongruity is removed". [Miller *et al.*, 1969, pp. 25–26]

That activity, of maintaining a presentation at the focus of attention, is the steering process previously referred to. In psychoanalytic terms it is the operation of ego and superego functioning. In terms of psychoneurological models it is the constant interaction of map and model "Yes, yes, you set yourself to think of a rhinoceros; good, good, that is what you are doing" and "No, no, you started thinking of planting a rosebush but now you are thinking about the Nile in Egypt, get back to rosebushes".

Allan Schore, compatibly along these lines of thought but in his hugely integrating fashion, favours a complex process he calls the dialogic self (1994, pp. 492 ff.). The small child begins to experience itself simultaneously as subject, through its awareness that it has wants and hopes and fears, and as object, through its awareness that other people react with kindness or unkindness to its wants and hopes and fears. (Schore considers shame to be the especially powerful element in these inner dialogues.) The child's activity is steered by the relative strengths of those two complex subject/ object elements in interaction; the level of complexity is such that there is no need for a separate construct like attention and how to steer it. Of course there are still problems about how to train oneself to be more able to "maintain a presentation at the focus of attention" as McDougall put it (1908, p. 209).

Summing up so far, and more on Schore's contribution

We can see the very different kinds of thinking reflected in the contributions from the different disciplines, though there seems now no real problem in reconciling them. From the one corner we get great quantities of experimentally verifiable evidence, ranging from neurology to cognition-based learning, which those in the psychoanalytic corner have tended to ignore until recently. The psychoanalytic corner meanwhile presents us with this useful concept of "introject", which helps us understand more about where our values and goals come from—the destinations on our maps, that beckon us on. To go back nearly a century:

> The essential mark of volition—that which distinguishes it from simple desire, or simple conflict of desires—is that the personality as a whole, or the central feature or nucleus of the personality, the man himself, or all that which is regarded by himself and others as the most essential part of himself, is thrown on the side of the weaker motive. [McDougall, 1908, p. 207]

In the 1990s a stunning book began to make its way into the libraries, written by a man who must surely have read nearly everything that up till then had a bearing on goal-directed behaviour, *Affect Regulation and Origins of the Self* (1994). Schore built up a very comprehensive account of how intentional behaviour might come about, using

> the integration of current developmental observations, data, and concepts from various fields that are studying the problem of socioaffective ontogeny—neurobiology, behavioural neurology, evolutionary biology, sociobiology, social psychology, developmental psychology, developmental psychoanalysis, and infant psychiatry. A special emphasis is placed on the application and integration of current developmental data from neurochemistry, neuroanatomy, neuropsychology, and psychoendocrinology into the main body of developmental theory. [Schore, 1994, p. 64]

Such a book cannot also be an easy read, but Schore does his best, with a good summary at the end of each chapter, and a brilliant summary of the whole book in five pages in Chapter five.

What happens in the brain, among the brain cells constantly transmitting and receiving impulses and constantly affected by changes in the secretions which are the physiological concomitants of emotion? Schore presents evidence of the emotional implications, for the baby, of changes in the mother's voice and movements. The pleasure or anxiety to which the baby is subject in the course of such experiences with the mother—being held in arms, being held in a mutually gratifying gaze, being shouted at or sung to and so on and so on—those circumstances activate lasting changes in the structure of the brain. Summarizing these processes in a little more detail, we may start with fortunate babies experiencing greater or lesser pleasure according to the mother's responses and initiatives. Then through repetition these associations acquire some permanence and then the fortunate baby learns to increase the number of occasions that produce such comfort or excitement or fun, either by involving the mother, or independently. And then it learns that, to an extent, these gratifying feelings can depend on its own initiatives, and this gives it the opportunity to regulate its own and to an extent other people's behaviour. With each successive year of life these opportunities become more complex and more varied, more independent of other people's intentions, and often more conscious. Just to give one more example of the immense learning that has gone into Schore's account:

> Using these principles as a springboard, in the second part of the book I present evidence to support the proposal that the maturation of this cortical area begins in a specific critical period which commences at the end of the first year of human infancy ... It is hypothesized that maternal regulated high intensity socioaffective stimulation provided in the ontogenic niche, specifically occurring in dyadic psychobiologically attuned, arousal-amplifying, face-to-face reciprocal gaze transactions, generates and sustains positive affect in the dyad. These transactions induce particular neuroendocrine changes which facilitate the expansive innervation of deep sites in orbitofrontal areas, especially in the early maturing visuospatial right hemisphere, of ascending subcortical axioms of a neurochemical circuit of the limbic system—the sympathetic ventral tegmental limbic circuit. [Schore, 1994, p. 65]

And so on. Apologies are in order for presenting such indigestible stuff. But every word counts and is backed by experimental work and careful reasoning. And Schore does take over a hundred pages just to explain what he means by that summary paragraph, and hundreds of pages to show his reasoning in detail. In one hundred pages he describes the processes by which what some might want to call the will is exercised, and how children learn self-control and goal-directed behaviour. Schore's word for the process is "affect-regulation" and it is Jane Austen's "moderation". (The process is briefly described on pp. 95–96 of the present book.)

What can a good (or bad) object do for a person?

Moralists and teachers have insisted for centuries that good things do not just happen through good fortune or Grace: exertion is required, and focused attention. But some mystics make no reference to the will at all. Their instructions call not for willpower, only for attention. "Look", they say, "Look at this wonderful good object—all the rest will follow". For them, as for many people, there would be no problem in not thinking about a rhinoceros—they were thinking of a hippopotamus anyway because it enthralled them more. How not to think of a rhinoceros? Be thinking of a hippopotamus. Current practice in Transcendental Meditation, if I understand it rightly, as well as much in Eastern traditions, encourages its practitioners to direct their attention first to breathing in and out, with perhaps a word or concept to focus on, until the consciousness of breathing fades and an ineffable something or nothing remains. These experts do not say "Use your will", they recommend that we pay attention and look at what we find worth looking at; all the rest will follow.

When we have introjected "good objects", i.e. ideas of desirable behaviour, of worthwhile pursuits or actions that give us pleasure or self-esteem, we possess something that makes us unhappy when we go against it. No willpower seems involved. Yet, under pressure of circumstances or in the heat of the moment, we may be overcome by some momentarily more alluring idea. Looking back later, we regret it. How can we in future be less vulnerable to immediate pressures and stay with more settled preferences? One way is to increase our susceptibility to the attractiveness of our internalised good objects, regarding them more, and training our attention.

On the other hand, internalized bad objects, damaging introjects, are likely to diminish our self-regard. Anxiously burdened people may have introjected what Fairbairn (1952) called "Exciting Objects", which lead people to expect that they can never have what seems desirable to them, or they may have introjected "Rejecting Objects" which leads them to think they ought not to have them; these latter people have what Fairbairn called an anti-libidinal ego (see also Klein, J., 1987, pp. 160ff.). People with such introjects are more likely to want to tinker with themselves and harass themselves so as to make themselves more acceptable to their unloving unaccepting introjects. Fairbairn was a Scot, and vulnerable to the Calvinist assumption that one is probably not acceptable. It is a striking fact that Fairbairn does not discuss subject–object relations of a warm, confiding, secure kind. More modern attachment theory is more inclusive, and allows that there are children with secure attachments to their introjected warm accepting understanding parents: these are more likely to become fortunate adults with the confidence to love their objects and expect to be loved in return. Less fortunate people find themselves in less secure attachments, with introjects that are impossibly demanding, unpredictably jealous, or madly incomprehensible, very powerful, and to be dreaded. Such people may pin their hopes on learning, by instruction, how to be the right sort of person and do the right kind of thing, so as to free the benevolence they have to hope their objects possess. They cannot expect goodness to be easily available. This makes for a very strenuous life, the life of *via negativa*. For Thomas à Kempis, for instance, a proponent of *via negativa*, discipline in establishing good habits is the only answer to the danger of misdemeanour.

> My child, you can never be perfectly free unless you wholly deny yourself. [*The Imitation of Christ*, Book iv, Chapter 32, 1]

Via negativa and ritual in psychoanalysis and religion

Psychotherapists with a psychoanalytic orientation rely to quite an extent on *via negativa* to focus the attention of the patient; they are careful about "maintaining the frame": the set hour for which both must wait even though both may be available ten minutes earlier or though another hour might suit both better on a particular occasion, the careful avoidance of bodily contact, the style of speech used, the choice of response to what the patient appears to be saying, and so on. It strikes those unfamiliar with the rationale as a ritualistic and forbidding way of going about things, but it does help to focus the attention, in the long run. Of course, in all religions there are people who fall in love with the ritual and overdo it, but abstinence and discipline and ritual do tend to focus the mind, the visible actions helping to focus on something otherwise too difficult to hold. Ritual helps to create and maintain what David Black (2000), a psychoanalyst with a major interest in religious attitudes and behaviour, has called a "position". A position is "the characteristic posture that the ego takes up with respect to its objects" (Hinshelwood, 1989, p. 363), "a constellation of anxieties, defences, object-relations and impulses" (*ibid.*, p. 363). Black refers to contemporary neurological theory to find neurological counterparts to "position" and, though he does not say so, these neurological structures are very like what might have been called habits of thought or feeling or emotion by psychologists a century earlier, and internal objects more recently.

> ... the religious object—Jesus, Mary, the Buddha, etc.—has no significant objective existence separate from the psychic world of the community of faith. What is achieved by worship, contemplation, prayer, meditation and so on, involving these objects, is a development, gradual or sometimes sudden, of a "position" in the mind which conforms to the structure of the founding vision of the religious community. Tradition and the community of faith ... have shaped and sustained the religious object. [Black, 2000, p. 16]

Black draws a parallel between the relation analyst/analysand and the relation of the worshipper to the religious object though, for reasons he makes clear, "it is a mistake to equate psychoanalysis with religion or to say that they operate in the same way or at the same level" (Black, 2000, p. 24). Black points out that, somewhat like the religious object, the analyst becomes an introject, creating a "position" in the analysand's psyche. Such introjects are thought to create benign changes in the mind. Psychoanalytic psychotherapy, working with transference phenomena, does not help through an intellectual understanding of one's motivation or of one's history. It helps by establishing or strengthening or freeing enough internal good objects so that one "naturally" does what one desires to do, without needing to will it or attend to it.

... like the transference of object in therapy, the objects of religion have a transitional character ... Their function is to be way-stations in understanding ... Contemplating, praying to, meditating on them is a means of opening the mind up ... to the area of experience they represent. [Black, 2000, p. 25]

That is the effect of internalised good objects—they help to establish good habits.

Keeping good objects in good health

Eva Hoffman (1989), writing about what may or may not be another ineffable process, describes precisely the two simultaneous but contradictory experiences of ease and freedom on one hand and, on the other hand, the disciplined practice that can make this apparent spontaneity possible. A talented girl is learning to play the piano well; her teacher is Pani Witeszca.

By some inexplicable process, the precise nuance of what I feel is conveyed through my arm to my fingertips, and then, through those fingertips, to the piano keys, which register with equal precision the slightest swerve of touch and pressure ... Expressing this musical speech involves a paradox. For if the spirit is to flow into the keys through the conduit of my arm and hand, it has to move in the other direction as well—from the keys into my arm and soul. Pani Witeszsca's ideal is to make the music sound as if it were playing itself. It is to that end that one has to relax ... so that one can become the medium through which the music flows as naturally as melting snow in the spring. [Hoffman, 1989, pp. 41–42]

But there is a further twist to the paradox:

Such receptivity can only be achieved through the rigor of controlled technique, if I don't have to worry about how I execute the passage, or whether I can manage a jump or trill. [ibid.]

Whatever technique we wish to improve, we know we must practise, practise, practise whether we feel like it or not, and so we have after all to draw on will power sometimes. The attractiveness of the object is hardly ever enough to keep us at it through thick and thin.

... Many different causes may lead us to break our resolutions ...
the slightest omission of any of our exercises scarcely ever happens
without some loss. [Thomas à Kempis, *The Imitation of Christ*, Book I,
Chapter 19, 2]

Our progress will be slow in proportion to our determination, and if
we mean to make great advances, we must show our earnestness. If
he who is strongly resolved often faints and fails, what of the man
who but seldom or feebly renews his purpose? [*ibid.*]

Unfortunately, practise, practise, practise whether we feel like it
or not, can make the exercise feel meaningless. Practice eventually
begins to feel "ritualistic", a good reason for abandoning it, though
less so for those to whom *via negativa* is congenial. In passing it may
be noted that in organized settings, where groups of people share the
ritual, the same unfortunate processes occur. With repetition, the
ritual symbolic act becomes more familiar and less transparent to the
reality beyond it; it becomes more concretely something you are
supposed to do and it gets done automatically. But then it no longer
holds the attention so well. This encourages a tendency to elaborate
the ritual further (or to simplify the existing forms) in an effort to get
the sense of transparency back into the experience. This may work,
or the resulting clutter may defeat the original intention of keeping
the attention focused. The group may then split into factions for
whom one or other practice feels most meaningful. Small wonder
that the history of psychoanalysis is strewn with splits and quarrels.

Fourteenth-century Walter Hilton's appropriately named in-
struction-book *The Ladder of Perfection* shows touchingly how
problems of attention and distraction can interfere with the much
desired contemplation of the good object. His writing shows a
complex interweaving of spontaneity and disciplined attention.
Book One, Chapter 14, describes, "How virtue begins in the reason
and the will, and is perfected in love". Because of reason and will ...

virtues which were formerly burdensome have becomes pleasant
and desirable so that he takes as much delight in humility, patience,
purity, temperance and love, as in worldly pleasures. [*The Ladder of
Perfection*, Book One, Chapter 14]

Book One, in the chapter, "On a firm and whole-hearted
intention", also emphasizes that you have to have a "firm intention

to please God, and then all the rest will follow" (Chapter 22). So far: *via positiva*. But it turns out that you do have to discipline yourself and do the required exercises until you come into line and these formerly difficult virtues cease to be burdensome. The argument appears circular, or perhaps the processes are in a benign spiral, as Chapter Seventeen in Book Two points out in its title:

> How reform of feeling and faith cannot be achieved all at once; it is effected by grace after a long time and with much bodily and spiritual effort.

Via negativa and *via positiva* are variously interwoven in the guidance given by the mystics and the spiritual directors, those inclined to follow *via positiva* being more tolerant of lapses of will, attention, or devotion. "When your heart is wandering and distracted", writes nineteenth-century St Francis of Sales,

> bring it back quietly to its point, restore it tenderly to its Master's side; and if you did nothing else the whole of your hour but bring your heart back patiently and put it near our Lord again, and every time you put it back it turned away again, your hour would be well employed. [*Instructions*, VI]

In the same vein, Brother Lawrence writes in the second letter included in *The Practice of the Presence of God*:

> If sometimes my thoughts wander ... by necessity or from infirmity, I am presently recalled by inward motions so charming and delicious that I am ashamed to mention them here ...

Brother Lawrence in particular is a good example of *via positiva*. For the first ten years as a monk he "suffered much", but that was twenty years ago. Eventually it all came easily to him. In the same letter he wrote:

> I have quitted all forms of devotion and set prayers but those to which my state obliges me. And I make it my business only to persevere in His holy presence, wherein I keep myself by a simple attention and a general fond regard to God, which I may call an "actual presence of God"; or, to speak better, a habitual, silent, and secret conversation of the soul with God, which often cause in me joys and raptures inwardly, and sometimes also outwardly ...

This he achieves by what he calls "faith" by which he seems to mean keeping his mind on the incomprehensibility and infinity of God as well as on His lovingness and nearness.

My most usual method is this simple attention, and such a general passionate regard to God, to whom I find myself often attached with greater sweetness and delight than that of an infant at the mother's breast: so that if I dare use the expression, I should choose to call this state the bosom of God, for the inexpressible sweetness which I taste and experience there.

CHAPTER ELEVEN

Narcissism—the mystics' remedy

O that I were an orange tree
That busy plant!
Then I should ever laden be,
And never want
Some fruit for him that dressed me.

George Herbert, 1593–1632, "Employment"

And half a century later:

Grant, I may not like puddle lie
In a corrupt security,
Where, if a traveller water crave,
He finds it dead, and in a grave;
But as this restless, vocal spring
All day and night doth run, and sing,
And, though here born, yet is acquainted
Elsewhere, and flowing keeps untainted;
So let me all my busy age
In thy free services engage ...

Henry Vaughan, 1622–1695, "The Dawning"

I n many cultures we find people who feel uncomfortably that perhaps they ought to be less preoccupied with themselves, even ought not to have a self, and that being preoccupied with money, consumer goods, being respected, even carrying on with the responsibilities of everyday living, might be obscuring some other

233

good thing, something ineffable. They are haunted by a sense of obligation. Should they love their neighbour more? Should they be kinder? Is the love of God compatible with being richer than others?

> As for the spirit of poverty, I do not remember any moment when it was not in me, although only to that unfortunately small extent which is compatible with my imperfection. I fell in love with St. Francis of Assisi as soon as I came to know about him. I always believed and hoped that one day Fate would force upon me the condition of vagabond and beggar which he embraced freely. Actually I felt the same way about prison. [Weil, 1950, p. 31]

and

> From my earliest days I always had the Christian idea of love of one's neighbour, to which I gave the name of justice, a name which it bears in many passages of the Gospel and which is so beautiful. [ibid.]

Worldly well-being is similarly distrusted by Dietrich Bonhoeffer, who wrote in his prison diary in 1944:

> July 16, God is weak and powerless in the world, and that is exactly the way, the only way, in which he can be with us and help us. Matthew 8.17 makes it crystal clear that it is not by his omnipotence that Christ helps us, but by his weakness and suffering. [Bonhoeffer, 1947]

Two days later, contrasting the behaviour of the conformist bien-pensant "religious man" with what he expects from Christians, he wrote:

> July 18, Christians range themselves with God in his suffering; that is what distinguishes them from the heathen. As Jesus asked in Gethsemane, "Could ye not watch with me one hour?" That is the exact opposite of what the religious man expects from God ... Man is challenged to participate in the sufferings of God at the hands of a godless world ... It is not some religious act which makes a Christian what he is, but participating in the suffering of God in the life of the world. [ibid.]

On July 21, he wrote that it is only by

... living completely in this world that one learns to believe. One must abandon every attempt to make something of oneself, whether it be a saint, a converted sinner, a churchman (the priestly type, so-called!), a righteous man or an unrighteous one, a sick man or a healthy one ... We throw ourselves utterly into the arms of God and participate in his sufferings in the world and watch with Christ in Gethsemane ... How can success make us arrogant or failure lead us astray, when we participate in the sufferings of God by living in this world? [*ibid.*]

Just now a circular from the Salvation Army comes through the door to remind us that every Salvation Army Officer, on being commissioned, promises:

for Christ's sake, to care for the poor, feed the hungry, clothe the naked, love the unlovable, and befriend the friendless.

Narcissism

Fresh spiritual movements have always had people who become uncomfortable at being situated at the centre of their personal universe. They do not want a preoccupation with esteem, money, goods, even family, to obscure their joy in the ineffable. They fear anything that might threaten this vital connection, and one threat, in the language of the psychotherapists, is the gratification of narcissistic needs, even when these needs are generally regarded as legitimately gratifiable. Thus pleasures that in previous chapters were seen as part of loving and being loved—recognition, trust, dependence, goodness always available, repose—are blighted by narcissistic anxiety: have I deserved them?

Narcissism is marked by an inability to love. People with strong narcissistic trends have to struggle to love themselves or others, have no sense of being lovable, cannot allow themselves to be loved. In a narcissistic state of mind, only one thing is deeply and immediately experienced: what happens to oneself. Some people, finding that this is how they are, do not like it. No wonder that some writings on mystical experiences read like manuals on how to counteract one's narcissistic ways or, as it used to be phrased, how to deny the self, or lose the self.

Buber (1947) gives an account of a childhood event that shows how a moment's self-preoccupation broke a boy's sense of mystical connectedness.

> When I was eleven years of age, spending the summer on my grandparents' estate, I used, as often as I could do it unobserved, to steal into the stable and gently stroke the neck of my darling, a broad dapple-grey horse. It was not casual delight but a great, certainly friendly, but also deeply stirring happening. If I am to explain it now, beginning from the still very fresh memory of my hand, I must say that what I experienced in touch with the animal was the Other, the immense otherness of the Other, which, however, did not remain strange like the otherness of the ox and the ram, but rather let me draw near and touch it. When I stroked the mighty mane, sometimes marvellously smooth-combed, at other times just as astonishingly wild, and felt the life beneath my hand, it was as though the element of vitality itself bordered on my skin, something that was not I, was certainly not akin to me, palpably the other, not just another, really the Other itself; and yet it let me approach, confided itself to me, placed itself elementally in the relation of *Thou*-and-*Thou* with me. The horse, even when I had not begun by pouring oats for him in the manger, very gently raised his massive head, ears flicked, then snorted quietly, as a conspirator gives a signal meant to be recognised only by his fellow-conspirator; and I was approved. [Buber, 1947, p. 41]

Then a moment's narcissistic self-consciousness appeared, and spoiled the experience.

> But once—I do not know what came over the child, at any rate it was childlike enough—it struck me about the stroking what fun it gave me, and suddenly I became conscious of my hand. The game went on as before, but something had changed, it was no longer the same thing. And the next day, after giving him a rich feed, when I stroked my friend's head, he did not raise his head ... [*ibid.*, pp. 41–42]

Buber contends that if one is too conscious of what one is doing, as if one were watching oneself on a stage or in a novel, important elements of the experience are lost: it has dwindled into a narcissistic experience. Self-consciousness, though obviously a great good, exacts payment. The Mariner, it will be remembered, blessed the serpents *unaware*. Buber calls the moment of narcissistic self-consciousness *reflexion*, which felicitously suggests that it is a moment of watching oneself as in a mirror. He also suggests that it is a moment when other people and things lose their quiddity.

> ... when a man withdraws from accepting with his essential being another person in his particularity ... and lets the other exist only as his experience, only as "a part of myself" ... then dialogue becomes a fiction, the mysterious intercourse between two human worlds only a game, and in the rejection of the real life confronting him, the essence of all reality begins to disintegrate. [*ibid.*, p. 43]

In practice, narcissism may be seen as a difficulty in experiencing other people as having an existence of their own, with their own inner world, with a capacity for suffering and joy in their own way independent of our needs or our views on the matter. Narcissism prevents us from relating to others in such a way that their sorrows and joys can cause us sorrow or joy, except by way of envy.

When other people's well-being is acceptable to me only if I can feel it as part of my self, I shall feel anger and envy whenever they seem better off than I. At best, envy prevents me rejoicing in their well-being; at worst I must deny their existence.

Some developmental antecedents of adult narcissism

Some well-intentioned self-centred people hate themselves, turning against the whole experience of having a self. This is rather different from the more common resolution to set one's face against what one fears may hinder the possibility of joy, bliss or goodness—the possibility of having a good object within, psychotherapists might say. Those who really hate themselves wrestle with anxiety and guilt about the selfish elements they notice in their every action, and that makes life very hard for them. Gerard Manley Hopkins (1844–1889) writes about this unhappy situation:

> I see
> The lost are like this, and their scourge to be,
> As I am mine, their sweating selves; but worse. [from "I wake and feel the fell of dark", 1953]

and:

> My own heart let me more have pity on; let
> Me live to my sad self hereafter kind,
> Charitable; not live this tormented mind
> With this tormented mind tormenting yet. [from "My own heart let
> me more have pity on", 1953]

Such people do not want to be as they are; they dislike themselves, their desires and phantasies feel too powerful to be contained by ego and superego. Maybe they were born more passionate than the norm? Maybe their normal-strength childhood impulses were not handled well by those who took care of them? Maybe something went wrong at the point where the infant's naturally rather autistic narcissism had to be abandoned for the reality-principles that rule the world we share with others. There is no greater boon parents can give, than to mediate reality to their child at the right time, in the least painful way, neither too brutally (as in "You've just got to put up with it and do it" or "If you can't do that, you're no good") nor too feebly (as in "Oh well, if you don't want to, never mind", which leaves the child with a grievance later in life—for though a parent may indulgently give way to demands, the later world is less likely to).

Differences in the degree of pathological narcissism must be attributable, at least in part, to differences in the way people's healthy narcissism was respected in childhood. If their littleness and dependence was taken into account, so that they found their grownups helpful rather than scornful, all may be well. But those whose littleness was used to make them feel needy, negligible, or exploited, may not find it easy to like other people's power, good fortune, goodness, richness. Fortunate children grow up into people who do not feel ashamed at being imperfect, at not being omnipotent. They are pleased that there is someone else who can be perfect. This being so among ordinary fortunate people, it is not surprising that, by extension, some people are effortlessly pleased to think that God is wonderful, and they have no problem in responding trustfully and cheerfully without going to much trouble. There are babies who had terrific fun when they were learning to use a spoon to eat with, who were allowed to push the goo into the mouth of whoever was willing to accept the stuff—a diagram of mutual pleasure-giving.

The proviso is: you must not be too hungry: Kohut writes that psychotherapists interpret appropriately in terms of drive-theory only when patients have been too damaged by deprivation or excess to be able to form gratifying object-relations (Kohut, 1977, Chapter 2, especially pp. 86–88). The more fortunate children will have been able to learn that it is almost as pleasant to hand out sweeties as to eat them yourself; something unhappy must have already happened to a child that feels it must have all the toffees. What fun to put socks on your baby brother's feet—if you don't feel deprived of parental care yourself.

Those unfortunates who did not learn the pleasures of exchange at the right time have more problems with greed, envy, selfishness, and such. They are in conflict much of the time, and have to make grand unnatural gestures. If they want to be good, they long to be hermits or martyrs in order to keep themselves from falling back into the greed and selfishness they dislike so much. More moderate fallible people apologize and are forgiven and received back into the fallible circle where they did their damage, as the Count does at the end of *The Marriage of Figaro*, and Baron Ochs at the end of the *Rosenkavalier*, when the Marshallin also acknowledges her limitations. In the same spirit are the moving reconciliations—improbable as they may be—at the end of *A Winter's Tale*.

At its best, the anti-narcissistic training recommended by many mystics is a training in getting into a mental attitude that is not easily destroyed by the knowledge of one's imperfection.

Via negativa and narcissism

The literature on mysticism shows two main approaches to the ineffable, depending among other things on how people feel about being the kind of person they are. Of course, much of what is written is a mixture of the two approaches—not always compatibly but that is the nature of the material, few mystics being logicians.

Via negativa recommends the systematic eradication of the self from the centre of action and consciousness. From this perspective, the self is regarded not as what you naturally live and love with, but as a hindrance to loving others and a hindrance to the source from which love flows. *Via negativa* is likely to be the self-prescription of people who feel plagued by their narcissism; they dislike being as they are.

> It comes to this, that we must surrender all that is dearest to us in the enjoyment of the senses and go through a dark night in which we live without their help and comfort. Then when this is accomplished we have to sacrifice the prerogative of our own way of thinking and willing, and undergo another still darker night in which we have deprived ourselves of all the supports which are familiar to us and make us self-sufficient. This is a kind of death, the making nothing of all that we are to ourselves; but the genuine mystic tells us that when all has been strained away our emptiness will be filled with a new presence; our uncovered soul will receive the contact of divine love ... [D'Arcy, 1951, p. 6]

Via negativa comes in two fairly respectable versions, plus some that may be regarded as perverse. One respectable version maintains that there is a God, or there is a life-style of ineffable value, so other that no gratifying encounter with it is available to ordinary people with ordinary senses and ordinary shortcomings. From this it is an easy step to believing that ordinary people need not apply. D'Arcy is a relatively sympathetic twentieth-century proponent of this view.

> The way is exceeding arduous, so arduous in fact, as to terrify all except the bravest lovers. [*ibid.*]

We may spot a tinge of elitism here as well as the narcissism which often goes with elitism. "God is so ineffable and I am so coarse, I had better get more refined if I want to get along with the Ineffable". This is one way in which people troubled by their narcissism hope to eradicate the self-regarding consciousness that plagues them. Incidentally, D'Arcy here makes a very characteristic mistake also made by great writers in the field of psychotherapy, and that is, to write as though what he has discovered about himself and his own psychic processes is universal truth applicable to all. D'Arcy must have found the way "exceeding arduous", so he expects everyone else to find it so, too. But perhaps much of the problem comes from the particular difficulty of talking about so ineffable an experience; the tinge of exclusiveness often disappears once we accept that the ineffable is bound to be difficult to find words for, and that some people are better at finding words than others are, and that is all. There need be no implication that we are not good enough, not as good as those who can find the words more easily, or that people better than us would find it all easier. Talking well about something is not the same as doing it well.

The second version of *via negativa*, also respectable, comes from the idea that we are so preoccupied with other interests that we do not notice or do not recognize bliss even when it is all around us. " 't is ye, 't is your estrangèd faces, that miss the many-splendoured thing", wrote the Edwardian Francis Thompson (1939) in "In no strange land". Seventeenth-century George Herbert (see pp. 111–112) has quite a few poems about not chasing glory, wit, social life, and so on, because God is more worth having. And at times a notion also creeps in that there is something intrinsically meritorious about "sacrificing" these things.

> Lord, in my silence how I do despise
>   What upon trust
> Is stylèd honour, riches, or fair eyes
>   But is but dust! [George Herbert, "Frailty"]

It is characteristic of this version of *via negativa* that Herbert appears to believe that being ill or in pain is the punishment for having turned his eyes to other pleasures: losing sight of the valued object does not, in itself, seem unhappiness enough for him. Projecting his own ideas of pleasure on to "the world", he finds that

> The merry world did on a day
>   With his train-band and mates agree
> To meet together where I lay
>   And all in sport to jeer at me. ["The Quip"]

In "The Quip", beauty comes to tempt the poet, then money, glory, wit and good conversation in turn, but his refrain each time is "Thou shalt answer for me, Lord"—he refuses them all, and expects reward for his refusal.

At the healthier end of the spectrum, what we are here considering is our difficulty in loving anything singled-heartedly for very long if it does not give continuous satisfaction. Most of us can accept, with greater or lesser reluctance, that this seems to be how we are constituted, but people who believe that there is nothing more worth while than loving God at all times may find it distressing to discover how little time they spend in loving anyone at all. If they are ambitious to get closer to ineffable glory, and find that love does not come easy, they may recruit for this purpose whatever pushy muscle has proved successful in other aspects of their life, and then they may get very near to perverted ideas of holiness. For instance, the fourteenth-century author of *The Cloud of Unknowing*, usually very acceptable to modern minds, starts off with a dissertation on the value of obedience and doing as one is told, in keeping with the ethos of the feudal system in which he grew up, but he occasionally gets carried over the top in a surprisingly neurotic-sounding style. In Chapter 24, he starts with

> Charity is nothing else than loving God for Himself, above all created things, and loving men in God as we love ourselves ... The perfect apprentice asks neither to be spared pain, nor to be generously rewarded, nor indeed anything but God himself ... For the perfect contemplative holds no man as such in special regard, be he kinsman, stranger, friend or foe. [*The Cloud of Unknowing*]

But then he goes further, and requires of the perfect apprentice that such a one

> ... considers all men his friends and none his foes. To such an extent that even those who hurt and injure him, he reckons to be real and special friends, and he is moved to wish for them as much good as he would wish for his dearest friend. [*ibid.*]

In Chapter 43 he goes quite a bit further still.

> Try to suppress all knowledge and feelings of anything less than God, and trample it down deep under the cloud of forgetting ... For it is the way of the perfect lover not only to love what he loves more than himself, but also in some sort to hate himself for the sake of what he loves. [*ibid.*]

John Donne (1573–1631), generally a man of strong feelings, can indulge in quite violent phantasies of overcoming narcissistic inclinations.

Batter my heart, three-person'd God: for, you
As yet but knock, breathe, shine, and seek to mend;
That I may rise, and stand, o'erthrow me, and bend
Your force, to break, blow, burn, and make me new. [Sonnet vi]

Not being a twentieth-century man, he can move unselfconsciously
into a quite explicitly masochistic mode later in the poem:

Take me to you, imprison me, for I
Except you enthrall me, never shall be free,
Nor ever chaste, except you ravish me. [*ibid.*]

Via negativa can take us into the realms of psychoneurotic
perversion, if it combines unfortunately with self-centredness,
sentimentality or self-hatred. Manic self-esteem may take a person
into unwarranted identification with a phantasized superlatively
good object, or, conversely, unwarranted identifications may take a
person into manic self-esteem when feeling in the presence of a
superlatively good, or at least strong, object, as perhaps Eigen and
some of his patients did (see pp. 176–178). The blurring of the
boundaries in the course of projection and introjection, explored in
previous chapters, may obliterate too painful a consciousness of
unworthiness and of the great gulf between oneself and an
overwhelming other. There is a non-religious version of this, which
simply worships hugeness, power, and the experience of being
overwhelmed. In the religious version it becomes tempting to argue
that "now I belong to this wonderful perfect God, I am as safe,
wonderful and perfect as God is". Worse, and more dangerously, "I
belong to this wonderful God and so I am always right in my
opinions and can do no wrong" or "I may be disgusting and other
people are certainly disgusting, but God is wonderful and if I
belong to God then I can do no wrong". In a novel by the historian
Edith Pargeter, writing as Ellis Peters, one of the characters asks
Brother Cadfael about St. Illtud, who had a wife . . .

a noble lady, willing to live with him simply in a reed hut by the river
Nadafan. An angel told him to leave his wife, and he rose up early in
the morning, and drove her out into the world alone, thrusting her
off, so we are told, very roughly and went to receive the tonsure from
Saint Dyfrid . . . Cadfael, I would ask, was that an angel who
commanded it, or a devil? [Ellis Peters, 1989, *The Potter's Field*, p. 203]

Grandiose postures are inevitably driven on by a suppressed wretched counterpart, "I am awful: No one would have anything to do with me if they knew me" (Klein J., 1987, pp. 216–218). Thomas à Kempis, the fourteenth-century author of *The Imitation of Christ*, though he writes mainly of calmer and less self-centred procedures, at times freely recommends hatred of oneself and of others, in a fiercely phobic way.

> We must not trust greatly in weak mortal man, however helpful to us and beloved. Neither should we take it too much to heart if we are sometimes thwarted and contradicted ... He that is with you today may be against you tomorrow, for men are often as shifty as the wind. Put all your trust in God; keep fear and love alike for Him alone ... [Book Two, Chapter 1, p. 3]

> Why do you so much as look round you in this world, when it is not to be your resting place? [Book Two, Chapter 1, p. 4]

The routinization of charisma

When we turn from the wilder extremes of *via negativa*, we can find people who regard self-centredness more calmly as a misfortune that can be remedied by good management, the wish to amend, good will, reason, a sense of proportion, and other rather appealing virtues of the Age of Enlightenment. Such qualities can also be taken to extremes, but those who possess them are attractive when contrasted with their more excitable and dramatizing compeers. On the other hand, those who have had to struggle against their own urgent narcissistic inclinations may at times find such complacency grating.

The term "routinization of charisma" was coined by Max Weber (1908) at the start of the twentieth century and came into prominence among English-speaking sociologists through the translating and editing work of C. Wright Mills and H. H. Gerth in mid-century. The routinization or bureaucratization of charisma denotes a stage in the process of social change, when change is initiated by remarkable personalities who have a gift for making what they advocate sound convincing to the general populace or to groups in power; major changes may then come about in belief-systems, the distribution of social goods, and the position of social groups relative to one another (Gerth & Mills, 1948). Weber called people who do this kind of thing "charismatic leaders", since it was by their charisma—the word means grace but carried for Weber a connotation of irresistible appeal—that these amazing changes came about. Weber considered that often, when these leaders aged or died, there would remain a set of devoted adherents who were by their nature followers and not innovators. They would tidy up the inconsistencies in their leader's pronouncements as these became apparent, and ensure that no one would deviate unknowingly from what had been revealed to them. This is the process Weber called the routinization or the bureaucratization of charisma. It is a term that easily comes to mind when reading some mystics' and theologians' material, and it may be seen as a perversion of healthier attempts to keep narcissism within limits.

Otto (1919, and thus incidentally more or less contemporaneous with Weber) was aware of this process; he perceived it *inter alia* in the tendency to formulate rules to govern our access to the Holy. In his chapter on "The Holy as a category of value", he considers how the bureaucrats of theology have attempted to define and prescribe what properly appertains to the Holy. Having expressed his distrust of their too ready association of moral merit with holiness, he goes on to say that non-moralizing attempts to trap the Lion may be equally unprofitable.

> The other ground of distrust is that usually in our theological systems an attempt is made to develop conceptual *theories* of these ideas, which are all pure intuitions, emotional rather than conceptual in character. They are thus made objects of speculation, and the final outcome is the quasi-mathematical "doctrine of imputation" and its drastic ascription, to the credit of the "sinner", of the "merit" of Christ, not to mention the learned inquiry whether this transaction involves an "analytic" or a "synthetic" judgement of God. [Otto, 1919, pp. 72–73]

Otto concludes that:

> the *tremendum* and *augustum* cannot be fully determined conceptually: it is non-rational, as is the beauty of a musical composition, which no less eludes complete conceptual analysis.

We know this, but seem often nevertheless tempted into definitions and prescriptions on how to live. Looking again at William Law's *Serious Call to a Devout and Holy Life*, we may indeed think for a while that if we could but follow his advice on how to pray—what to focus on at the sixth hour (gratitude and joyful devotion), what at the ninth hour (humility) and so on—we might be safe from narcissism once and for all. How sensible and practical he is, suggesting when we should pray, how, about what, when to praise, when to intercede for others, and, incidentally, how to educate both girls and boys. All in his adult ego-and-superego-based way, and of course inevitably in danger of routinization, and of the amazing lack of imaginativeness that so often accompanies bureaucratic routines:

> By love, I do not mean any natural tenderness, which is more or less in people according to their constitutions; but I mean a larger principle of the soul, founded in reason and piety, which makes us tender, kind and benevolent to all our fellow creatures as creatures of God, and for his sake.

> It is this love, that loveth all things in God, as His creatures, as the images of His power, as the creatures of His goodness, as part of His family, as members of His society, that becomes a holy principle of all great and good actions. [Law, *A Serious Call to a Devout and Holy Life*, Chapter 20]

However true and worthy this statement, it is a little chilling. What we may call the Holy-Living Party needs a wary as well as a sympathetic eye. The excesses of bureaucratic formulation about what is right and how to live in all eventualities (all eventualities tending to be regarded as potentially morally threatening) can kill good feelings. However, in the climate prevailing at the time of writing, we are equally in danger from the anything-goes-as-long-as-you're-sincere-and-don't-think party.

Holy living, or even just living in a happy harmless friendly social way with a proper concern for others, may be possible for long stretches of time if there have been long stretches of happiness in childhood that still resonate in the adult's unconscious processes. Otherwise, like the depressive position, it can be rather tiring and, in its pathological form, severe and sado–masochistic. On the other hand, if there is too little moral earnestness, too little encouragement to develop adult ways and concentrate the mind on reason, and evaluate and plan ahead, we get babyish ways.

Holy silliness as an anti-bureaucratic anti-obsessional remedy for narcissism

In the Table of Contents of *The Little Flowers of St. Francis of Assissi*, who lived from 1181 to 1226, we find:

Chapter Three: How St. Francis, having allowed an evil thought to arise in his mind against Brother Bernard, ordered him to place his foot three times upon his neck and his mouth ...

Chapter Eleven: How St. Francis made Brother Masseo turn round and round like a child, then go to Siena ...

Chapter Twenty-One: Of the most holy miracle of St. Francis in taming the fierce wolf of Gubbio.

The wolf, writes the author, after hearing St. Francis preach, ate only vegetables for the rest of its life; it was fed by the charity of the townspeople of Gubbio, and it followed St. Francis everywhere.

Part Two of *The Little Flowers* is about Brother Juniper, and uncritically reports him acting much dafter than St. Francis and, it may be thought, with less point. For instance, one of the brothers was very ill and in his fever longed for some pork. So Juniper hurried away and cut the leg off a local live pig so that his brother might have some pork. The owner of the pig is furious and shouts at Juniper.

Brother Juniper, who delighted in insults, cared nothing for all this abuse but, marvelling that anyone should be wroth at what seemed to him only a matter for rejoicing, he thought he had not made himself well understood, and so he repeated the story over again, and then flung himself on the man's neck and embraced him, telling him that all had been done out of charity, and inciting him and begging him for the rest of the swine also; and all this with so much charity, simplicity and humility, that the man's heart was changed within him.

So off went the owner, killed the pig and gave it to the friars.

Then St. Francis, considering the simplicity and patience under adversity of this good brother Juniper, said to his companions and those who stood by: "Would to God I had a forest of such Junipers".

What remedies are there for narcissism?

"Silly" and "simple", now carrying very different connotations, were used interchangeably for centuries. Our ways of seeing have lost something by the divergence. "Punks" have emerged partly in response to this loss, though they carry more anger than Francis and his friends seemed to.

Bureaucratic rules and holy silliness are extreme self-help solutions to the problems of narcissism, but people may be drawn to them by the dilemma in which they feel caught. For one may feel grand and in control in the confident narcissistic mode but, nagging at the threshold of consciousness, there is also the depressing knowledge that one is not permanently perfect. Yet behind every cry deploring one's inadequacy lies also a hidden conviction of unacknowledged potential. Neither the wretchedness nor the grandeur can be felt quite sincerely. Narcissism is a delusional state.

In their obsessive preoccupation with perfection and imperfection, people may resort to extreme measures to get rid of the self. They flinch from other people and isolate themselves because of their shame and guilt and fear, or they protect themselves with rules that disregard their many harmless needs or, resorting to holy silliness, make fun of the whole predicament, like the punks. No wonder that ever since the trait was first delineated, narcissism has proved difficult to modify, either through psychoanalytically-based talking-cures or through other therapeutic measures.

Via negativa advocates repression and superego control. The problem then is that with these agencies at the centre of personality organization, the self is the focus of attention. That is no way of getting rid of obsession with the self: struggling by these means to eradicate the self, we fall from self-absorption into self-obsession.

Can self-forgetfulness work? It is much commended by the mystics. But people with pathological narcissism cannot forget themselves; they are compelled by their distresses to take themselves too seriously. Self-acceptance first, then? But self-acceptance, that healthy-minded prescription, cannot work if people cannot forget themselves. Presumably, not having felt accepted by those who took care of them in earlier days, they cannot accept themselves as they are now, nor can they accept other people as *they* are now without anger, shame or guilt. If they could accept the facts of good and bad intermixed, they might be able to forget and, for a while at least, live with their imperfections and sometimes downright nastinesses without obsessing about them.

In the quaint language of psychoanalysis—no more quaint than the language of the mystics, though—there are three great realities we deny at our peril. They were first enunciated by Money-Kyrle (1971) and lately brought back into more general circulation by John Steiner (1985). In this more recent version, the three great realities we want to deny, but deny at our peril, are the goodness of the breast, the sexual intercourse of our parents, and our mortality. These three considerations freeze the blood in our narcissistic veins:

— we depend on others for our survival;
— we did not create ourselves, and the people on whom we depend do not exist just for us but have interests apart from us; and
— everything and everyone must die and eventually come to an end.

To anticipate our final conclusion, what appears essential is that there should be someone of importance who is willing to put up with the narcissistic tiresomenesses of the person in distress; what is needed is someone who continues to believe unsentimentally in the other person's potential for good, when there appears little evidence of it. This must be someone whose well-being is ultimately independent of what the sufferer is up to—it must not be a spouse, a parent or child or too devoted friend, or anyone who is at risk of being personally implicated—"co-dependent" is the current term— lest their involvement adds to the narcissistic person's guilt or shame or sense of importance. The fate of this helpful figure must not be entirely in the hands of the sufferer.

Culture clashes

The mystics, those psychotherapists of earlier days, contribute something to the discussion of narcissism that is not totally new to the modern mind but highlights some aspects that might otherwise not be seen in their full significance. The misdeeds for which their culture is responsible may tempt us to turn away, and the language is often unfamiliar, based as it is on a different view of what life is about, but if we are to learn from the experiences of people from another culture, we have to overcome the embarrassment or antagonism (or sentimental idealized attachment) we may have about that culture's language. If we do so, we may find support for some tentative modern ideas about narcissism and its remedies. In any case, remedies may be efficacious even when we do not share the assumptions (in this case theological Christian assumptions) on the grounds of which a remedy is recommended. For the assumption may not affect in any relevant way the relationship between sufferer and therapist on which the remedy depends. It is possible to learn from another culture without taking it over wholesale.

Via positiva is a remedy but . . .

In *via positiva* people characteristically look at, or relate in some way to, a blissful other. This is what Charles Williams meant by a Beatrician moment, and the Lady Julian by her report that

> . . . he said again and again: It is I, it is I who am most exalted, it is I whom you love. It is I whom you delight in . . . It is I whom you serve; it is I whom you long for, whom you desire; it is I whom you mean; it is I who am all. [Twelfth Revelation, Chapter 26]

This would not leave a person much space for other preoccupations. *Via positiva* is a prophylactic and a remedy for narcissism; it is based on the idea that blissful communion is the most natural thing in the world. *Via positiva* does not tell people that they are wonderful or wicked, it tells them that it does not matter whether they are or not. Then they can stop obsessing. "I would beside my Lord be watching", sings the tenor in Bach's *St. Matthew Passion*, "And so my sin would fall asleep". That is, it will not keep him awake.

At its best, the recommended anti-narcissistic training of the mystics is a training in knowing what you are, and looking beyond that. Knowing what you are is also an avowed aim of psychotherapy —indeed, the two trainings, mystical and psychotherapeutic, have interesting elements in common, as several of the passages that follow will show.

It has to be acknowledged that there are some pre-conditions, some of which require hard work. Those fortunate people who can just forget about themselves often write as if lack of self-concern and a happily loving life are as easy as breathing, but as a regular thing it is probably only achieved after much experience of breath-management. Doubtless most of them had times when they needed to direct their attention consciously and conscientiously to the source from which they derived their sense of well-being. Very few of them can have maintained their concentration indefinitely without support. Many of them lived very disciplined lives, in their solitary hermitages, in their religious communities, amid family demands or other commitments. They would have had to have recourse to Weil's implicit forms of the love of God (see p. 124), encouraged by the beauty of nature, by ritual, or by communal living. Probably these resources at times failed them, but we do not know about it because they picked themselves up again and carried on. Or they lived with it as a dark night of the soul. Or they fell away, we do not know.

There is bound to be tension between the extremes of *via positiva* and *via negativa*, between the all-you-need-is-love camp and the love-is-not-enough brigade who think that, because people are easily lazy, greedy, short-sighted, etc., an internal bureaucrat needs to be installed. William Law's prescriptions usually strike a pleasant balance. Clearly in favour of internal bureaucrats, he recommends them with a verve and common sense that makes them less unattractive. What is needed is a reasonably disciplined life and good habits.

> And if anyone was to ask himself, how it comes to pass, that there are any degrees of sobriety which he neglects, any practices of humility which he wants, any method of charity which he does not follow, any rules of redeeming time which he does not observe, his own heart will tell him that it is because *he never intended* to be exact in those duties. For whenever we fully intend it, it is as possible to conform to all this regularity of life, as it is possible for a man to observe times of prayer ... [*A Serious Call to a Devout and Holy Life*, 1728, end of Chapter 2, my italics]

Intention—the use of attention and will—is Law's notion of motivation.

This doctrine does not suppose that we have no need of Divine
Grace, or that it is in our own power to make ourselves perfect. It
only supposes, that through the want of a sincere intention of
pleasing God in all our actions we fall into such irregularities of life
as by the ordinary means of grace we should have power to avoid
... *We have not that perfection* which our present state of grace makes
us capable of, *because we do not* so much as *intend to have it.* [*ibid.*]

Law's recommendations are directed to steadying one's intentions. His anti-narcissistic prescriptions may be summed up as, first,
to establish a disciplined way of life and adhere to a routine so as to
be able to resist impulses that have doubtful antecedents, and,
second, to love other people in a practical way whether you feel
much for them or not, and , third, to get some self-knowledge.

Lastly, you are not to content yourself with a hasty general review
of the day, but you must enter upon it with deliberation, begin with
the first action of the day, and proceed, step by step, through every
particular matter that you have been concerned in, and so let no
time, place or action be overlooked.

An examination thus managed, will in a little time make you as
different from yourself, as a wise man is different from an idiot. It
will give you such a newness of mind, such a spirit of wisdom, and
desire of perfection, as you were an entire stranger to before. [Law,
1728, Chapter 23]

Self-knowledge and self-forgetfulness need each other

It will not do simply to laugh at William Law's sobriety, for the
refreshing lack of interest in one's virtues and/or shortcomings, so
characteristic of *via positiva*, may not endure indefinitely, just as new
insights in the course of psychotherapy often seem to lose their efficacy:

When a man is experiencing in his spirit this nothing in its nowhere,
he will find that his outlook undergoes the most surprising changes.
As the soul begins to look at it, he finds that all his past sins,
spiritual and physical, that he has committed from the day he was
born, are secretly and sombrely depicted on it. They meet his gaze
at every turn, until at last, after much hard work, many heartfelt
sighs and many bitter tears, he has virtually washed them all away.
[*The Cloud of Unknowing*, Chapter 69]

Walter Hilton gives similar sensible warnings about this process of "working through" an insight, before he comforts and encourages:

> Nevertheless, there is one work in which it is both very necessary and helpful to engage, and which—so far as human efforts are concerned—is a highway leading to contemplation. This is for a person to enter into himself, and to understand his own soul with all its powers, virtues and sins. In this interior examination you will come to recognise the honour and dignity proper to the soul at its creation, and the error and wretchedness into which you have fallen through sin. This realisation will bring with it a heartfelt desire to recover the dignity and honour which you have lost. You will be filled with disgust and contempt for yourself ...

but also you will

> resolve to humble yourself and destroy everything that stands between you and that dignity and joy. [Hilton, *The Ladder of Perfection*, Book One, Chapter 42]

And then comes the interesting advice:

> However vile a wretch you are, and however great the sins you have committed, forget yourself and all that you have done, both good and bad. Ask for mercy with humility and trust. [*ibid*., Chapter 44]

After self-knowledge may come humility, and humility can bring self-forgetfulness.

One may note, in passing, Hilton's therapeutic respect for the typical narcissistic inflation of self-importance, "However vile you are ...", together with the instruction that both good and bad have to be forgotten—the remedy lies in looking away from oneself.

Twentieth-century Florence Allshorn's language is nearer to our times than that of many of our sources, which makes her more easily accessible. She seems to have been rather like a twentieth-century abbess: she founded a community in Sussex—St Julian's—which started as a guest-house for missionaries on furlough, and for others needing a retreat. Following an old tradition, her friends and colleagues collected and published some of her lectures and instructional meditations. Well-read in the mystics, she often paraphrased her sources without explicit references—why should she, in the course of group meditation, but it can be inconvenient for more academic readers of her *Notebooks* (1957). She is clearly paraphrasing fourteenth-century Jakob Boehme, for instance, when she writes that "there are still deep longings in us, which hold us back from doing everything in love" and again when she refers to the "passions, resentments and pride" which we have to "drag into the light" so that we may

> ... recognise their ugliness, and their deep roots, desiring that no pride or fear shall blind us to our condition. [Allshorn, 1957, p. 66]

We need "faith that, in bringing them to the light, they can be changed"—a belief that psychotherapists also have—and she warns that this "means death to all our carefully built-up self-esteem and self-defence". (*ibid.*)

Allshorn takes up Boehme's phrase "self-naughting" to describe the process that psychotherapists call "working through": allowing oneself, in the supportive presence of another person, to find and reconsider more and more, those things in oneself that make for unease and guilt or shame.

> The whole of the ascent is summed up in this "clearing of yourself" as St. Paul calls it; this "know yourself" of the saints; to discover every impulse in you of self-love and self-assertion; then to let them go into the ready helping hands of a Saviour, knowing a great self-emptying ... [*ibid.*, p. 66]

Then

> at the root of you, instead of the old unease, the old feeling of guilt, the lovelessness, there is the constant happy shining, whatever comes, a great and smiling content. [*ibid.*, p. 67]

Dependence on a good object

Dependence on a good object is Allshorn's (Boehme's) specific remedy for narcissism; and Boehme is also Allshorn's source for her moving descriptions of our need to love and be loved, and of the dreadful void left in the psyche of those whose capacity for loving and being loved has been stunted or abraded. First, Allshorn points to what appears to be an everyday fact for Boehme, that love is the natural condition of life.

His creatures must always be desirous, because the flame of His desire entered into them at their creation. It is their energy and their elation. If they let go of Love, they let go of life and go out where darkness and death are, and have nothing but anxious and unsatisfied desires. [*ibid.*, p. 65]

If ... we were made to love, then every creature is desirous of finding this disinterested love, ... and all the unhappiness, the struggle to make oneself felt, anger, self-assertion ... dryness and depression are only desire robbed of love. [*ibid.*, p. 65]

Here narcissism, which is an obsessive putting oneself in the centre of attention, is considered both a cause and a consequence of lack of love at the centre. People afflicted in this way cannot let go, cannot forget themselves, are compelled to take themselves seriously, in order to have a centre at all. The remedy is humility.

Via positiva relies on dependence, conscious or unconscious, on a good internal object. When we feel that ultimately all will be well, because we have resources with which to meet all eventualities, it is easier to do without the immediate gratifications that greed, vindictiveness, or throbbing genitals can provide—and also without the consolation of despising oneself for being such a remarkable sinner. There are more hopeful ways of feeling good if we think we have access to unfailing resources. We need not at this point ask if they are located within us or elsewhere, though the old mystics had no doubts about it.

"A soul conformed to the likeness of Jesus desires nothing but him", wrote a fourteenth-century friar, Walter Hilton, whose reliance on faith in grace is indeed Lutheran in tone.

Humility says "I am nothing, I have nothing". Love says "I desire only one thing, which is Jesus". [*The Ladder of Perfection*, Book Two, Chapter 21]

If only you could understand this, you would see that Jesus is everything and Jesus does everything. You yourself do nothing; you simply allow him to work within your souls, accepting sincerely and gladly whatever he deigns to do in you. [*ibid.*, Chapter 24]

Some centuries later, the Protestant Tersteegen was to write:

The easiest and most correct way to holiness is to contemplate God in Christ, and to forget oneself and all one's own miseries ... Through this gazing upon God and His Divine Perfections the soul is wonderfully illuminated, strengthened, satisfied and, as it were in sleep, sanctified, and that indeed in a way more thorough than we could have imagined; because the impression of God's Presence, Majesty, All-sufficiency and Perfection so penetrates the soul that it feels everything that is not God to be small and insignificant. [Tersteegen, 1697–1769. *The Way of the Servants*, letter VI]

He is our resting-place; when we come to Him we have nothing else to search for, or to desire, or to disquiet ourselves with at all; and then our soul perceives that it is has reached the haven where it would be; it has found the place where it can rest ... In this one Good we have all that is good. [*ibid.*]

The *via positiva* mystics point at bliss and say "look how blissful, how comforting, how good, how much love is here". "Look what fun I have", says St. Francis. "Look how happy I am", says Brother Lawrence.

And it was observed that in the greatest hurry of business in the kitchen he still preserved his recollection and heavenly-mindedness. He was never hasty nor loitering, but did each thing in its season, with an even uninterrupted composure and tranquillity of spirit. "The time of business", said he, "does not with me differ from the time of prayer, and in the noise and clutter of my kitchen, while several persons are at the same time calling for different things, I possess God in as great tranquillity as if I were on my knees at the Blessed Sacrament". [Brother Lawrence, *The Practice of the Presence of God*, end of Fourth conversation]

Relationship as part of the remedy

Accept the facts; forget the fuss. It may be possible for people to forget themselves after they have faced some facts about themselves that they had been trying hard to ignore but until they can do this, one fact is that they are at times unacceptable to themselves and others and they have to live with that. The solution suggested by these mystics is to be in a relationship with a good object, to experience being appreciated without prior conditions, to begin to feel kinship with other people who are also imperfect, eventually recognizing that they may have something you need and that you may also have something to offer.

This speaks directly to the sense of wretchedness and uselessness against which the narcissistic hype is a defence. The more attractive *via positiva* mystics regarded narcissism as a misfortune to be managed into diminution until there was hardly any left, and , as a way of learning to manage it, they suggested self-knowledge, a cast of mind in which people get used to seeing themselves and their imperfections not alone but in company, in a relationship with others, or one Other, concerned and able to bear the inevitable dependence such a relationship creates.

Modern remedies against such obsessions as alcohol-dependence, or other substance-abuse, follow the same lines. An upbeat confident note characterizes much of their advice: if you can accept that you are as you are and that you depend on the kindness of good objects inner and outer, your obsessions will diminish. Often another person, who may also have been addicted, is provided to help you develop the capacity to be honest with yourself and with others. Believing that you can be rescued by another's efforts is good medicine for narcissism.

The same process can at times be found in the modern consulting-room, with some psychotherapists and perhaps more often with counsellors, whose training until recently tended to discourage them from too much busy-ness, for this work needs a great deal of un-oppressive patience.

From the sufferer's side there is also a proviso: an insistently self-satisfied client is an incurable one. Patients with narcissistic problems, before they can work well in therapy, require that modicum of self-knowledge or insight that tells them there is something amiss over and above their own sinfulness or the injustice of other people. But granted even just an occasional discomfort about their condition, relationship with another person becomes crucial—the rest of the requisite self-knowledge will follow later, though probably slowly. The relationship with the psychotherapist, well managed, may make possible a person's growing consciousness of narcissistically-based problems as they arise in that relationship and elsewhere, and this can then lead to increased self-understanding and acceptance.

All this is now well-understood, and that makes it all the more interesting that trained professionals can still sometimes find the narcissistic personality so blindingly irritating that, famous and rightly respected though they may be, they can lose their cool, and more than a hint of annoyance can creep into their tone. Perhaps our own pressure to put the annoying patient right gets so strong that we cannot help making the relationship disagreeable to the patient, and of course the narcissistically wounded patient then becomes more tiresome than ever. Otto Kernberg's understanding and intentions are flawless when he describes, in *Severe Personality Disorders* (1984), what is likely to happen when the therapist tries to help people with strong narcissistic tendencies. For instance, a patient who has been talking about something that has engaged his or her interest, may find the therapist cuts across this with a comment that is meant to throw new light on the patient's underlying personality dynamics. By doing this, the therapist fails, as Kernberg put it, "to fulfil the patient's expectation for admiration and reconfirmation of the grandiose self". True, though not a very nice way of putting it to the patient. Such events, Kernberg writes,

> ... typically evoke anger, rage, or a sudden devaluation of the analyst and his comments. Similar reactions characteristically follow times when the patient has felt important understanding and help coming from the analyst, understanding and help that painfully bring him to an awareness of the analyst's autonomous, independent functioning. The analyst's tolerance of such periods of rage or devaluation, his interpretation of the reasons for the patient's reactions, gradually permit the patient to integrate the positive and negative aspects of the transference: to integrate idealization and trust with rage, contempt, and paranoid distrust. [Kernberg, 1984, p. 198]

Even in this passage, a perhaps oversensitive reader might be uncomfortable at the tone of Kernberg's account: no reference is made here to the pain of the dilemma facing such patients, who are required to give up, bit by bit, the habits of thinking of a lifetime, habits they have lived by, however uncomfortably. Kernberg's account is almost entirely in terms of the patient's recalcitrant envy. On subsequent pages, where many of the narcissistic patient's feelings are impeccably accurately described, the note of resentment is unmistakeable. Here, for instance, is part of an explanation of a patient's rage:

... periods of emptiness and the patient's feeling that "nothing is happening" in the treatment situation may often be clarified as an active, unconscious destruction of what the patient is receiving from the analyst, a reflection of the patient's inability to depend on the analyst as a giving maternal figure.

The patient's avid efforts to obtain knowledge and understanding from the analyst in order to incorporate them as something forcefully extracted rather than something received with gratitude contribute to the unconscious spoiling of what is received, a complex emotional reaction first clarified by Rosenfeld (1964) and one that usually takes a long time to resolve. Typically, lengthy periods of intellectual self-analysis, during which the patient treats the analyst as absent (which may elicit negative countertransference in the form of boredom), are followed by or interspersed with periods when the patient eagerly expects and absorbs interpretations, attempts to outguess the analyst, rapidly incorporates what he has received as if he himself knew it all along, only once more to feel strangely empty, dissatisfied, as not having received anything after this new knowledge has been, as it were, metabolized.

By the same token, the patient typically, by projection, assumes that the analyst has no genuine interest in him, is as self-centred and exploitative as the patient experiences himself to be, and has no authentic knowledge or convictions but only a limited number of tricks and magical procedures which the patient needs to learn and incorporate. The more corrupt the patient's superego, and the more he needs to project devalued self and object representations, the more he suspects the analyst of presenting similarly corrupt and devalued characteristics. The gradual emergence or breakthrough of more primitive transferences may shift this overall picture into the expression of paranoid distrust and direct aggression in the transference. [*ibid.*]

Regular contact with a good-humoured therapist, who can identify with narcissistic reactions, and bear them with a warmer equanimity, allows a person to be less fearful and, little by little, to let go of these unpleasant defences against self-knowledge. Interestingly, it was the counselling ethic of empathic listening and unconditional acceptance, and of reflecting back without the overtones of a judgmental need to put the client right, that made it possible for some sufferers to find relief in the middle of the twentieth century, when psychoanalytic techniques were still focused almost exclusively on interpretation and the achievement of intellectual insight. Kernberg, of course, knows this. In the same book from which the above excepts were taken, different types of psychotherapy are recommended for different casts of mind, and classical psychoanalysis recommended only for people with the kind of personality-structure Kernberg thinks can bear it (Kernberg, 1984, pp. 206 ff. and 147 ff.; see also Klein J., 1995, p. 157 ff.)

Finally: recognition

What happens in fortunate relationships with good psychotherapists not too plagued by having to protect their own narcissistic pains, is that people feel recognized and accepted. This makes possible a diminution of self-consciousness, of what Buber called "reflexion" (see p. 237). As people with narcissistic problems become more able to tolerate their imperfections because they feel recognized and accepted, there will also be a diminution in their tense fault-finding disapproval of others.

The secret ingredient for narcissistically afflicted people, as for others, was discussed in Chapter Five under the heading "Recognition". Recognition is the natural opposite of narcissistic loving. For narcissistic patients this means that their good qualities are seen with appreciation and pleasure, not judgmentally, scornfully or spitefully. Also their own arrogance and spite are understood and respected as defences against the pain that the fear of their own imperfection inflicts on them.

The therapist may have to assume that the pain is there, for there may for a while be little evidence of this repressed or split-off-life. Not that the therapist has to conceal his or her knowledge of the patient's spiteful dealings, but if it can at all be managed, the patient must be kept secure in the therapist's recognition that he or she is a potentially whole person, whose history contains much hidden and often unconscious shame, guilt, and pain. Until these are clearly known by both patient and therapist—which requires a lot of work—the therapist cannot be fully experienced by the patient as "knowing the patient", and during this time the therapist has to accept the patient without full knowledge of all circumstances. But that seems in any case an inescapable condition of honest living.

REFERENCES

Ainsworth-Smith, I. (2001). Conference Convener: *Mental Anguish and Religion*. Brighton: Mole Conference, 26 Church Road, Portslade, Brighton, BN41 1LA.

Allshorn, F. (1957). *The Notebooks of Florence Allshorn*. London: S.C.M. Press.

Allwein, G., & Barwise, J. (1996). *Logical Reasoning with Diagrams*. Oxford & New York: Oxford University Press.

Andrewes, L. (1555–1626). See Higham, F.

Arden, M. (1985). Psychoanalysis and survival. *International Journal of Psychoanalysis, 66*: 471–480.

Arden, M. (1993). Thoughts on the healing process. *International Forum on Psychoanalysis, 2*. Stockholm.

Armstrong, K. (1983). *Beginning the World*. London: Macmillan.

Ashworth, A. (1998). *The Oblique Light: Poetry and Peak Experience*. Quaker Universalist Group, Pamphlet No. 28.

Austen, J. (1811). *Sense and Sensibility*. Published in many paperbacks e.g. Corgi, Everyman, Pan, Signet.

Balint, A. (1939). Love for the mother and mother love. In: M. Balint (1965).

Balint, M. (1959). *Thrills and Regressions*. London: Hogarth Press.

Balint, M. (1965). *Primary Love and Psychoanalytic Technique*. London: Hogarth Press.

Baradon, T. (1998). Michael: a journey from the physical to the mental realm. In: Anne Hurry (Ed.), *Psychoanalysis and Developmental Therapy*. London: Karnac Books.

Bell, C. (1914). *Art*. London: Chatto and Windus.

Bell, C. (1932). *Civilisation*. London: Chatto and Windus.

Betjeman, J. (1958). In a Bath Tea-room. In: *Collected Poems*. London: John Murray.

Bion, W. R. (1967). *Second Thoughts*. London: Heinemann.

Bion, W. R. (1970). *Attention and Interpretation*. London: Karnac Books, 1984.

Biven, B. (1982). The role of skin in normal and abnormal development, with a note on the poet Sylvia Plath. *International Review of Psychoanalysis, 9:* 205–206.

Black, D. (1993). What sort of a thing is religion? A view from object relations theory. *International Journal of Psychoanalysis, 74:* 613–625.

Black, D. (2000). The functioning of religions from a modern psycho-analytic perspective. *Mental Health, Religion, and Culture, 3:* 13–26.

Boehme, J. (Sixteenth-century mystic) *The Way to Christ (and other writings)*. P. Erb (Trans.). New York: Paulist Press, 1970.

Bollas, C. (1987). *The Shadow of the Object*. London: Free Association.

Bomford, R. (1999). *The Symmetry of God*. London: Free Association.

Bonhoeffer, D. (1947). *Letters and Papers from Prison*. (Various Trans.). London: SCM Press, 1953.

Bouyer, L. (1956). *Life and Liturgy*. London: Sheed and Ward.

Bowlby, J. (1969). *Attachment*. London: Hogarth Press [reprinted London: Pelican, 1971].

Bowlby, J. (1973). *Separation*. London: Hogarth Press [reprinted London: Pelican, 1975].

Bowlby, J. (1980). *Loss*. London: Hogarth Press [reprinted London: Pelican, 1981].

Brazelton, V. B., Koslowski, B., & Main, M. (1974). The origins of reciprocity in mother–infant interaction. In: M. Lewis & L. A. Rosenblum (Ed.), *The Effect of the Infant on its Care-givers*. London: Wiley Interscience.

Britton, R. (1989). The missing link in parental sexuality. In: J. Steiner. (Ed.), *The Oedipus Complex Today*. London: Karnac Books.

Brother Lawrence. (Seventeenth-century Mystic). *The Practice of the Presence of God*. H. Martin (Ed.). London: SCM Press, 1956.

Buber, M. (1923). *I and Thou*. Edinburgh: F. T. Clark, 1937.

Buber, M. (1946). *Moses*. East–West Library. Oxford: Phaidon Press.

Buber, M. (1947). *Between Man and Man*. R. G. Smith (Trans.). London: Routledge and Kegan Paul [reprinted Fontana, 1961].

Buber, M. (1957). Distance and relation. *Psychiatry, 20*: 97–104.

Buchan, J. (1941). *Sick Heart River*. London: Hodder and Stoughton.

Bunyan, J. (1628–1688). *The Pilgrims Progress*. R. Sharrock (Ed.). Harmondsworth: Penguin.

Clark, M. (1998). God could be something terrible. In: I. Alister & G. Hauke (Eds.), *Contemporary Jungian Analysis*. London: Routledge.

Clark, M. (in press). Women's lack: the image of woman as divine. In: A. Duncan & T. Adams (Eds.), *The Feminine Case: Jung, Women's Language and the Creative Discourse*. London: Karnac Books.

Cloud of Unknowing. (Fourteenth-century author, not known). C. Wolters (Trans.). Harmondsworth: Penguin, 1961.

Coleridge, S. T. (1772–1834). The Rime of the Ancient Mariner. In: *The Oxford Book of English Verse*. Oxford: University Press, 1939.

Conference on Mental Anguish and Religion. (2001). *q.v.* Ainsworth-Smith, Hamilton, Powell, Ross.

Cummings, E. E. (1960). *Selected Poems 1923–1958*. London: Faber and Faber; London: The Penguin Poets, 1973.

Dante, A. (1265–1321). *The Divine Comedy*. Dorothy Sayers (Trans.), *Hell* (1949), *Purgatory* (1955), *Paradise* (1962). Harmondsworth: Penguin.

Dante, A. (1992). *Vita Nuova*, M. Musa (Trans.). Oxford: University Press.

D'Arcy, M. C. (1945). *The Mind and Heart of Love*. London: Faber and Faber; London: Fontana, 1962.

D'Arcy, M. C. (1951). *Poems of St John of the Cross* [Preface] *q.v.* St John of the Cross. London: Harvill Press.

Davies, Robertson. (1976). *The Manticore*. Harmondsworth: Penguin Books.

Davies, Robertson. (1983). *The Deptford Trilogy* (comprising i.a. *The Manticore*, 1972). London: Penguin.

Dillard, A. (1975). *Pilgrim at Tinker Creek*. London: Jonathan Cape.

Donne, J. (1572–1631). Holy Sonnet vi. In: *The Oxford Book of Christian Verse*. Oxford: University Press.

Drever, J. (1963). *A Dictionary of Psychology*. Harmondsworth: Penguin.

Duns Scotus. (c. 1264–1308). *Principles of Individuation and The Theory of Knowledge*. A. Wolter (Ed. & Trans.). London: Nelson's Philosophical Texts.

Durkheim, E. (1915). *Elementary Forms of Religious Life*. Joseph Ward Swan (Trans.). London: Allen and Unwin.

Ehrenzweig, A. (1967). *The Hidden Order of Art*. London: Weidenfeld and Nicholson.

Eigen, M. (1998). *The Psychoanalytic Mystic*. London: Free Association.

Eliot, G. (1876). *Daniel Deronda*. London: Dent.

Emde, R. N. (1990). Mobilising fundamental modes of development: empathic availability and therapeutic action. *Journal of the American Psychoanalytic Association, 38*: 881–913.

Emde, R. N., & Gaensbacher, T. (1981). Some emerging models of emotion in human infancy. In: K. Immelman, G. W. Barlow, L. Petrinovitch & M. Main (Eds.), *Behavioural Development, the Bielefeld Interdisciplinary Project* (pp. 562–602). Cambridge: University Press.

Fairbairn, W. R. D. (1952). *The Psychoanalytic Study of the Personality*. London: Routledge and Kegan Paul.

Fenichel, O. (1948). *The Psychoanalytic Theory of Neurosis*. London: Routledge and Kegan Paul.

Field, N. (1996). *Breakdown and Breakthrough*. London: Routledge.

Fonagy, P. (1995). Playing with reality. *International Journal of Psychoanalysis, 6*: 39–44.

Fonagy, P., & Moran, G. (1991). Understanding psychic change in child psychoanalysis. *International Journal of Psychoanalysis, 2*: 15–22.

Forster, E. M. (1907). *The Longest Journey*. London: Edward Arnold [reprinted Penguin, 1980].

Freud, S. (1891). *On Aphasia: a Critical Study*. New York: International Universities Press, 1953. [This is cited by Rizzuto in her bibliography for the *International Journal of Psychoanalysis 1990, 71*: 270, but it is not in the Standard Edition as such, though references to aphasia appear throughout *S.E., 1*].

Freud, S. (1914). On narcissism. *S.E., 14*: 67–102.

Freud, S. (1923). *The Ego and the Id. S.E., 19*: 12–66.

Freud, S. (1924a). The economic problem of masochism. *S.E., 19*: 159–170.

Freud, S. (1924b). The dissolution of the Oedipus complex. *S.E., 19*: 171–179.

Freud, S. (1930). *Civilisation and its Discontents. S.E., 21*: 64–145.

Freud, S. (1933). The anatomy of the mental personality. In: *New Introductory Lectures in Psychoanalysis. S.E., 22*: 5–182.

Freud, S. (1950b). Jokes and their relation to the unconscious. *S.E., 8*: 167–176.

Friedman, M. (1955). *Martin Buber—the Life of Dialogue*. Chicago: University Press.

Gardner, W. H. (1953). *Gerard Manley Hopkins—Poems and Prose*. Harmondsworth: Penguin.

Gerrard, J. (1996). Love in the time of psychotherapy. *British Journal of Psychotherapy, 13*: 163–173.

Gerth, H. H., & Mills, C. Wright (Ed.) (1948). *From Max Weber: Essays in Sociology.* London: Routledge and Kegan Paul [this is a translation and commentary on Max Weber *q.v.*].

Gimello, R. M. (1978). Mysticism and meditation. In: S. T. Katz (Ed.), 1978. *q.v.*

Greenson, R. (1967). *The Techniques and Practice of Psychoanalysis.* New York: International Universities Press.

Grotstein, T. (1995). Orphans of the "real": some modern and post-modern perspectives on the neuro-biological and psycho-social dimensions of psychosis and primitive mental disorders. *Bulletin of the Menninger Clinic, 59*: 312–332.

Grotstein, T. (1997). Bion, the Pariah of "O". *British Journal of Psychotherapy, 14*: 77–90.

Hamilton, N. (2001). Transpersonal psychotherapy: psychotic voices and voices of inner guidance. *q.v.* Conference.

Harris-Williams, M. (1997). Inspiration: a psychoanalytic and aesthetic concept. *British Journal of Psychotherapy, 14*: 33–44.

Hayek, F. von (1952). *The Sensory Order.* London: Routledge and Kegan Paul.

Hebb, D. O. (1958). *A Textbook of Psychology.* Philadelphia and London: W. B. Saunders.

Hebb, D. O. (1949). *The Organisation of Behaviour.* New York: John Wiley [reprinted London: Chapman and Hall].

Hebert, A. G. (1961). *Liturgy and Society.* London: Faber and Faber.

Herbert, G. (1593–1632). Frailty. *Oxford Book of Christian Verse.* Oxford: University Press. Employment, *ibid.*; The Quip, *ibid.*; A True Hymn, *ibid.*; Discipline, *ibid.*

Hick, J. (1999). *The Fifth Dimension, an Exploration of the Spiritual Realm.* Oxford: One World.

Higham, F. (1952). *Lancelot Andrewes.* London: SCM Press.

Hilton, W. (Fourteenth Century). *The Ladder of Perfection.* L. Shirley Price (Ed. & Trans.). Harmondsworth: Penguin Classics.

Hinshelwood, R. (1989). *A Dictionary of Kleinian Thought.* London: Free Association.

Hoban, R. (1973). *The Lion of Boaz-Jachin and Jachin-Boaz.* London: Jonathan Cape

Hoffman, E. (1989). *Lost in Translation—Life in a New Language.* London: Heinemann.

Hopkins, Gerard Manley. (1953). *Selected Poems*. London: Heinemann.

Hopkins, J. (1995). The spiritual connection: a dilemma for psychotherapists? *British Journal of Psychotherapy*, 11: 601–604.

Hunt, L. (1784–1859). Abou Ben Adham. *Oxford Book of English Verse*. Oxford: University Press.

Hurry, A. (Ed.) (1998). *Psychoanalysis and Developmental Theory*. London: Karnac Books.

Jacobs, M. (2000). *Illusion, a Psychodynamic Interpretation of Thinking and Belief*. London and Philadelphia: Whurr.

James, W. (1891). *Principles of Psychology*. London: Macmillan.

James, W. (1892). *Psychology*. London: Macmillan.

James, W. (1902). *The Varieties of Religious Experience*. The Gifford Lectures in Natural Religion. London: Collins, Fontana.

Jefferies, R. (1883). *The Story of my Heart* (1912 edn) (p. 104). London: Duckworth.

Joseph, B. (1975). The patient who is difficult to reach. In: P. L. Giovacchini (Ed.), *Tactics and Techniques in Psychoanalytic Therapy, Volume 2* (pp. 205–216). New York: Jason Aronson.

Julian of Norwich. (Fourteenth-century mystic). *Revelations of Divine Love*. H. Backhouse & R. Pipe (Ed.). London: Hodder and Stoughton.

Jung, C. J. (1954). *The Practice of Psychotherapy*. In: *Collected Works, 16*. London: Routledge and Kegan Paul.

Jung, C. J. (1959). The archetypes and the collective unconscious. In: *Collected Works, 9*. London: Routledge and Kegan Paul.

Kardiner, A. (1945). *The Psychological Frontiers of Society*. New York: Columbia University Press.

Katz, S. T. (Ed.) (1978). *Mysticism and Philosophical Analysis*. London: Sheldon and Bess.

Kernberg, O. (1976). *Object Relations Theory and Clinical Psychoanalysis*. New York: Jason Aronson.

Kernberg, O. (1984). *Severe Personality Disorders*. New Haven and London: Yale University Press.

Kipling, R. (1901). *Kim*. London: Hodder and Stoughton.

Klein, J. (1987). *Our Needs for Others and its Roots in Infancy*. London: Routledge.

Klein, J. (1995). *Doubts and Certainties in the Practice of Psychotherapy*. London: Karnac Books.

Klein, M. (1930). The importance of symbol formation in the development of the ego. *International Journal of Psychoanalysis*, also in *The Writings of Melanie Klein Volume 1*, R. Money-Kyrle, B. Joseph, E.

O'Shaughnessy & H. Segal (Eds.). London: Kegan Paul, 1975.

Klein, M. (1957). Envy and Gratitude. In: *Envy and Gratitude and Other Works* (pp. 264–267). London: Hogarth Press.

Knox, R. (1958). *Autobiography of a Saint*. London: Harvill Press.

Kohut, H. (1977). *The Restoration of the Self*. New York: International Universities Press.

Koslowski, B. (1974). The origins of reciprocity in mother–infant interaction. In: M. Lewis & L. A. Brazelton (Ed.), *q.v.*

Krieger, L. (1976). *The Theory of Criticism*. Baltimore: Johns Hopkins University Press.

Lacan, J. (1966). *Ecrits*. Paris: Seuil [reprinted 1949–1969, A. Sheridan (Trans.). New York: W. W. Norton, 1977].

Laing, R. D. (1970). *Knots*. London: Tavistock [reprinted Penguin, 1972].

Laplanche, J., & Pontalis, J. B. (1988). *The Language of Psychoanalysis*. London: Karnac Books.

Law, W. (1728). *A Serious Call to a Devout and Holy Life*. London: Wyvern, 1966.

Lewis, C. S. (1955). *Surprised by Joy*. London: Geoffrey Bles.

Lewis, C. S. (1960). *The Four Loves*. London: Geoffrey Bles, Fontana.

Lewis, M., & Rosenblum, L. A. (Eds.) (1974). *The Effect of the Infant on its Care-givers*. London: Wiley Interscience.

Likierman, M. (1989). The clinical significance of aesthetic experience. *International Review of Psychoanalysis, 16*: 133–150.

Likierman, M. (1993). Primitive object-love in Melanie Klein's thinking. *International Journal of Psychoanalysis, 74*: 241–274.

McDougall, W. (1908). *Social Psychology*. London: Methuen.

McDougall, W. (1912) *Psychology. Home Universities Libraries*. London: Williams and Norgate; New York: Holt.

McDougall, W. (1923). *Outline of Psychology*. London: Methuen.

Main, M. (1974) The origins of reciprocity in mother–infant interaction. In: M. Lewis & L. A. Brazelton (Eds.), *q.v.*

Marvel, A. (1621–1678). Thoughts in a garden. *Oxford Book of English Verse*. Oxford: University Press.

Maslow, A. H. (1968). *Towards a Psychology of Being*. Princeton, NJ: Van Nostrand.

Matte Blanco, I. (1975). *The Unconscious as Infinite Sets*. London: Duckworth.

Mautner, T. (1997). *The Penguin Dictionary of Philosophy*. Harmondsworth: Penguin.

Mehta, G. (1979). *Karma Cola*. London: Jonathan Cape, 1980 [reprinted London: Minerva].

Meissner, W. W. (1992). *Ignatius of Loyola, the Psychology of a Saint*. New Haven and London: Yale University Press.

Meltzer, D. (1973). *Sexual States of Mind*. Strath Tay, Perthshire: Clunie Press.

Meltzer, D. (Ed.) (1978). *The Collected Papers of Roger Money-Kyrle*. Strath Tay, Perthshire: Clunie Press.

Meltzer, D., & Harris-Williams, M. (1988). *The Apprehension of Beauty*. Strath Tay, Perthshire: Clunie Press.

Melville, H. (1851). *Moby Dick*. Many editions.

Mendoza, S. (2003). The emerging religious dimension of knowing in psychoanalysis. In: *The Edges of Psychotherapy, Volume 3. Psychotherapy in Practice*. B. Bishop, J. Klein & V. O'Connell (Eds.). London: Karnac Books.

Miller, G. A., Galanter, A., & Pribram, K. (1969). *Plans and the Structure of Behaviour*. New York: Holt.

Money-Kyrle, R. (1971). The aim of psychoanalysis. In: D. Meltzer (Ed.), *The Collected Papers of Roger Money-Kyrle*. Strath Tay, Perthshire: Clunie Press, 1978.

Ogden, T. (1979). In projective identification. *International Journal of Psychoanalysis*, 60: 357–373.

Ogden, T. (1982). *Projective Identification and Psychotherapeutic Technique*. New York: Jason Aronson

Ogden, T. (1994). The analytic third: working with intersubjective clinical facts. *International Journal of Psychoanalysis*, 75: 3——19.

Ogden, T. (1996). Reconsidering three aspects of psychoanalytic techniques. *International Journal of Psychoanalysis*, 77: 883–900.

Otto, R. (1917). *The Idea of the Holy*. J. W. Harvey (Trans.). Pelican, 1959 [reprinted Oxford: University Press, 1923].

Peters, E. (1989). *The Potter's Field*. London: Headline Books.

Pope, A. (1688–1744). *An Essay on Man*. M. Mack (Ed.). London: Methuen, 1950.

Powell, A. (2001). Inspiration and persecution—messages from the self and beyond. In *Conference, q.v.*

Redfearn, J. (1985). *Myself, My Many Selves, Volume 6*. London: Library of Analytic Psychology, Academic Press.

Reeves, J. (1994). *Introduction to the Works of Gerard Manley Hopkins*. London: The Wordsworth Poetry Library.

Richards, V. (Ed.) (1996). *The Person who is Me*. Winnicott Monograph Series. London: Karnac Books.

Ridler, A. (1945?). *Cain*. London: Faber and Faber.

Rizzuto, A.-M. (1990). A proto-dictionary of psychoanalysis. *International Journal of Psychoanalysis, 71*: 261–270.

Ross, A. (2001). Psychotherapy and religion. In: *Conference, q.v.*

Rowe, D. (1993). Book review. *British Journal of Psychotherapy, 10*: 284–285.

Ruysbroek, J. van (1293–1381). *The Spiritual Espousals.* E. Colledge (Trans.). London: Faber and Faber, 1952.

Rycroft, C. (1968). *A Critical Dictionary of Psychoanalysis.* London: Nelson [reprinted Penguin, 1972].

Sayers, D. L. (1949, 1955, 1962). *q.v.* Dante.

Schleiermacher, E. (1821–1822). *Der Christliche Glaube ...* (The Christian Faith Systematically Presented according to the Principles of the Protestant Church.) No English version found but see e.g. *A Prince of the Church*: Schleiermacher and the Beginnings of Modern Theology. Philadelphia, 1984.

Schore, A. (1994). *Affect Regulation and the Origin of the Self.* New York: Hillsdale and Hove, UK.

Searles, H. (1960). *The Non-Human Environment in Normal Development and in Schizophrenia.* New York: International Universities Press.

Searles, H. (1965). *Collected Papers on Schizophrenia and Other Subjects.* New York: International Universities Press.

Searles, H. (1979). *Countertransference and Related Subjects.* New York: International Universities Press.

Segal, H. (1957). Notes on symbol-formation. In: *The Works of Hannah Segal.* New York: Jason Aronson, 1981.

Shand, A. F. (1914). *The Foundations of Character.* London: Macmillan.

Shirley-Price, L. (Ed.) (1952). *The Imitation of Christ* by Thomas à Kempis. London: SCM Press.

Smart, C. (1732–1771). A Song to David. In: *The Oxford Book of Christian Verse.* Oxford: University Press, 1931.

Smart, N. (1996). *Dimensions of the Sacred: an Anatomy of the World's Beliefs.* London and New York: Harper Collins.

Snow, C. P. (1952). *The Masters.* London: Macmillan [Harmondsworth: Penguin, 1956].

Sprott, W. J. H. (Trans.) (1937). *New Introductory Lectures on Psychoanalysis* by Sigmund Freud. *q.v.* International Psychoanalytical Library. London: Hogarth Press.

St. Catherine of Siena. (Fourteenth Century). *Letters.* Suzanne Noffke (Trans.). Binghampton, New York: University of New York, 1988.

St. Francis de Sales. (1567–1623). *Introduction to the Devout Life.* Alan Ross (Trans.). London: Burns Oates, 1930.

St. Francis of Assisi. (1181–1226). Canticle to the Sun. In: B. Fahy (Trans.), *The Writings of St. Francis of Assisi*. London: Sheed and Ward, 1964.

St. Francis of Assisi. (1181–1226). *The Little Flowers of St. Francis of Assisi*. Dom Roger Huddleston (Trans.). London: Burns Oates and Washbourne Ltd, 1926.

St. John of the Cross. (1542–1591). *Poems*. Roy Cambell (Trans.). London: Harvill Press, 1951.

St. Teresa of Avila. (1515–1582). *The Life of the Holy Mother Teresa of Jesus*. E. Allison Peers (Trans.). London: Sheed and Ward, 1946.

St. Teresa of Lisieux. (1873–1897). *Biography*. Trans. by Ronald Knox as *Autobiography of a Saint*. London: Harvill Press, 1958.

Steiner, J. (1985). Turning a blind eye: the cover-up for Oedipus. *The International Review of Psychoanalysis*, 161–172.

Steiner, J. (1989). *The Oedipus Complex Today*. London: Karnac Books.

Steiner, J. (1993). The relationship to reality in psychic retreats. In: J. Steiner (Ed.), *Psychic Retreats*. London: Routledge.

Stern, D. (1985). *The Interpersonal World of the Infant*. Boston: Basic Books.

Stout. (1899). *A Manual of Psychology*. London: University Correspondence College Press.

Suso, H. (Fourteenth-century mystic). *The Little Book of Eternal Wisdom* and *The Little Book of Truth*. J. M. Clark (Trans.). London: Faber and Faber, 1953.

Tersteegen, G. (1697–1769). *The Way of the Servant*. Norwich: Pelegrine Trout in assoc. with Pilgrim Books, 1986 [reprinted London: Watkins, 1918].

Thomas à Kempis. (c. 1380–1471). *The Imitation of Christ. q.v.* L. Shirley-Price, 1952.

Thomas, D. (1954). *Under Milk Wood*. London: J. N. Dent.

Thomas, R. S. (1993). *Collected Poems 1945–1990*. London: J. N. Dent [reprinted London: Phoenix, 2001].

Thompson, F. (1859–1909). The Hound of Heaven. In: *The Oxford Book of Christian Verse*. Oxford: University Press, 1941.

Thompson, F. (1859–1909). In no strange land … In: *The Oxford Book of English Verse*. Oxford: Clarendon Press, 1939.

Traherne, T. (1636?–1674). Desire. In: *The Oxford Book of Christian Verse*. Oxford: University Press.

Turquet-Milnes, G. (1926). Baudelaire. In: *From Pascal to Proust*. London: Jonathon Cape.

Underhill, E. (1936). *Worship*. London: Collins, Fontana, 1962.

Vaughan, H. (1622–1695). The Dawning. In: *The Oxford Book of Christian Verse*. Oxford: University Press.

Voltaire, F.-M. (1759) *Candide*. J. Butt (Trans.). Harmondsworth: Penguin Classics.

Weber, M. (1908). *Wirtschaft und Gesellschaft*, see Gerth, H. H. & Mills, C. (1948). *From Max Weber: Essays in Sociology*, Wright (Ed.).

Weil, S. (1950). *Attente de Dieu (Waiting on God)*. Translated from French by Emma Craufurd. First published 1951, Routledge & Kegan Paul Ltd; issued Fontana Books, 1959.

Welldon, E. (1988). *Mother, Madonna, Whore*. London: Free Association Press.

West, R. (1991). *This Real Night*. Reissued London: Virago, 1992.

Williams, C. (1930). *War in Heaven*. Re-issued 1988 Eerdmens *sup*.

Williams, C. (1931). *Many Dimensions*. Harmondsworth: Penguin Books, 1952.

Williams, C. (1932). *The Greater Trumps*. London: Victor Golancz.

Williams, C. (1933a). *Shadows of Ecstasy*. Re-issued by Eerdmans, *sup.*, 1980.

Williams, C. (1933b). *The Place of the Lion*. Re-issued by William B. Eerdmans, *sup.*, 1956.

Williams, C. (1937). *Descent into Hell*. London: Longman Green.

Williams, C. (1939). *The Descent of the Dove*. London: Longman Green [reprinted Faber and Faber 1950; Fontana, 1963].

Williams, C. (1941). *All Hallows' Eve*. Re-issued 1981 by William B. Eerdmans Publishing Co., Grand Rapis, US.

Williams, C. (1943). *The Figure of Beatrice*. Re-issued by D. S. Brewer, 1994. Woodbridge, UK and Rochester, US: Boydell and Brewer.

Winnicott, D. W. (1958). *Collected Papers: Through Paediatrics to Psycho-Analysis*. London: Tavistock Publications [reprinted London: Hogarth Press, 1975]. This collection contains "Hate in the countertransference", first published in 1947; and "Transitional objects and transitional phenomena", first published in 1951 and also found in *Playing and Reality q.v.*

Winnicott, D. W. (1964). *The Child, the Family, and the Outside World*. London: Penguin. A large part of this material was originally published in two volumes by Tavistock Publications (1957), in *The Child and the Family* and *The Child and the Outside World*.

Winnicott, D. W. (1965). *The Maturational Processes and the Facilitating Environment*. London: Hogarth Press. This collection contains "Ego integration in Child Development", first published in 1968, "The development of the capacity for concern", first published in 1963, which re-appears in a different version under the title "The capacity for concern" in *Playing and Reality q.v.*, and "Ego distortion in terms of true and false self" first published in 1960.

Winnicott, D. W. (1969). The use of an object and relating through identifications. *International Journal of Psychoanalysis, 50*: 21–31.

Winnicott, D. W. (1974). *Playing and Reality*. Harmondsworth: Penguin.

Wittgenstein, L. (1922). *Tractatus Logico-Philosophicus*. London: Routledge.

Wodehouse, P. G. (1933). The story of Webster. In: P. G. Wodehouse (Ed.), *Mulliner's Nights*. London: Herbert Jenkins.

Wolters, C. (Trans.) (1961). *The Cloud of Unknowing*. Harmondsworth: Penguin.

Wright, K. (1996). Looking after the self. In: V. Richards (Ed.), *The Person Who is Me*. Winnicott Studies Monograph Series. London: Karnac Books.

Wright, K. (1991). *Vision and Separation between Mother and Baby*. London: Free Association Press.

Wyon, O. (1943). *The School of Prayer*. London: SCM Press.

Yeats, W. B. (1990). Vacillation. In: *Collected Poems*. London: Macmillan.

Xenophanes. (c. 500 B.C.). *Early Greek Elegy*. T. H. Williams (Ed.). Cardiff: University Press, 1926.

Zaehner, R. C. (1957). *Mysticism, Sacred and Profane*. Oxford: University Press.

INDEX